Theories of Social Capital

Political Economy and Development

Published in association with the International Initiative for Promoting Political Economy (IIPPE)

Edited by
Ben Fine (SOAS, University of London)
Dimitris Milonakis (University of Crete)

Political economy and the theory of economic and social development have long been fellow travellers, sharing an interdisciplinary and multidimensional character. Over the last 50 years, mainstream economics has become totally formalistic, attaching itself to increasingly narrow methods and techniques at the expense of other approaches. Despite this narrowness, neoclassical economics has expanded its domain of application to other social sciences, but has shown itself incapable of addressing social phenomena and coming to terms with current developments in the world economy.

With world financial crises no longer a distant memory, and neo-liberalism and postmodernism in retreat, prospects for political economy have strengthened. It allows constructive liaison between the dismal and other social sciences and rich potential in charting and explaining combined and uneven development.

The objective of this series is to support the revival and renewal of political economy, both in itself and in dialogue with other social sciences. Drawing on rich traditions, we invite contributions that constructively engage with heterodox economics, critically assess mainstream economics, address contemporary developments and offer alternative policy prescriptions.

THEORIES OF SOCIAL CAPITAL

Researchers Behaving Badly

Ben Fine

PlutoPress

www.plutobooks.com

First published 2010 by Pluto Press
345 Archway Road, London N6 5AA and
175 Fifth Avenue, New York, NY 10010

www.plutobooks.com

Distributed in the United States of America exclusively by
Palgrave Macmillan, a division of St. Martin's Press LLC,
175 Fifth Avenue, New York, NY 10010

British Library Cataloguing in Publication Data
A catalogue record for this book is available from the British Library

ISBN   978 0 7453 2997 0   Hardback
ISBN   978 0 7453 2996 3   Paperback

Library of Congress Cataloging in Publication Data applied for

10   9   8   7   6   5   4   3   2   1

Designed and produced for Pluto Press by
Chase Publishing Services Ltd, 33 Livonia Road, Sidmouth, EX10 9JB England
Typeset from disk by Stanford DTP Services, Northampton, England
Printed and bound in the European Union by
CPI Antony Rowe, Chippenham and Eastbourne

Contents

Acknowledgements

This is the first book in the IIPPE Series and offers the opportunity to appreciate all of those who have made IIPPE possible and who continue to contribute to its growth, success and influence. The book itself has in part been designed to help research students in going about their research, and I can also thank numerous students for rewarding interactions, hopefully reciprocal, over the years. Last, and more immediate, thanks to Pluto staff for launching the series with this volume, and to Anthony Winder in particular for his conscientious copy-editing leading to improvements on each and every page.

Preface

To say that capital is social is not at all the same thing as saying
that the social is capital.
(With due acknowledgement to the Mad Hatter and the March Hare.)

The story is told (it is almost certainly false) that Queen Victoria
was so taken by *Alice in Wonderland* that she requested its author,
Lewis Carroll (aka Charles Dodgson, a lecturer in mathematics at
Christ Church, Oxford), to send her a copy of his next published
work. She duly received *An Elementary Treatise on Determinants*.
Now the divide between fantasy and mathematics is not so great
that it cannot be bridged by a single individual. But social science
and social theory have become marked by a number of less easily
bridged divides – not least those of methodology, method and
subject matter. This is so much so that it is relatively rare for a
topic to find a presence across all disciplines and, even where
there are exceptions, the topics concerned tend to be treated and
understood in entirely different ways. This is hardly surprising if,
for example, we focus on the relationship between economics and
the other social sciences. The dismal science has, with some notable
exceptions where rational choice is involved, a totally different
concept of the individual than that of social theory, a consequence
in part of the equally yawning gap between the methodologies
associated with axiomatic deduction as opposed, for example, to
postmodernist deconstruction of identity. By the same token, the
ways in which society is addressed are at odds with one another,
reflecting methodological individualism on the one hand rather
than some form of systemic analysis on the other.

Nonetheless, we do all live in the same world even if we
experience and interpret it differently. Some general concepts are
almost unavoidably shared, apart from individual and society, most
notably the state and the market. And others, such as globalisation,
enjoy a prominence when we reflect what is taken to be the ethos
of a particular stage in our commonly shared history. That history
and our existence are now dominated by capitalism, however this
is itself understood as an economic and social category. In the age
of neo-liberalism, there has been a thrust to convert as much as

possible to market forms in general and to the control of capital in particular. This has reinforced, rather than introduced, a tendency to treat all, and not just commercial, resources as if they were a form of capital. Most notable has been human capital in the past. It has been complemented by environmental capital as the way in which we do, or do not, sustain the globe's ecology. 'Mental capital' is a recent addition – incorporating the idea that we should treat our own well-being as a sort of asset, sharing characteristics with the factory if not the bank account (see Chapter 2), and no doubt minds as well as banks can go toxic.

This is all a blatant example of a sort of generalised commodity fetishism in which all social relations, and not just those attached to the market, appear as, indeed, they are in part, a material relation between things that have some worth or, at least, some effect. Everything from our abilities to our states of mind becomes capital-like. In this light, it is hardly surprising that each and every social relation or interaction should become seen as a form of capital, something to be accumulated and to be deployed for advantage if not profit. And this is exactly why the notion of social capital has emerged and shot to prominence over the past 20 years (although why this should happen now, with the content and incidence that it has across the social sciences, is addressed in what follows). So, if I were to be asked to give a definition of social capital, it would be *any* aspect of the *social* that cannot be deemed to be economic but which can be deemed to be an asset. As will be seen, it can be anything from your personal acquaintances (not what but who you know) and family, through communal or associational activity, to your identity or culture and trust in police, politicians or others, and so on.

And so the social becomes capital and the capital is no longer social despite our opening (invented) quote. Let us leave the last word to Alice herself, who could well have been dreaming of social capital.

> If I had a world of my own, everything would be nonsense. Nothing would be what it is, because everything would be what it isn't. And contrary wise, what is, it wouldn't be. And what it wouldn't be, it would. You see?

For Lily

1
Introduction

This book has been many years in the writing and even more in the making. For there is a prehistory that will be more or less put aside (but see Chapter 2), ultimately leading to the publication of *Social Capital versus Social Theory* (Fine 2001a). After that, within a year or so, I vowed to go cold turkey on what was becoming an obsessive attention to social capital. The rewards of my continuing addiction had diminished considerably and might even have become negative. One event more than any other persuaded me to change my mind: the appearance of the article by Bebbington, Guggenheim, Woolcock and Olson (Bebbington et al. 2004). I had seen an earlier draft in 2002 but was, I thought, reliably informed, to my disappointment, that it was not to be published. But there it was in print after all, a remarkable testimony to the momentum behind, and role of, social capital in the World Bank and, to that extent, more widely and generally so. As detailed in Chapter 6, this account of social capital is so revealing, and yet so flawed, that I was drawn back into the study of social capital – or, perhaps I should say, 'social capital', as, in a sense, there is no such thing, other than in the minds of the scholarly careless and/or opportunistic.

It was and remains hard, at least for me, to resume the critique of social capital in a half-hearted way, not least because I have always sought to command both its position as a whole across the social sciences and how this has evolved, and continues to evolve, with its rise and fall within the World Bank particularly emblematic if not entirely representative. So, in 2004, I once again searched over the literature, not having done so for a number of years. The stockpile was intimidating, and the subsequent flow equally so. Just to catch up was a monumental task, inevitably selective and only partially completed. And so it has remained. But it did mean that my knowledge of social capital ranged far beyond the triggering mechanism derived from and around the account of the World Bank's social capitalists.

From then until now has been a cycle of beginning to draft chapters for the book, only to be interrupted by other commitments and finding a new round of literature to absorb upon resumption. To my shock, I found that ten months had passed from the beginning of January 2008 until I was able to resume what has now proved to be the final stage of this labour of Sisyphus. In the interim, of course, the literature had continued to accumulate, more in spread of subject matter than depth of analysis. This meant that I was faced with the daunting task of organising my discussion of the material, both incorporating the new into the old framework of what had been confronted before and stretching that framework to accommodate as comfortably as possible what I chose to include. This has not simply been a matter of principle but of practice since, as already indicated, the literature has been expanding faster than it can be read and absorbed, let alone be written about.

Having published so much about social capital already, I was also determined to explore new themes and motivations, and to write a new book rather than merely updating the old one. Of course, some of the themes from the old book are retained, the most important being that social capital is the degradation of, not a contribution to, social science. It is worth laying out the features of social capital that were recognisable even after a short life of little more than a decade.

First is the breadth and scope of social capital across a number of dimensions. As will become apparent, what it is ranges over all forms of individual interaction (with the partial exception of those within market and global relations and those within the state – why not who you know within the state bureaucracy and the international elite in particular?). The same applies to other non-individualistic forms of interaction or collectivity as embodied in institutions and culture, widely conceived and ranging equally extensively from the family or household through to all other levels below the international (with the exception again of the state, as before, and with the curious absence of the global as a sphere of application for social capital; but see Chapter 7). The applications of social capital have also been astonishingly diverse, with some presumption that its presence offers potential benefits to outcomes. And the spread of social capital across disciplines is also extraordinarily impressive, much like, if to a lesser extent, the presence of globalisation across the social sciences – which, interestingly, has experienced a similar timing in emergence and drive to prominence (Fine 2004a).

Second, though, this marriage between social capital and social theory has been an unfortunate one. For social capital has both reduced and distorted the contributions that are available from the rich traditions across the social sciences. In short, social capital has been parasitical, only prospering in its own degraded and degrading way through drawing upon social theory selectively and, inevitably, at its expense.

In part, third, this is because 'social capital' is itself a sort of oxymoron. It presumes that there can be a capital that is not social. It is rarely made explicit what this asocial capital is, where the boundary lies between it and social capital, and what role is played by that other capital in itself and as complement to, or constraint upon, its alter ego. Not surprisingly, despite the terminology, the relationship between social capital and capitalism is usually glossed over.

Fourth, as a result, the economy, and economic theory, tend to remain unexamined in the context of social capital. There is some loosely formulated presumption that markets cannot work at all or cannot work perfectly in the absence of social capital. This opens the potential for (more) social capital to enhance the working of the market, just as it enriches non-economic behaviour and outcomes through benevolent collectivity.

Fifth, whilst the economy only occupies a shadowy existence across the other social sciences, it offers a highly attractive analytical fix for economics itself, as a *residual* theoretical and empirical factor. Differences in economic performance had traditionally been seen as the consequence of different quantities of capital and labour. The former had been refined to incorporate various types, such as physical, financial, environmental and human capital. Social capital, for economists in their own limited departure from neo-liberalism, could be added to capture anything else that might contribute to performance, with the non-market such as social capital understood as the path-dependent response to market imperfections.

Sixth, it is not only within economics that social capital finds a natural home as a type of capital to represent a residual explanatory factor that fills out the social as opposed to the economic. Social capital has generally served so much as a residual explanatory factor for other disciplines and applications that it has frequently pushed itself forward to become a leading explanatory factor. This can only be so through setting aside what are other, arguably more powerful, determinants of economic, social and cultural life. Generalising over such an extensive literature as is offered by social capital is dangerous; but omissions (apart from the economy other than as something given but to be enhanced), despite being significant elements in social interaction, include class, the state, trade unions, and political parties, substance and organisations. For, although there is a healthy literature on social capital and political activity as such, it is remarkably removed from the substance of politics itself, whether by content or nature of activity (other than whether voting or not – but in support of what, how and with what beliefs?). Not surprisingly, social capital has appealed across the spectrum of conventional politics, from Bush to Blair, so anaesthetised and yet flexible is it in its political and uncritical content. And, by the same token, from scholarship through to rhetoric, cooperation and collectivity for mutual gain have been emphasised at the almost absolute expense of power, oppression and conflict.

Seventh, the policy perspective induced by social capital, although never put in these terms, is self-help raised to the level of the collective. However good or bad things might be, they could be better if people interacted more, trusted one another, and cooperated. Social capital offers the golden opportunity of improving the status quo without challenging it. Everything from educational outcomes through crime prevention to better psychological health can be improved if neighbours and communities would only pull together and trust and interact with one another.

Eighth, Bourdieu is acknowledged to have been an early purveyor of social capital, and he placed considerable emphasis on both its class dimensions and its contextual content. He offered a much deeper understanding of social capital than what has followed, but also a narrower definition, as he distinguished it from cultural and symbolic (and economic) capital. These differences have been lost in subsequent literature by rounding up the symbolic and the cultural into the social, whilst equally dropping the class and contextual content for universal notions of any collectivity across time, place and application. In place of Bourdieu, the rational choice or individualistic foundations of other renditions of the concept of social capital, drawing on the influence of the rational choice sociologist James Coleman, have come to the fore, although these have been disguised, since acknowledgement of them would reduce the appeal of social capital to those other than of a neo-liberal bent. And the most recent literature has begun to bring Bourdieu and context back in and to stand aloof from rational choice. Yet this renders the concept different in every application, so that transposability between case studies and analytical categories relies upon a leap of faith. In this respect, social capital is treated as if it were capital in money form, along with presumptions of fluidity between its various components and effects (something of which Bourdieu himself was guilty). This all renders the relationship between social capital and neo-liberalism to be complex and shifting; see below and later chapters.

Ninth, social capital has become so prominent so rapidly as a result of what can only be described as an intellectual malaise within academic life, although it is a moot point whether this has worsened over the concept's lifetime as a result of the pseudo-commercialisation of research activity. Precisely because of its amorphous, all-encompassing nature, social capital is an ideal example, for want of a more tempered term, of the hack academic ('hackademic'?). To put it bluntly, social capital has prospered at the expense of intellectual integrity, as publications, research grants and popular punditry have been exploited for gain, academic, personal or otherwise. Social capital plus topic X has been the route to open new avenues and close others, generally both replicating and reducing what we knew about X previously and adding to the forward momentum of social capital in scope of definition and application.

Tenth, proponents of social capital have exhibited a stunning capacity to absorb criticism, when recognising it, by continuing to move forward. Opposition is readily perceived as seeking the addition of an otherwise missing variable or method, so that the remedy is to incorporate what is otherwise absent. Where criticism is offensive to the core values of social capital, it is usually simply ignored, especially in relation to the points already elaborated. This is so much so that those contributions that do acknowledge criticism do so selectively, for the purpose of supporting their own particular contributions.

Eleventh, as should be apparent, irrespective of other criticisms, social capital has become definitionally chaotic, as it is imbued with so many different variables, approaches and applications. Again, this has frequently been acknowledged in the literature, only for another definition or approach to be adopted, compounding rather than resolving the collective conceptual chaos (the social capital of social capital!). There is a significant, if heavily outweighed, literature that is critical of social capital and, almost certainly, a body of social scientists who will have nothing to do with it because of its conceptual chaos and incoherence. Yet this aversion to social capital inhabits a parallel universe with limited dialogue with, or response from, the ranks of the social capitalists themselves.

Last, social capital has thrived in the particular intellectual context peculiar to the 1990s, in which there has been a reaction against the extremes of both neo-liberalism and postmodernism. Social capitalists have rejected the belief that markets work perfectly and have embraced the idea of getting real about how people go about their (daily) lives. This is also characteristic of social capital's counterpart, globalisation, which in many other respects is both the complement and the opposite to social capital. As already indicated though, the global is notable for its absence from the world of social capital; the latter is more about communities accepting the world as it is and bettering themselves on this basis as a form of 'participation' and 'empowerment'. Thus, and further, the 'dark side' of social capital, as in corruption and community or racist violence for example, is often acknowledged only to be brushed aside. This places social capital in a peculiar relationship to neo-liberalism, although some see it as an instrument and cloak for it.

These features of social capital form the starting point from which a further ten years of literature have been assessed, not only to track the most recent developments but also to explore new themes. Since I have been a tutor for research students for 30 years or so, it seemed appropriate to use that experience to offer advice on how (not) to do research. This is made explicit in Chapter 2, where lessons are drawn from my social capital work to address the task of how to go about writing a literature survey. One central lesson offered is to find one or more organising 'pegs' on which to hang a survey to give it analytical as opposed to descriptive content. And the chapter itself takes up the peg of the degradation of social science that is perpetrated by social capital, further deploying the metaphor of McDonaldisation.

The chapters that follow can in part be interpreted as having one or more pegs of their own, not always made explicit. Chapter 3 examines the history of social capital as a concept and, equally, the constructed history that has been imposed upon it. It shows that social capital does not have a history of any substance – and for good reason given its legion faults. Indeed, it is necessary to explain why social capital should have become so prominent, and so rapidly so, at the end of the second millennium and, yet, was so pale in presence previously. And, to the extent that social capital does have a history, it is with a content that is the opposite of the one that has been discovered or invented to support the substance of this bloated orgy of literature confined to the late twentieth century. For social capital has previously been perceived to be an economic category, not one of civil society, signifying both the aggregate capital as a whole and the systemic properties to which this is attached. In other words, social capital in history has been about the political economy of capitalism and not about civil society detached from the economy.

Despite its short history, social capital has had a rich and rapid evolution. As previously documented in my earlier book and by many others subsequently, its origins in the radical sociology of Bourdieu were discarded for the rational choice functionalism associated with James Coleman before this, in turn, was veiled by an expanding scope of definition and application and a multidisciplinary spread. Inevitably, the result was to expose the deep limitations of the concept for the tasks it was being asked to accomplish, especially by omission of many of the standard variables across social theory. As is now all too apparent, this did not lead to the rejection of social capital. On the contrary, the omissions provided the foundations for the continuing expansion of social capital by adding what had previously been missing, with limited care and attention to individual, let alone collective, coherence. The result, as documented in Chapter 4, has been what might be termed the 'bringing back in', or BBI, syndrome, itself a peg of wider potential applicability than to social capital alone. The chapter demonstrates this process for social capital in general and across particular topics, such as BBI class, gender, race and context. The ultimate irony is provided by BBI Bourdieu, or BBBI. But, whatever Bourdieu's merits and deficiencies in positing the category of social capital, BBBI restores at most a pale version of his original intent and content – other than with a few exceptions that prove the rule. This is hardly surprising since what was left out, and so is subsequently open to BBI, is the radical and critical content of social theory. And this can hardly be satisfactorily grafted on as an afterthought or qualification to a stock that is so disregarding of such considerations.

Such a state of affairs has not been without its positive side, as illustrated in Chapter 5, where the curious absence of social capital from the discipline of history is observed and explained (although the historical application of social capital by non-historians is far from rare). The resistance by historians to the unsubtle charms of social capital is explained differently as far as social history and economic history are concerned. For the former, sensitivity to context and to the major factors in historical change that social capital has tended to overlook has meant that the discipline has cold-shouldered the concept, not least in light of the previous, if light, tradition of perceiving social capital to be economic capital as a whole or to be social and economic infrastructure. In principle, though, social capital is far more attractive to economic history, especially cliometrics in its newer form of emphasising that institutions matter in light of market imperfections. But, as no more than an accident of timing, 'institutions' as the all-embracing category to capture the non-economic had already attained prominence within economic history before social capital emerged as a potential alternative residual concept to occupy the putative space between market and state (and the state itself has also been reduced to the status of institution, designed like any other to respond to path dependence, market imperfections, and so on). So, whilst social capital might have been an ideal conduit for the newer (market imperfections) economic history, it had already been eclipsed by the new institutional economics in that role.

The relationship between social capital and (the discipline of) history offers a case study of social capital within a discipline, one in which social capital has failed to establish a stronghold, not least because of its limited capacity to deal with context and the major determinants of economic and social change in any convincing fashion. This is the first of three case studies, each distinctive (and suggesting the adoption of pegs along the lines of why social capital should have different impacts across different and within specific disciplines), with the two others following in Chapters 6 and 7. The World Bank (and, to a lesser extent, development) and social capital is covered in Chapter 6. Social capital was, of course, well established at an early stage within the World Bank, and this benefited from extensive coverage in my earlier book, which teased out the Bank's own particular amalgam of scholarship, rhetoric and policy. The Bank warrants a return visit in this volume because of the extraordinary analytical acrobatics offered by its social capitalists, not least in both accepting, if after the event, the criticisms of social capital that had prevailed whilst social capital was heavily promoted by the Bank and justifying this as an honourable compromise in order to shift the Bank's economists to take the social seriously. It is argued that these stances lie somewhere across the divide between dishonesty and delusion, with unwitting self-deception as possibly the kindest inter-pretation. The chapter also offers the opportunity to treat social capital more fully as a buzzword within development, a peg that is constructed across a number of different aspects. Moreover, whatever the impact of social capital within the Bank, there is the broader impact outside to assess.

Management studies and social capital are the focus for Chapter 7. The pairing offers a different case study from history (a relative absence) and development and the World Bank (an early and heavy presence and promotion), since social capital appears on the management studies scene relatively late, and within the critical or heterodox branch of the discipline, but has more recently proliferated across the discipline's orthodoxy. For this, as for the other case studies, it is found that social capital degrades the rich mix of elements, occasionally heterodox and radical, that have informed the discipline.

Both Chapters 8 and 9 give some indication of the recent developments across social capital, with greater depth of treatment in the first of the two. Chapter 8 begins with an account of what has been an accumulating, even overwhelming, weight of literature that is critical of Robert Putnam across any number of grounds – conceptual, theoretical, empirical, as well as in his representation of the past and past thinkers. Whilst Putnam, to deploy his metaphor, is far from bowling alone, there have been many willing to ambush him in the alley. These even include economists who are shown to have incorporated social capital into their own preconceived technical framework; but, narrow though this framework might be, it does expose both definitional and empirical conundrums for the concept. And this in turn allows for a consideration of the way in which social capital has conceived the individual and trust. As before, the lack of depth and sophistication is striking.

Chapter 9 covers in passing some new (and old) topics that have fallen within the social capital compass, from disaster relief through to religion. This is all offered both as a warning of what is to come and as an invitation to resist it. There is also an account of the extraordinarily limited impact social capital has had on policy formulation as opposed to furnishing rationalisation for it, a strong theme across critical literature. And the book closes with a renewal of the appeal to engage fully with social capital through critical rejection, itself a point of departure for more constructive analysis. This is primarily an appeal for a different orientation in collective, and thereby individual, action. For, as is already apparent, whilst there has been much critical work on social capital, including some that is of the highest quality, this tends to continue to accept the concept as legitimate as long as it is suitably modified and refined. But what is possible for the individual does not prevail across the literature as a whole, which can even be strengthened in its degradation of social theory by legitimising itself through incorporation of dissent. The thrust of critical contributions taken together point to the need to reject social capital.

This is all the more urgent in light of current material and intellectual developments. Previously, for the latter, I have emphasised how social capital has been a particular contribution to, and reflection of, the dual retreat from both postmodernism and neo-liberalism. Scholars, and others, are concerned about the nature of contemporary capitalism, for which the virtual worlds of perfectly working markets and subjective interpretation are no longer appropriate. This has been brought home with extreme force in view of the current financial crisis. It has exposed the contradictions within neo-liberalism, with extensive state intervention being adopted precipitously to shore up the banking and financial systems.

Elsewhere, I have argued that financialisation – not only the proliferation of financial markets but also their increasing penetration into more and more aspects of our economic *and* social lives – lies at the heart of neo-liberalism (Fine 2007b, 2008c and 2008d). Initially, in a first phase of neo-liberalism, the state supported this financialisation through a variety of interventions designed to promote the spread of the market in general and, as a consequence, of finance in particular. More or less synonymous with the rise of social capital has been the second phase of neo-liberalism, in which the state has been intervening, both to sustain financialisation and to respond to the excesses in economic and social life that this has brought about. The response to the current crisis is a sharp illustration of this.

This has significant implications for the location of social capital in the contemporary world. In rhetoric and scholarship it is not neo-liberal, for it is not entirely anti-state, and it does not believe that markets work perfectly, although it primarily does seek remedies outside of, at most in conjunction with, both the market and the state. On the other hand, social capital, as already hinted, does offer an ideal frame for neo-liberal policy in its second phase – to improve the workings of the economy and society more generally by promoting ameliorative action within civil society – and without attention to the broader and deeper forces that both create dysfunction and constrain its correction.

This book has been a hard and, more than often than not, an unrewarding intellectual slog over many years. I hope to have passed on my stamina and commitment to the reader through the medium of good humour. Research is hard work but it can also be fun. The main title of the book is taken, with due modesty, with an eye to Marx's *Theories of Surplus Value*. His monumental assessment of the classical political economy of his time is full of insights that he gained from the material he covered, even if accompanied by sharp criticism. But there, as indicated in the subtitle of my book, the parallel begins to break down. Social capital is more interesting for what it excludes than for what it includes, and, for the latter, what it contributes to its own dissolution.

2
From Rational Choice
to McDonaldisation

2.1 INTRODUCTION

The purpose of this chapter is to offer an initial overview of some
of the general features of the social capital literature, and to draw
out the lessons that can be learned from doing so for undertaking a
literature survey on other topics. Section 2.2 suggests that the best
way to enrich a survey with some analytical depth is to organise it
around one or more themes, or 'pegs'. The particular theme chosen
in Section 2.3 for social capital is how the literature has degraded
the social theory that it has itself incorporated, reducing rather
than enhancing scholarly value through its contributions. In Section
2.4, this theme is explored in more detail by pointing to a number
of other pegs and by selective reference to the literature itself.
The concluding remarks point to the diversity of the content and
direction of social capital across disciplines and topics, something
to be addressed, if not fully, in the remainder of the book.

2.2 PEGGING A SURVEY

The best starting point for research is a literature survey. This
presumes that a topic has already been suitably identified, something
that can prove difficult. And the topic has to be appropriately
reduced to key word(s) or the like for a literature search. Mercifully,
at least in most respects, such searches can now be undertaken
electronically, with the corresponding need to identify a database.
But one problem is to find key words and databases that do not
overlook important contributions but also do not include too many
that are irrelevant or marginal. Books might be found through title
or subject search of the catalogues of major libraries.

Once in researching labour market segmentation (Fine 1998a),
I employed 'labour&segment*' as a search string; this had the
interesting result of throwing up numbers of articles on Caesarean
section. On the other hand, the search in response to a request to

give a lecture on gender and consumption, using 'gender&consu*',[1] provided a disproportionate number of contributions on alcoholism, drug addiction (especially cigarette smoking) and eating disorders. In light of my interest in food, the latter fortuitously offered an avenue of research that I had not foreseen (Fine 1995a and 1998b).

In this way, the literature search can, at an early stage, change the topic of research in unanticipated directions. Subject to numbers of items from the search, it is best to make a quick skim of titles, followed by their abstracts, which are normally, but not always, freely available electronically. From this, a choice must be made of which pieces to obtain, hopefully easily, and to read in full. An obvious starting point is one or more survey articles if available. The sooner a 'feel' is found for the literature the better – what are its main methods, content, results, controversies and dynamic. The contrast between an early and a late contribution can be revealing.

Ideally, the literature search will yield a significant but manageable number of contributions. But just one article can be sufficient if it is good (or bad) enough. Looking at the South African coal industry, I found a piece that examined technical change through measuring and explaining total factor productivity over time. Although universally used, this technique is known to be flawed for theoretical reasons. But, in addition, it depends upon a number of assumptions that are totally unreasonable, such as full employment of all factors of production, and perfect competition in input and output markets. It was possible to take these assumptions as the point of departure to display an industry that depended upon an apartheid labour market system, tied government contracts to state-owned power stations for domestic markets, and state allocation of quotas for export through state-owned transport facilities (Fine 1992b)![2]

At the opposite extreme to a single, judiciously selected contribution, is to be confronted with a mountain of literature. Such is the case with social capital. An IngentaConnect search on 'title/keywords/abstract containing "social capital"' in December 2007 offered 4,158 articles running back to 1968 – although, significantly, all but 18 of these are more recent than 1990! Here is a ready indication of the extent to which social capital is a phenomenon of at most the last 20 years;[3] its imagined history prior to then is discussed in Chapter 3. Even so, despite its late start, the weight of social capital literature is formidable. Further, in debate with me over the intellectual origins of social capital, Farr (2007, p.54) reports that '[a]n internet search records some 6 million items, among them the names of the Social Capital Foundation, Social

Capital Partners, Social Capital, Inc., and a new self-help book, *Achieving Success through Social Capital* [Baker 2000]'.[4] At a more academic level, I had previously undertaken full-scale literature searches on four occasions, 1999, 2002, and towards the ends of both 2006 and 2007. For each, I have amongst other means made use of BIDS, at www.bids.ac.uk, and I have sought to access as much of the material as possible and as seemed reasonable. But this has become increasingly taxing and difficult, with over a thousand new items for the third search, together with a hundred or more new books discovered through reference to library catalogues. And a fifth search, undertaken only a year later in view of my not being able to embark upon this book in the interim, left me 400 articles in debt, with numbers of new books at least in proportion.[5] Keeping up with the literature has proved almost impossible.[6] I have found that new literature is added faster than I can read it, let alone prepare what I am writing about it, and, inevitably, there must be a cut-off point in considering both old and new contributions. How this is done surely reflects the researcher's degree of patience (or obsession), personal idiosyncrasy and sheer pragmatism.

When literature to be surveyed is so voluminous, this makes essential what is in any case something that is desirable, taking the feel for the topic one or more steps further forward. This is to filter the literature through one or more themes. These have to be selected in dialogue with the literature itself, and so there are no golden formulas for doing this as they will be research-topic (and researcher) specific. At least, though, some useful ideas of possibly more general applicability can be teased out from other literature surveys. For a review of new growth theory for example, which itself only dates back to the mid 1980s, the literature expanded exponentially in both empirical (so-called Barro-type regressions) and theoretical content, but the contributions for the latter could be organised into how various market imperfections were utilised to yield increasing returns to scale (Fine 2000, followed by 2003b and 2006). Contributions were readily perceived to project randomly and speculatively selected *microeconomic* factors into *macroeconomic* outcomes. And, then, the Barro-type approach simply and illegiti-mately ran multiple regressions across any combination of those microeconomic factors, including those drawn from outside the boundaries of economics traditionally conceived. In the most recent literature, the appalling nature of the empirical work is now recognised, but with the added irony that this literature draws critical conclusions from the evidence, which contradict the theoretical assumptions on which that evidence is constructed – so that we need to explain why there are growth spurts and collapses, for example, when the theory is based on steady-state growth paths.[7]

Globalisation provides an even greater volume of literature than social capital. Both concepts originate from the early 1990s, with globalisation heavily in the lead initially and continuingly so, both in quantity, breadth and speed of take-off, although social capital has narrowed the gap, which remains large (see Chapter 5). A BIDS search in December 2007 offered 10,319 articles with title/keywords/abstract containing 'globali*', if only going back to 1991, with, interestingly, none listed for 1990, and only three before then in total. One way of organising and reading this literature was through its both representing and contributing to what I have termed the dual retreat from the extremes of both neo-liberalism and postmodernism (Fine 2004a most explicitly, but see also Fine 2002a and Fine and Milonakis 2009). In other words, contributions could be understood in terms of a wish to move beyond the analytical agendas of state versus market (set by neo-liberals) and of decon-struction of meaning (set by postmodernism) and to get to grips with the nature of contemporary capitalism, especially in light of the collapse of the Soviet bloc and the emergence of the 'new world order'. In addition, because of the rapid expansion of the literature as a form of academic fashion, it could be sifted through the extent to which it genuinely added new insight or simply refashioned the old, such as modernisation theory, through the prism of a new trendy term.

These two examples of globalisation and new growth theory have already offered a few themes, and there are many others, by which they might be critically assessed, such assessment itself ideally addressing both the nature of the literature in light of the themes and reflecting back upon the themes themselves. Before returning to the issue of themes, and in the context of social capital, consider the following advantages of deploying them. First, it allows the literature to be categorised and organised for the purpose of survey and, where the contributions are impossibly large, the researcher can weed out, or violently disregard, what is not wanted or not to be covered. This also helps to get through a voluminous literature more quickly and, in this respect, more efficiently. Texts can be read, even skimmed, for their relevance to themes, and notes taken accordingly, hopefully avoiding the need to revisit them at a later stage on becoming aware of a lack of appropriate earlier attention (although this cannot and should not be avoided where knowledge of, and thinking on, the literature evolves).

Second, relative to the themes, both the strengths and weaknesses of the literature can be highlighted – what it does or does not do and, possibly, what it can or cannot do. Third, it avoids the dull presentation of the literature survey as a glorified annotated bibliography of who said what or as a simple descriptive narrative of the chronology of the subject matter (each of which does, nonetheless, require at least some simple form of selection). Fourth, there is the prospect of some originality in presenting the literature in these terms, especially through implications for the themes, and the weaknesses or even absences in the literature which can be highlighted. What is particularly pleasing is if these insights can then be deployed in your own contribution in moving beyond the literature survey, thereby offering some originality both in how the literature has been presented and in addressing what it has not presented or what it has misrepresented. You say, as it were, 'the survey shows that the literature has these absences and faults; I will correct them and/or move beyond them'.

The advantages of early and judicious selection of themes are probably uncontroversial. But there are potential disadvantages that should be highlighted. Suppose, to go to the extreme, you have already made up your mind about the literature and you are convinced that your own approach is correct and appropriately exhaustive. There is then the clear danger of discarding what you cannot see through the prism of your own approach and interpreting all that you do see through that prism and through that prism alone. If you have decided that you are the enemy of functionalism (or instrumentalism or structuralism) then you are liable to read any text, especially if it refers to social functions (instruments or structures) as if it were functionalist. If you oppose the notion of Fordism, you will interpret any deviation from an idealised form of mass production as if it supported your case. It is essential to avoid reducing the literature to preconceived and rigid elements, although it is equally impossible to avoid preconceptions.[8] At least the latter should be as transparent as possible both to yourself and to your eventual readers (who will, no doubt, however consciously, impose their own preconceptions upon you in any case).

I like to dub as 'pegs' the themes used on which to hang a literature survey. The preceding discussion has opened up the issue of how to select pegs in doing research, especially if wishing both to draw upon and contribute originally to what has gone before. As already mentioned, there are no general answers and it is more a matter of the proof of the pudding being in the eating, leaving open the selection of the various ingredients that might be considered in making sure that we are at least eating the right, and a nutritious, pudding and not the dog's dinner of scraps.

With social capital – and the same is even more true for globalisation, if not for the narrower methodological and analytical terrain of new growth theory – the literature is so extensive that it is a matter not of searching out appropriate pegs but of choosing between the embarrassment of riches on offer. When I began to categorise the literature from searches according to themes, I found that I had straddled four separate sheets of paper with a dozen or more themes on each. As such, the social capital literature does offer any number of examples that might be of use in other applications. Let me begin with two, lying at the opposite ends in time of my own work on social capital.

2.3   SOCIAL CAPITAL AS McDONALDISATION[9]

My own interest in social capital arose accidentally, although it was possibly an accident waiting to happen. In the mid 1990s, I had begun to study the relationship between mainstream economics and the other social sciences. I had become convinced, on evidence that was initially casual but was soon to be cumulative, that the imperialism of economics (or the discipline's colonisation of the subject matter of other social sciences) had entered a new, aggressive, wide-ranging and yet more palatable and successful phase. Consequently, I was understandably intrigued to find that two individuals at the opposite extremes of social science, a radical sociologist, Pierre Bourdieu, and one of the most orthodox of mainstream economists, Gary Becker, were both using the term 'social capital'. Significantly, Becker was and remains the leading practitioner of an economics imperialism of an older, longer-standing kind. Becker's form of economics treats all economic *and* social phenomena as if they could be reduced to optimising individuals interacting as far as possible as if a (more or less perfect) market were present. His so-called 'economic approach' to social science has obvious affinities with rational choice, differing only in subject matter (and in the extent of its considered incorporation of non-economic literature).[10]

In this respect, social capital does offer an example of economics imperialism, which can be used as a peg, since it has served as a conduit for economics to incorporate the 'social'. I have dealt with this extensively in earlier contributions, not least as economics imperialism has itself progressed from the phase dominated by Becker (as if markets work perfectly and the non-market can be treated as if a market were present) to a new phase in which the social is seen as the response to market imperfections. But, like other examples of economics imperialism, whether by discipline or topic, the incorporation of the social through social capital has its own special features. One of these is the extent to which economics imperialism has other means of introducing the social on a generalised basis, through the new institutional economics, for example, with the result that the presence of social capital is thereby diluted; see Chapter 5 for implications for the otherwise surprising absence of social capital from economic history. But what is also special about social capital as economics imperialism is that the concept is itself colonising of social theory without the need for a push or even a contribution from economics. Indeed, social capital has flourished across the social sciences to a large extent by omitting proper consideration of the economic.

One peg for social capital, then, is to examine its presence in, and implications for, cross-disciplinary study. In my own work, from the simple question of how could the two Bs be deploying the same concept, I became embroiled in the meteoric rise of social capital across the social sciences. My investigation bordered on the obsessive as I meticulously sought out literature on social capital, ultimately culminating in an earlier book (Fine 2001a). After this, given the rapid growth and massive weight of the literature and its generally moderate quality in all respects, I tried to curb what was proving to be an intellectually unrewarding addiction to the topic. I limited myself to a casual watching brief, complemented by the occasional assault on the literature, usually prompted by specific requests to contribute. I was asked in the early 2000s, for example, to review social capital and its application to Africa as well as its then continuing adoption, if not fanatical promotion, by the World Bank (Fine 2002c and 2003c).[11]

By then, moving far beyond and away from the two Bs' conundrum, I had already adopted and consolidated as an organising peg the idea that social capital represented first and foremost individual and, especially, collective degradation of scholarship. This is also fully documented in earlier work. I would have left it there but for further stimulus and invitation to engage, and this peg, in particular, has continued to be a guiding thread in assessing subsequent literature. Put more neutrally, the issue is one of how social capital has reflected and drawn upon the strengths and weaknesses available within social theory.

Here the machinations at the World Bank around social capital have been especially revealing. First, in carrying the story of social capital forward, it is important to report that the social capitalists at the World Bank, stunningly and remarkably, responded to critics, including myself, by essentially accepting all the intellectual arguments that had been levelled against them, as if they had always been aware of them, but excusing their stance on the strategic grounds of civilising less intellectually rounded economists at the Bank (Bebbington et al. 2004; their book followed in 2006). As someone who was heavily embroiled in debating and comprehending the scholarship of the Bank and its relationship to rhetoric and policy, both for social capital and more widely,[12] I felt obliged to respond to what I perceived to be apologetics for self-confessed scholarly degradation (see Fine 2008a and Chapter 6).

But, second, I would not even have known about the publication of this shift in the stance of the Bank's social capitalists but for the request to contribute to a special issue on buzzwords in development, for which 'social capital' is a pressing candidate (Fine 2007d and Chapter 6). For, third, at more or less the same time, I was invited to address the topic of social capital as a plenary speaker at the biennial Critical Management Studies (CMS) conference. This all tipped the balance in drawing me back into undertaking a review of the literature once more, at the end of 2006 as previously indicated, both to see how social capital was progressing in management studies, and to situate this relative to the more general evolution of social capital across the social sciences (Fine 2007a and Chapter 7).

As chance would have it, one of the other two plenary speakers at the CMS conference was George Ritzer. He and I had long shared an interest in consumption, and he had achieved fame for his McDonaldisation thesis, in which the humble hamburger serves as a model for understanding modern capitalism, and not just consumption (Fine 2002a for some discussion; also Fine 2007c). As I had agonised over how to present something new to the conference, over and above the role of social capital in management studies, or how to present the same subject matter in a new and entertaining way, McDonaldisation offered an ideal solution. For my degradation peg could be translated into the plenary message that social capital is the McDonaldisation of social science; do not consume it if you value your intellectual health or you will be consumed by it. This is so for all, both as individuals and as collectives of scholars. There is, by the way, a tradition of attaching mutually contradictory metaphors to social capital – the missing link, the glue that binds society, the lubricant that moves it, the bonding, bridging, linking and (relatively rarely) bracing, and so on.[13] And you may already have realised that my pastiche places me in the role of film-maker Morgan Spurlock, famous for having suffered the ill health of relying on a diet of McDonald's. I have been on a very heavy diet of this social capital stuff, and believe you me, it makes you intellectually sick if not soon rejected.[14]

And, just to reinforce the point, with apologies to Philip Larkin's classically expressed antipathy towards children, the peg of McDonaldisation is poetically brought home by the following (first appearing in Fine 2002b, but also made available at 'The Voice of the Turtle',[15] www.voiceoftheturtle.org/show_article.php?aid=387, accessed 20 March 2009).

> They fuck you up with social cap.
> They may not mean to but they do.
> They fill you up with faults on tap
> And add some extra, just for you.
>
> But they were fucked up in their turn
> By fools in rational hats and coats,
> Who half the time were soppy-stern
> And half at one another's throats.
>
> Man hands on social cap to man.
> It deepens like a coastal shelf.
> Get out as early as you can,
> And don't have any for yourself.

2.4   THE McDONALDISATION MENU

To establish the legitimacy of the approach to social capital as McDonaldisation of social theory, it is only necessary to run the concept through the hamburger machine – but backwards in order to identify its ingredients. This is not as easy a starting point as might be imagined. For what social capital is, just as might be said of a hamburger, is not so easy to define. Apart from variation in ingredients and size from outlet to outlet, is it beef or mad cow disease, both or somewhere in between, and what about its cultural content and meaning (Fine 2007c)? For, the simple mantra from the university of life, 'it's not what you know but who you know', which is widely taken up as an initial definition of social capital, opens up a deluge of interpretations as far as what we mean by knowing and how we know, from family and neighbours to the whole of civil society, and from individual acts of reciprocity to cultural norms of trust. And, equally, applications of such knowing and known have blossomed without apparent limit, forming a corporate enterprise of many affiliates across the academic world.

As a result, social capital has developed a gargantuan appetite in terms of what it is, what it does, and how it is understood. Almost any form of personal and social interaction has the capacity to be understood as social capital. As a positive resource, it is presumed to have the capacity to facilitate almost any outcome in any walk of life, and to be liquid or fluid across them to a greater or lesser extent. And it is equally adaptable across subject matter, disciplines, methods and techniques, as far as the social sciences are concerned. In short, in principle, and to a large degree in practice, social capital can be anything you like. It has established a major presence in most of the major disciplines, especially sociology, politics, economics, and business, development, education, health and management studies, as well as within and across these as in sub-disciplines and topics such as crime, housing, the environment and migration.

So social capital is to social science as McDonald's is to gourmet food. At the largest McDonald's in the world, in Gurnee, Illinois, covering a floor space of 32,000 square feet, is to be found the spoofed 'Not Quite Perfect' (NQP) outlet (*The Onion* 2005). Here are sold at an eighth of the price the misshapen and mis-manu-factured, from one-foot long chips to grey milkshakes. 'I'll never take my children there again', said Anita, mother of three, 'They opened up the Happy Meal and there were headless figurines in there. It scared the bejesus out of them'. But, equally for sale, are the misconceived, such as the ten-gallon buckets of McRib sauce for home consumption. Even the US appetite for obesity did not stretch this far, and the product failed and so was placed at the NQP counter. Are we to believe that such monstrosities cannot occur in the academic world, whether in the use or making of ideas? Of course, history teaches us otherwise, but we do tend to have a firmer belief in the infallibility of the present. And there is also the issue and temptation of whether NQP social capital can be made better if not perfect – something to be strongly challenged in subsequent chapters.

Further, with social capital, like McDonald's, you can always find a local outlet unless you are very unlucky, even in the most unlikely of places. My favourite examples shift over time with the spread of social capital itself, as the novel becomes mundane. In the past, it was that social capital could explain the differential survival of holocaust twins. More recently it has been the impact of social capital on the incidence of dental caries in Brazil (Pattussi et al. 2006). The more social capital you have, the better are your teeth, one of the most favoured applications of social capital being to health (Fine 2008e). Not having social capital makes you sick as well as having bad teeth. Although we might view the ingredients of the hamburger with some suspicion, I am reminded more of what might be termed the Coca-Cola-isation thesis, especially its advertising campaigns over the years and, at times, its self-representation as the real thing, although what is real and what is the thing can be shifted to suit.

The most recently covered literature, though, has excelled itself in the bejesus stakes. Social capital has been tied to each of the following: whether second homes solicit keen neighbourliness or shunned newcomers (Gallent 2007); the colour of skin: the lighter it is the better you get on, especially with marriage prospects (Smith 1995 and Hunter 2002); the language you speak, with Pomerantz (2002) locating Spanish as a form of economic and social capital, since it serves as a marker for status in an increasingly bilingual United States rather than as a genuine gain of linguistic competence;[16] in preventing deforestation (DesRoches et al. 2007); accruing gains from festivals (Arcodia and Whitford 2007), as well as whether casinos are good or bad for the community (Griswold and Nichols 2006; Steffensmeier and Ulmer 2006 – presumably there will be a London Olympics and social capital study before long); and, my current leader of the pack, pets as a source of social capital (L. Wood et al. 2005 and 2007).[17] Further, as I report across the literature on the reputed benefits for health from social capital (and so for those who network with me in the campaign against social capital), it will improve mental and self-reported health, health at work, life satisfaction and well-being, and children's health; and lower risk of violence, accidents, suicide, coronary heart disease, cancer, teen pregnancy and 'risky' and pre-marital sexual activity, fatalism, being overweight, chances of drug (ab)use (apart from cannabis!) and addiction (but enhance successful withdrawal), being a depressed mother of young children, low birth weight of children, excessive alcohol consumption, and so on. Social capital is truly a wonder drug.

The point here is not so much to mock the notion that such objects of study should be taken seriously but to question whether social capital as such serves the purpose of furthering knowledge in these instances. And, in the bigger picture, when we have so many of these studies of less esoteric subject matter, what do they do to the substance of social capital itself as a concept deployed so freely across the social sciences and other disciplines? First, though, from reading across the literature, it is very easy to see how social capital has spread and grown. It started off by way of 'middle-range theory', in which social capital is connected to outcome (see Figure 2.1). The idea is that social capital, however it is defined (perhaps as having a 'good' family or living in a 'good' neighbourhood), allows you to gain a more favourable outcome: educational achievement for example. As a middle-range theory,[18] that is one that is pitched somewhere between a systemic understanding and methodological individualism (especially rational choice), it is possible to ignore wider considerations and deeper determinants and other consequences. For social capital, and possibly more generally, this has the effect of allowing such omitted factors to be introduced on a piecemeal basis (see Chapter 4), whether drawn from the macro or the micro, and also to translate middle-range concepts more or less directly into observable and measurable categories so that empirical evidence can be brought to bear.[19]

Figure 2.1

Thus, middle-range theory has the practical advantages of putting aside a deeper understanding, of the nature of the family and of educational achievement for example, and of allowing the immediate investigation of hypotheses on this basis, subject to the availability of appropriate data. It has the corresponding disadvantage of its results being entirely subject to the qualification of what has been omitted. This simple observation is a devastating indictment of social capital for numerous reasons that will emerge through the rest of the book; for, at best, middle-range theory should serve as a mode of investigation as opposed to a mode of arguing towards conclusions, asking questions rather than answering them.

For the moment, though, consider that major parts of society have been collapsed into the simplicity of Figure 2.1. Such diagrams and those that follow are to be found in various forms littered across the literature, if not always with the same transparency and rarely with the same degree of critical interpretation. Not surprisingly, each of the boxes in the diagram is bursting to break out of its narrow confines and to restore the fragmented multiplicity of causes and consequences from which it derives. In deference to presentation, I have limited the number of these to three each, as presented in Figure 2.2. But in the case of social capital, hundreds of variables have been used, ranging from whether you engage in communal weeding through to whether you trust your politicians, quite apart from the presence of pets, as previously indicated. And, as also observed, the favourable consequences of social capital have been equally legion, from holocaust (or Titanic) survival to good teeth.

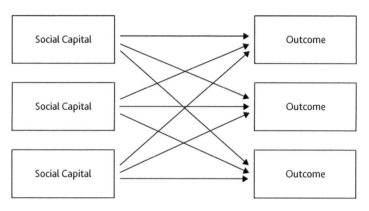

Figure 2.2

There are now multiple arrows connecting the social capital box or boxes to the outcome boxes, with the metaphor of the mess and mass of telephone wires across a telephone exchange being apt. As Keating (2001, p.217) puts it, even if in the specific context of source of 'leadership' in local regional development, there is no simple relationship between 'culture, institutions, social relations and leadership', and so there can be no presumption that this is resolved by, or with the addition of, social capital. But, to revert to our mangle-of-wires metaphor, this immediately suggests, like a conversation, that the arrows could go in either direction – is social capital cause or consequence or even simply correlate (see below)? In addition, there is the issue of how the network of wires got to be put in place, and how conversations or effects get to be triggered. This has been recognised in the literature in terms not only of what social capital is, but also how it is created and how we distinguish what it is from what it does. Thus, Letki concludes from data from 38 countries that

> confidence in political institutions and their objective quality are the strongest predictors of civic morality [i.e. social capital]. At the same time, the findings show that the recently popular claims about the importance of social capital for citizens' moral standards are largely unfounded. (2006, p.305)

Similarly, Diani (2001) finds that social movements are a source of social capital (networks) rather than vice versa, and also for Rossteutscher (2002) associations are not the source of civic-ness but its reflection. Rothstein and Stolle ask:

> What is the relation between, on the one hand, social capital in the form of norms about reciprocity and, on the other hand, the Social Democratic type of encompassing and universal welfare state? Is there something special about the types of mechanisms that are behind the abundance and maintenance of social capital in Scandinavia? (2003, p.1)

And they offer the following answer:

> It is argued that the high level of social capital in the Scandinavian countries can be explained by (a) the high degree of economic equality, (b) the low level of patronage and corruption and (c) the predominance of universal and non-discriminating welfare programmes.

But, if accepting this to be so, would it not be the case that factors (a) to (c) would themselves have more direct impact on outcomes than would social capital as an independent influence?

Such issues have been addressed by Durlauf (2002b), predominantly in technical statistical terms. For him, the problem here is, for example, that differences in outcomes for those with and without social capital may be due to the differences in the factors that have created the differences in social capital in the first place. Are the (favourable) outcomes due to the presence of social capital or to some other variable (see also Chapter 8). This is not exactly rocket science, but it has been overlooked all too frequently by the social capital literature. In addition, apart from the problem of presence and direction of causation, there is the matter of whether its effects are, indeed, positive. It is universally acknowledged, other than by those definitionally precluding this, that social capital is not necessarily a good thing, since it can be used for undesirable purposes or lead to undesirable outcomes. As such, it has variously been described as dark, perverse or negative – as with corruption, the Ku Klux Klan, mafia, racism, nepotism, etc.

One way of representing these conundrums is to recognise that, as a middle-range theory, social capital necessarily sets aside the qualifying variables, A and B, within which it is situated, as illustrated in Figure 2.3. For simplicity, the fragmentation of the social capital and outcome boxes have been erased. This is in order to highlight that outcomes are necessarily the consequence not only of the direct impact of social capital itself but also of variables A and B. A acts directly, and indirectly through B and through social capital. A variables are in some sense more fundamentally causal than both B variables and social capital that serve as parallel middle-range variables. Of course, there are also interactions within the boundaries of the bundles of variables represented by A, B and social capital (and the outcomes). More specifically, if trade unions, classes and the state are important to outcomes alongside social capital, and do themselves create or condition social capital, then their exclusion from consideration (not, as will be seen, entirely hypothetical for much of the social capital literature) will tend to bias, probably overstate, the role of social capital. The latter might just be a proxy or a conduit for more important determinants. In crude and extreme empirical terms, this would be the case if social capital and outcomes were independent of one another but each was a product of something else – a situation derived from Figure 2.3 by deleting variable B and its connecting arrow as well as the one between social capital and outcomes. Thus, Abom (2004, p.342) points to 'a complex and diverse range of social, cultural, political and economic issues that contributed to low levels of "broad-based" social capital', including violence, corruption, authoritarian state, and top-down non-participatory practices of NGOs in an urban settlement in Guatemala. This is a long list of A and B type variables. They are liable in and of themselves to have a much greater effect on outcomes than social capital itself!

From the point of view of organising a literature survey, this discussion offers the opportunity or peg of what is termed the

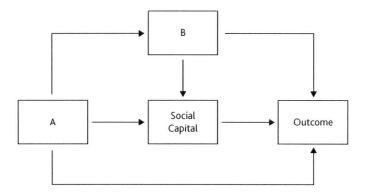

Figure 2.3

'nesting of social capital' hypotheses. Whether in theoretical or empirical terms, Figure 2.3 offers a more general theory in which those theories that involve social capital exclusively as an explanatory factor can be assessed as special cases. Thus, is it legitimate to set aside the independent and/or prior influence of A and B variables in the assessment of social capital? This is, in part, nothing more than a cautionary tale of not conflating correlation with causation and of taking full account of otherwise omitted variables and relations between them. In particular, there is the issue of how social capital is created and sustained, something that is recognised widely within the literature to have been subject to relative neglect. Inevitably, as the literature has evolved, the salience of A and B variables to outcomes has come to the fore, whether for theoretical reasons or because case studies or empirical work more generally have rendered accounts of these variables unavoidable.

But the response of the social capital literature to nesting has been somewhat unusual, both individually, and often consciously so, and collectively, if necessarily unconsciously, in terms of overall effects from individual contributions taken together. Essentially, rather than correcting for factors A and B in assessing the nature and impact of social capital, the latter has been widened in scope of definition to incorporate these factors. Rather than taking gender or ethnicity, for example, as prior or conditioning variables, these are seen themselves to be sources of social capital. In other words, the social capital box both internally fragments in terms of its constituent elements *and* expands to incorporate other elements from A and B.

It follows not only that social capital has a gargantuan appetite in terms of its scope of application, but the same is true of its definitional content. And the more elements are added to what social capital is, the more it becomes definitionally chaotic, a feature widely acknowledged within the literature. For Johnston and Percy-Smith, both using and deploring metaphor,[20]

> [s]ocial capital is the contemporary equivalent of the philosopher's stone. Just as alchemists pursued the secrets of turning base metal into gold, academics, policy makers and politicians have allegedly unpacked the mysteries of effective communities and collectivities … However, we would argue that the social capital debate lacks the level of minimal agreement about the meaning of the key operational concept to sustain meaningful debate and dialogue. Indeed, the status of social capital as a concept should more accurately be characterised as chaotic, while at times it operates as little more than a warm metaphor or a vaguely suggestive heuristic device. (2003, p.332)

Paradoxically, though, when this chaos is commented upon in the literature in a typical article, it is often followed by a new definition appropriate to the intended application, adding some new element or other, or selecting one as most appropriate. The effect is to push the chaotic momentum further forward. And there are two further immediate consequences of this definitional chaos. One is to expand social capital so that, as previously observed, it comes to incorporate any social variable. The other, as we have also already seen, is to homogenise unduly under a single concept what is an extraordinarily wide range of diverse applications. It is as though not only are all hamburgers treated as if they were the same, but everything else is considered to be hamburger-like. Not surprisingly, then, in a late and unusually reflective special issue on social capital, Knorringa and van Staveren (2007, p.6) seem to observe approvingly as editors of their collection that 'none of the contributions spends a lot of "ink" on defining social capital'.[21] And Meulemann (2008a, p.9) agonises over how to define social capital, and eventually suggests that 'social capital consists of the relations of persons, it basically is *relational capital*'.[22] But then he proceeds to see it as underpinning '*system capital*'. Further, it is recognised that social capital is both cause and consequence. And the chapters that follow in the collection often make little reference to social capital as opposed to trust, citizenship or whatever, and point to the need for other variables to be taken into account as well as the micro-, macro- and multi-level linkages involved.[23]

Further, apart from adding to the definitional chaos surrounding social capital, some attempts have been made to reimpose some categorical order rather than positing their own further chaos-inducing idiosyncratic definition. This is done through placing different types of social capital under broader definitional umbrellas. One popular form is the division into three types of social capital: relational, cognitive and structural. This is innocuous as far as it goes, presuming the divisions to be reasonably hard and fast, but it does not go very far and could be said to be characteristic of any approach to social theory. Even blander has been the attempt to re-aggregate across the hundreds of variables that have made up social capital. This has been done by reference to social capital as bridging (within groups), bonding (across groups) and linking. The latter is used variously, and at times ambiguously, to refer to links across hierarchies, power relations, and from 'lower' to 'higher' levels, as in connecting the state to civil society or local government. There tends to be some presumption that bonding capital may be bad (as it can lead to coercion), but that bridging capital is good (as it signals cooperation), as is linking capital (since the state supports or sustains such cooperation). The problem is that bonding, bridging and linking, BBL, cut across the traditional variables of social theory – such as class, gender, race and so on – and, as a result, overlook the fact that one person's bond is another person's bridge, etc., depending upon context and issue. Such tensions and conflicts within society cannot be wished away by aggregating social divisions and complexities into the otherwise neutral, bland and universal categories of BBL. Further, as Arneil (2006, pp.179–80) argues, the desire for bridging to predominate over bonding social capital runs the potential risk of homogenising across rather than respecting minority differences.

This all adds up to chaos, not only in definition of social capital, but also across its favoured analytical framework or middle-range starting point of deriving positive outcome from some element of social capital (Figure 2.1). Expanding Figure 2.1 into Figure 2.3, by way of the intermediate step of the multifarious fragmentation across the various boxes barely hinted at in Figure 2.2, involves multiplicities of arrows with differing directions and signs of causation. It becomes apparent how much (often implicit) homogenising and flawed reasoning is involved in deriving results for the impact of social capital. More specific aspects of such flawed reasoning will be taken up in later chapters. But, more generally, just as societies are divided along the lines of socio-economic and sociocultural status, so the potential to form 'social capital', however it is defined, and the potential to use it or for it to have an effect, will be highly variable, mixed and shifting according to what might be taken to be more fundamental underlying determinants – whether you are young or old, educated or not, male or female, employed or unemployed, rich or poor, rural or urban, and so on.

Of course, it is precisely the suppression of such variables, their location as conditioning rather than determining, or their incorporation into the universal notion of social capital, that imparts to the concept the property of being able to reinterpret all previous social science through its prism. Hence, social capital has been presumed to be a more general approach than that individually attached to notions such as networks, trust, linkages, and so on. Through its prism, though, these concepts and their lineages are bowdlerised. Social capital is equally at home as a residual or complementary category, putatively explaining what was previously inexplicable in its absence. Thus, for example, social inclusion might be a form of social capital, it might be explained by social capital, or it might reinforce the effects of social capital (with social exclusion as the corresponding dark side). Inevitably, though, the social capital prism filters out more light than it lets through, in drawing simplistically upon basic categories of social analysis, stripped of their rich traditions and contested meanings.

To a large extent, this homogenisation of social science is appropriately reflected and embedded in the term 'social capital' itself, since this refers to anything other than the individual (the social) that is a resource (the capital). In this respect, social capital is terminologically something of an oxymoron. If there is some capital that is social, there must be some other capital that is not social. Generally, the presumption is that what is presumably asocial capital is either personal or private or, very different, economic. Possibly, this is some terminological quibble, but it does allow the notion of social capital to gloss over a proper understanding of capital as attached to a definite historically developed form of economic and social organisation, and to a definite *economic* moment within capitalism. Both economic capital and personal capital are always socially situated. Otherwise, social capital is simply a resource, like physical or human capital, for example, and as such, paradoxically, it is weak in its understanding of itself, both as social and as capital

(Smith and Kulynych 2002a; Bankston and Zhou 2002; Roberts 2004; Pawar 2006; and Arneil 2006, for example).

Social capital might, then, be the counterpart to economic capital (asocial?), the state, or even personal capital. In what respect it is *social* and/or *capital*, and hence distinctive as such, is underexplored, or, more exactly, overgeneralised and homogenised as the social and as a resource that is deemed to be capital-like (when, in fact, what is intended is something that is not capital at all, whether within capitalism or not). Significantly, this use of social capital reflects a more general syndrome of capitalising, if you like, on any resource used for whatever purpose or effect, and dubbing it capital, to give rise to what has been termed a 'plethora of capitals' (Baron and Hannan 1994). Within economics itself, we have physical, economic, human, personal, environmental, financial, natural capital, and so on. These have been complemented by a range of other capitals, garnered from across the other social sciences, such as the symbolic, cultural, organisational, intellectual (for which there is a dedicated academic journal), religious, moral (ethical and socio-moral), (embedded) career, bootstrap, and, in one contribution alone, club capital, envisioned capital, virtual capital, working capital, and black economy capital (McGonigal et al. 2007), although my current favourite is 'mental capital'.[24] And these capitals have also been variously combined with social capital, to give rise to a plethora of social capitals – bonding, bridging, linking, bracing (new on the block), expert, innovation, intellectual, organisational, cognitive, structural and relational and, most apposite, imagined (Quinn 2005) – the social capital you have with soap operas for example and, one suspects increasingly, reality television. As Kanazawa finds, women watch more TV than men and thereby believe they have more friends:

> My contention and the supportive evidence presented here suggest that, contrary to Putnam, there is nothing shallow about the community we experience by watching TV, or so our brain thinks. Watching TV *is* our form of participating in civic groups because we do not really know that we are not participating in them. (2002, p.171)

This usefully raises the issue of whether social capital is, indeed, imaginary in our own minds let alone those of its scholarly proponents. Do we bowl alone and/or together in reality or in our dreams? And are our dreams enough to make us change our behaviour and feelings, to trust one another (or not in case of a bad dream) and act accordingly?

In this proliferation of capitals – in which the failure to address capital as such, other than as a neutral resource, tends to be pervasive – social capital stands out as an exception in one major respect. Whereas the other capitals are more and more narrow in their range of application, in search of the specificity of the resources, exactly the opposite holds for social capital. It gobbles up all the other capitals, but for the economic, and treats them as special cases of itself. But the more social capital expands the less, certainly proportionately and paradoxically, it addresses the economy – other than in economics itself (see Chapter 8).

This in part reflects another feature of social capital, the way in which its understanding of society is structured. Basically, it takes a tripartite division between economy (or market), the state and civil society as unproblematic. Its focus is within civil society, in and of itself, or in its (beneficial) interaction with the other two. There is a presumption that such is an appropriate way to undertake causal analysis as opposed to focusing initial attention on other variables such as class, gender, race, and so on as mutually determining the tripartite structure itself. Further, there is the issue of how the separate elements of the structure mutually condition one another, as already raised by Figure 2.3. Thus, Evans et al. (2006), Lowndes et al. (2006a and b) and Smith et al. (2004) all indicate that, in the context of local government/participation, social capital is always conditioned, if not dominated, by other factors such as institutional capability, vision and governance, with the state capable of promoting as well as of responding to social capital in a top-down process of engagement that runs against the grain of the bottom-up ethos of social capital. And, once again, there must be questions over whether the direct impact of the (local) state is more important than any effect it has indirectly through social capital.[25]

This all has the further consequence of endowing social capital with its McDonald's-like ubiquity through its attachment to what I have dubbed hack academia or 'hackademia'. With all social theory reinterpreted through its prism, a common feature of a typical social capital article can be its adoption of the form social capital plus X, or vice versa. Whatever I, or even somebody else, published before, I can publish again as if a new contribution (something equally characteristic of much of the globalisation literature). Of course, this may be disguised by new case study or empirical analysis, but these could equally have been done, and often have been, before social capital had ever been heard of. In addition, social capital opens access to research grants and other marks and perks of academic life.

But, despite their mutual potential for hackademia, there are two features that social capital does not have in common with globalisation which, to some extent, explains why the latter is even more prominent and extensive. For, first, despite its wide scope of definition in principle, social capital in practice has exhibited a number of no-go areas, even though these are at the core of social interaction. Generalising unduly, these include class, the state, trade unions and the substance of politics (as opposed to neutrally perceived participation, especially voting and/or trusting).There has also been a neglect of gender, race and ethnicity, with these beginning to force their way onto the agenda after complaints of neglect alongside a number of other aspects of inequality.

The reasons for these omissions are to be found in the analytical location of social capital structurally. As a middle-range concept, it seeks to occupy a space within civil society, interacting with but having its own independent effect on some aspect of society more generally. Consequently, the more obvious and standard determinants of economic and social functioning fade into the background. And with them go the standard variables of socio-economic analysis, such as power, class, conflict and hierarchy, as emphasis is placed upon the possibility and virtues of cooperation and collectivity. For the ideological and policy consequences of this, see Chapter 9.

Second, whilst the globalisation literature has stimulated extensive and continuing debate and critique across varieties of positions, much the opposite is the case for social capital. This is not to suggest that there has been little criticism. Quite the contrary, there has been much, even if only a small minority in terms of the number of contributions, and it has been devastating in many respects (see especially Chapter 8). But, again by drawing on a typical article, critical commentary, whether within or of social capital, has tended to be referenced piecemeal and in passing and as a rationale for justifying a further contribution. In other words, social capital has deployed criticism as legitimacy, a sort of repressive tolerance, and not critical engagement for analytical advance. My own treatment by the literature is significant here. References to my work, which are quite extensive, primarily fall into two types. One is to pick up a single issue of criticism as a point of departure for continuing to use social capital by way of correction. The other is to place me in the position of being extreme for rejecting social capital altogether, thereby making the alternative of accepting social capital appear reasonable, albeit with reservations and/or piecemeal qualifications and modifications. But if there are two options – to accept or reject – each is as extreme as the other, even if it's only one that is presented as extreme!

The issue ought to be settled on substance and through debate and not on whether one or other position is 'extreme' or not (consider rejection of cannibalism or racism for example). Personally, I have found lack of debate so frustrating that I began to preface the frequent seminars and so on that I have given on social capital with the explicit challenge to the audience that they indicate where I am wrong or where there is disagreement. This has rarely solicited a public response. But, in private, individuals say they agree with me, but that they are going to use social capital anyway as a means of furthering their own contributions, to which they would, nonetheless, make corrections in the light of my criticisms. And, it would be claimed, at least economists are being civilised by bringing non-economic factors into their considerations. The problem, though, is less a matter of persuading economists to be civilised by continuing their colonisation of the other social sciences and more one of constituting an alternative economics. In short, social capital has created a *cordon sanitaire* around itself through which criticism is ignored and incorporated, apparently strengthening the idea through acknowledging opposition. In place of the global, the economic, class, the state, conflict, gender, power and so on, social capital offers a bland alternative, highly conciliatory in principle and practice with more humanely presented forms of neo-liberalism, with token incorporation on narrower terms of other *buzzwords* such as empowerment and participation[26] (see Chapter 6).

2.5   CONCLUDING REMARKS

Jokes, like metaphors, should not be allowed to run and run as they become tedious and hackneyed. It is time to move on from the idea or peg of social capital as the degradation of social theory through McDonaldisation. With one irresistibly compelling example in Chapter 8 and more than a few passing references, I shall not follow this advice in the remainder of this book. For the McDonaldisation peg for appraising the literature has a number of mini-pegs, ranging from nesting to hackademia, and, as will be seen, more can be added more or less without limit. This is because whatever social capital is used to address (or to avoid) can be turned back upon social capital to expose its limitations. Nonetheless, for the moment, it is appropriate to observe that, like McDonald's within and across locations, social capital does not get everywhere both within and across disciplines and topics. In some places, it is or has been excluded altogether, whilst in others it resides, if not side-by-side, at least in parallel with other cuisines. And, where it does manage to locate itself across social theory, social capital does not have the same content and impact and, over its short life of 20 years, nor does it have the same chronology. Possibly, it is helpful to move from the metaphor of social capital as McDonaldisation to that of Disneyisation (Bryman 1999). Social capital not only homogenises and degrades, it also attaches itself to theming across numerous products and outlets within the academic world and more widely, just as the film is accompanied by the DVD, the toys and artefacts, and so on.[27]

Where and how social capital goes in practice remains an open question, given that in principle it can be more or less anything and be universally applied. To some extent, an answer to where it does not go is to be found in the story of the omitted factors from the world of social capital, those mentioned previously: the state, trade unions, the economy, conflict, power and the standard socio-economic and sociocultural categories such as class, race and gender. But, as addressed in the next chapter, the story is a little more complicated than this, and the relationship between what is or is not included in the world of social capital is not only of interest, but is also both changing and waiting to be discovered as the literature and its applications evolve.

3
The Short History of Social Capital

3.1 INTRODUCTION

It is said, with unconfirmed attribution to Winston Churchill, that history is written by the winners. Whilst this has a strong ring of truth about it, there are exceptions. In economics and development studies, for example, the history tends to be retrieved as much as written by the vanquished, as the winners have little or no interest in recalling the past, or their interpretation of it, let alone in celebrating it. The orthodoxy's own version of history could only be written by too transparent a misrepresentation of how it came to prevail (Milonakis and Fine 2009 and Fine 2007f). Sometimes the history is better for the orthodoxy if it is forgotten altogether rather than (re)written.

Such is both true and false of social capital and, to that extent, it does conform to the nostrum, suitably modified to allow for both rewriting and writing out. For the winners out of social capital certainly have offered a history in which, somewhat incredibly on the face of it, the explosive growth in use of the concept over the past two decades can apparently be traced back to its origins in earlier contributions. This can only be done, however, by *not* writing two other histories – one, as is already apparent, about how little social capital has been used in the past, and the other about how, when it *was* used, it was predominantly used in different ways than it has been recently. In particular, in the latter history, the main, if limited, use of social capital in the past was as an *economic* category (see Section 3.3). Since social capital, despite its name, has in its recent reincarnation tended to be located *apart* from the economic, its history as an economic category, other than as a benign influence, has to be overlooked in order to purvey a contemporary non-economic alternative predominantly situated within civil society. Further, the relative absence of social capital in the past reflects a continuing and pervasive commitment to rejecting the attachment of 'capital' to anything that is not an economic category and to acknowledging, in any case, that the economic is itself social – so how can social capital be a non-economic category?

Whilst this might suggest an alternative narrative for the history of social capital, it only partially explains why it should have had the (differently interpreted) rhythm and content that it does. Section 3.2 suggests an answer in terms of a number of factors. The least important from a proximate point of view, though it is structurally decisive, derives from the discipline of economics and its relations to the other social sciences. Because the social (and the historical, methodological and much else besides) had been taken out of economics by the beginning of the post-war period, this laid the basis for social capital to prosper within the other social sciences, but with a limited economic content. This could hardly have occurred to the extent that it did had a genuine interdisciplinary political economy exerted an influence within and from economics as a discipline. Nonetheless, it took time for social capital to emerge and, when it first did so, it was, uncomfortably for orthodoxy, associated with the radical sociology of Pierre Bourdieu from the early 1980s. But with the increasing influence of both neo-liberalism and a rational choice methodology, especially in US sociology and political theory, social capital abandoned Bourdieu for the rational choice perspective most closely associated with James Coleman. Ironically, for idiosyncratic reasons, this also placed crude economics imperialist, Gary Becker, in the forefront in the use of social capital. But the intellectual climate was already changing by the early 1990s, with the dual retreat from the excesses of both neo-liberalism and postmodernism. The result has been to allow social capital to emerge as a buzzword in social theory, chronologically alongside, and without intersection with, globalisation. Putnam becomes the leading proponent of social capital, and the opposite extremes of Becker and Bourdieu are discarded, as well as the rational choice overtones associated with Coleman.

The rest, as they are inclined to say, is history and will, to some extent, be charted in future chapters. We shall find that social capital seeks to compensate for its early history by bringing back in all those elements that it was necessary for it to take out, especially those associated with Bourdieu, in order to endow it with its own peculiar character. And, whilst a leopard cannot change its spots, it may be able to disguise them to deceive. As revealed in the concluding remarks, if we are to accept that social capital has a history, then it is one that might be traced back to a bearded gentleman with very different ideas of both the social and capital.

Very few have speculated on why social capital should have emerged to such prominence so rapidly. Even fewer have offered sensible answers, since to do so almost inevitably requires a critical rejection of the concept and an acknowledgement that it has little earlier history and practically none of the sort that is now so popular. As a sociology of knowledge applied to social capital, my own explanation remains sorely inadequate. But it does have the positive features of bringing together both developments within the material world and the ways in which they are, or are not, captured in the intellectual world. As argued in Chapter 1, social capital offered a timely if limited response to the second phase of neo-liberalism. But this is not simply to conform to a relative theory of knowledge, that social capital is a reflection, a tool even, of neo-liberalism. The nature of neo-liberalism itself across time and across scholarship, rhetoric, policy and (mis)representation of reality is too contradictory to allow for this. But nor is this to subscribe to an absolute theory of knowledge, in which the emergence and evolution of social capital is determined by its own disciplinary logics. As may be useful for other concepts and topics, it is important to peg social capital to both relative and absolute accounts of the sociology of knowledge.

3.2   'TWIXT BECKER AND BOURDIEU

My own personal involvement with social capital begins in the mid 1990s with its paradoxically shared use by Becker and Bourdieu. As will be seen, these are no longer central figures in the concept's evolution, with Becker enjoying at most a fleeting if significant cameo. By contrast, Bourdieu is universally acknowledged as a pioneer in the rise of social capital, before being joined, and sidelined, by rational choice sociologist James Coleman, who was then superseded by the more rounded if proselytising Robert Putnam as central figure. Currently, though, Bourdieu is experiencing something of a revival in the literature, even if predominantly at the margins and, to a large degree, in distorted form (Chapter 4). How is all of this to be explained?

Bourdieu was already deploying the term 'social capital', albeit in French, at the beginning of the 1980s (see Fine 2001a for a fuller account and Chapter 4 for a critical assessment of Bourdieu). He belonged to the tradition of high French theory. As implied in previous chapters, the dual retreat from the extremes of postmodernism and neo-liberalism was, at that time, only on the distant horizon. Bourdieu neatly if unwittingly anticipated this through combining material with cultural analysis, allowing some concession to postmodernism by examining closely the meaning of categories of analysis, as in his classic work *Distinction* (1986) – why, for example, is culture high or low in terms of its class origins and practices? But he also remained resolutely opposed to the invented myths of mainstream economics and its presumed beliefs that the world could or should be left to the market as suggested by laissez-faire ideology.[1]

In this light, there is much to commend in Bourdieu's approach to social capital. First, he sees it as one amongst a number of capitals, alongside the cultural, symbolic and economic, all but the last of which have tended to be subsumed under social capital in the subsequent literature. Second, whilst appeal to these different types of capital is generalised across a huge historical range, from the Sun King to contemporary French society, Bourdieu is adamant that each application is context-specific, for which he posits his own investigative apparatus involving habitus and field, corresponding notions notably absent from other social capital literature. Third, Bourdieu is focused upon questions of class, power, conflict and the way in which different capitals are formed and play a role in reproduction and transformation. Again, the contrast with the subsequent literature is striking.

In this way, it can be readily seen that Bourdieu's construction of social capital belongs to a method of social theory entirely at odds with that associated with the other, equally universally recognised if slightly later, pioneer of social capital, James Coleman (Fine 2001a for full account). For him, the explicit rationale for social capital is the single-minded promotion of rational choice theory. But this does itself have to be set in intellectual context. For, despite the success of rational choice as promoted by James Buchanan and his colleagues and the interpretation of politics on this basis as public choice, rational choice initially garnered significant if limited scope of application across the social sciences even in its favoured location, the United States (see Amadae 2003 for an outstanding account of the context, origins and stumbling blocks in the rise of rational choice over the post-war period). Even economists, in a Keynesian era and a general climate of greater state intervention, were less than confident in extending the model of rational economic man beyond the boundaries of microeconomics, itself complemented by a macroeconomics and other fields not initially grounded in models of individual utility maximisation (Fine and Milonakis 2009). Instead, US social science was heavily endowed with much less theoretical content than its French counterpart and, by way of compensation, depended much more upon statistical investigation and case studies.[2] For Coleman, social capital helps to explain relative performance in educational achievement according to family and neighbourhood characteristics, a far-flung approach from a Bourdieu-type treatment as a field for reproducing hierarchy and power.

But, whilst Bourdieu's approach to social capital can be seen to have anticipated intellectual developments, Coleman's remains rooted in the past, in the effort to promote rational choice across the social sciences just as the intellectual and material environment was turning against it, if not closing it off. Here what is of importance, if totally overlooked in the literature almost without exception (other than in some references to his empirically flawed accounts of the relationship between social capital as family and neighbourhood and educational attainment),[3] concerns the origins of social capital for Coleman himself. Coleman was a late participant in the social *exchange* debate that began in the 1960s and that sought to base social theory on aggregation across individual interactions, primarily basing its methodological individualism on psychological motivation. Over its short life, like rational choice, social exchange had the best chance to prosper in a neo-liberal environment. But it failed to establish itself, and the attempt exhausted the time during which neo-liberalism was both at its peak and its most extreme. Yet, just as the leading proponents of social exchange admitted defeat, for good reasons (the anatomy of society cannot be found in the anatomy of the individual), so Coleman adopted the remarkable expedients of switching from *psychological* to as-if-(rational)-*economic* motivation, and terminologically switching from social *exchange* to social *capital*. This both launched the latter and detached it from the humiliation of social exchange, to which Coleman himself never made any reference in his promotion of social capital.

In addition, newly discovered for this volume are the earlier rational choice origins for social capital in the work of James Buchanan, the Nobel Prize winner in economics for public choice theory. For him, '[t]he simple exchange of apples and oranges between two traders – this institutional model is the starting point for all I have done'.[4] Whether everything in politics, from corruption through to war, can be understood in terms of the market for fruit is a moot point but,[5] significantly, Buchanan is not dismissive of the social as such as opposed to the individual as if trading fruit, for he is wary of the loss of America's idealised tradition of liberty:

My diagnosis of American society is informed by the notion that we are living during a period of erosion of '*social capital*' that provides the basic framework for our culture, our economy, and our polity – a framework within which the 'free society' in the classically liberal ideal perhaps came closest to realization in all of history.[6] (1986, p.108)

The essay in which this appeared was traced back and, revealingly, found to have first been published by Buchanan in 1981, almost a decade before Coleman offered up social capital. And the quote continues: 'My efforts have been directed at trying to identify and to isolate the failures and breakdowns in institutions that are responsible for this erosion'.[7] In effect, putting this provocatively, especially in light of a shared and reactionary nostalgia for an idealised America of the past,[8] this makes Coleman a plagiarist of Buchanan (with Putnam to follow Coleman) – not least as Coleman and Buchanan were heavily involved together in the Public Choice Society from its origins, suggesting that it is unlikely that Coleman would not know of Buchanan's account of social capital.

So, initially at least, there were two sources for social capital, Coleman and Bourdieu, essentially running in parallel, although they did come together for a dialogue of the deaf on one remarkable occasion (Bourdieu and Coleman 1991). Some of the early US literature did reference and even deploy Bourdieu in its own empiricist way, but there can be no doubt that Coleman had triumphed as the continuing inspiration for social capital into the 1990s. As a result, like the simple hamburger's revenge on sophisticated French cuisine, social capital has tended to eschew certain classical ingredients of social theory, at least initially – those such as class, power, conflict, trade unions, the state, gender and race, and politics (other than participation in electoral democracy).

But, in this respect, Coleman's successful influence is in part pyrrhic. For, as social capital was on the point of being adopted, and as a precondition for it to be so, both neo-liberalism and rational choice were in general if not universally on the wane, at least across the social sciences. In a sense, there is in any case a tension for rational choice in its application to neo-liberalism if it is going to adopt social capital. For it is necessary both to emphasise the perfect workings of the market, not least through individual pursuit of self-interest, and also to accept the imperfect working of the market as a rationale for the positive role that can be played by the non-market presence of social capital. Idahos and Shenton (2006, p.68) perceptively point to 'the historical moment of the 1980s and 90s when, in the West, adherents of doctrines of neo-liberalism and communitarianism battened on to one another in a usually tacit but mutually buttressing fashion'.

Correspondingly, the use of social capital offers an unwitting replication of Buchanan's neo-liberalism. Mayer too (2003) recognises that social capital is treated as if it were economic but is not so. But, as such, it fits neatly into a growing reaction against both excessive statism and excessive neo-liberalism, exhibiting a discomfort with adversarial politics (which is either ignored or implicitly perceived as a lack or decline of civility) and the causes for this for which community self-help serves as a remedy. So, in complementing the market with the community, a wedge was created for social capital to be interpreted and deployed in a fashion that was less complicit with neo-liberalism. In retrospect, the results are strikingly revealed by the rare but remarkable wish of modern-day neo-liberals Meadowcroft and Pennington (2007) to rescue social capital from social democracy and restore it to its rightful place, in a world in which the sparingly minimal non-market forms of organisation within civil society will spontaneously arise as long as the state remains heavily contained and constrained.[9]

In other words, with this contribution as the exception that proves the rule, and coming 20 years after Coleman first hoisted social capital onto the neo-liberal bandwagon (and nearly 30 years after Buchanan's essay), social capital could both in principle and in practice best prosper upon entering the 1990s only in an environment in which pure forms of neo-liberalism and rational choice were rejected. As Castle (2002, p.347) almost accidentally recognises of social capital, 'some [unattributed] sociologists have resisted embracing the concept because they regard it as based on rational choice modelling widely used in economics, and they fear the imperialism of economics'. But acceptance has predominated over resistance by the simple expedient of a collective amnesia over the rational choice and neo-liberal origins of social capital, and economics imperialism has also been studiously avoided rather than confronted (see below).

This is beautifully illustrated by the fate of Becker as pioneer, even more than and, to some extent, by comparison with the fate of Bourdieu (see Chapter 4 for bringing Bourdieu back in, BBBI). For, although this involves a digression into economics and economics imperialism, it is worthy of note that Becker himself is unambiguously a rational choice social theorist from a foundation within economics. Significantly, he ran a joint seminar with James Coleman at the University of Chicago from the late 1980s. This, no doubt, introduced him to the term 'social capital'. But, both for social capital and more generally, Becker has fallen entirely out of the picture. He is an embarrassment because of his honest and fanatical commitment to the principle of utility maximisation as the single explanatory factor for all economic and social phenomena in an as-if-perfectly-working market environment. As George Akerlof (1990, p.73) quipped, in line with Samuelson's critique of Friedman's monetarism, Becker knows how to spell b-A-n-A-n-A but does not know where to stop.

Nonetheless, there are features of Becker's understanding of social capital, as opposed to his bananarama, that are shared by his supposedly more rounded fellow economists. These are that social capital should serve as a residual explanatory factor for any, usually collective, resource. As such, it can range over more or less anything in the context of a market imperfections approach to economic and non-economic phenomena, so that social comes after physical, natural, human, financial and any other type of capital that is attached to an individual. The major difference with Becker over the past two decades has been the emphasis on market *imperfections* as point of departure. These, especially asymmetric information between buyers and sellers, are used to explain why markets might not work perfectly – fail to clear, fail to be efficient, even fail to exist. As a result, the non-economic or non-market, everything from guarantee schemes for second hand cars through custom, culture, institutions and the state, are explained as the non-market response to market imperfections – as opposed to Becker's explanation of the non-market as if it were a perfectly working market, as for human capital, intra-family relations, crime, even drug addiction and cultural preferences by generation.

Over the last decade, I have emphasised how the shift amongst economists in explaining the social from Becker's as-if-perfect market to the as-if-non-market response to market imperfections has given rise to a new phase in economics imperialism.[10] Becker's is the self-confessed old style – everything is reducible to utility maximisation in a world of as-if-perfectly-working markets, whereas the new phase is one of non-market responses to as-if-imperfectly-working markets. Without going into details, the results have been to unleash a tidal wave of economics imperialism, the colonisation of the other social sciences by economics, with a whole host of 'new' fields around the borders of economics – the new institutional economics, the new development economics, the new political economy, the new economic geography, the new economic sociology, the new financial economics, the new industrial economics, the new labour economics, the new welfare economics, and so on – although these might be better termed newer (as if market *imperfection*) as opposed to new (as if market perfection).[11] In addition, these are presented to colonised disciplines in more palatable forms, since it is now accepted that markets do not work perfectly and that institutions, habits, customs, history, etc, do matter (and we can prove it in a mathematical theorem).

Not surprisingly social capital has thrived amongst economists in this environment, not least for another reason: the increasing capacity to deploy econometrics so as to incorporate variables at will into a regression to explain economic performance, such as growth or poverty alleviation. Whilst I have probably written more about economics imperialism than I have about social capital, I want to bring this back to the previous chapter's peg of McDonaldisation. In putting forward the thesis, Ritzer perceives it to be a consequence of a Weberian drive for modernist rationality, although his later work tempers this with considerations of postmodernist aspects. Such a perspective can be extrapolated from the material world to that of social theory, for the drive to modernist rationality is the epitome of economics par excellence. But it also creates a tension across the social sciences with how the 'irrational', broadly conceived, is perceived and incorporated. That tension goes to the heart of economics imperialism in particular and the relations between economics and the other social sciences. This is especially so when we note the dualism within modernism itself – between a putative science and reason, on the one hand, and art and culture as its rejection, or alter ego, on the other.

In a longer perspective, with the marginalist revolution of the 1870s, economics set itself the task of underpinning itself with the perfect (rational choice/utility maximisation) hamburger, although the old marginalists, such as Marshall, did realise that there was much more to an intellectual diet than this. In broad conceptual terms, this task was heavily symbolised by the redefinition of economics by Lionel Robbins in the early 1930s as the allocation of scarce resources between competing ends. At the time, this definition was so clearly inadequate to the nature of economics as it then was as well as to the economic problems of the day, that other branches of economics prospered, not least Keynesianism, American Institutionalism, and development economics, and were recognisably mainstream at that time at least. Nonetheless, as a discipline, economics set itself the task of establishing itself as the science of economic behaviour through attention to the technical details of utility optimisation. This became a goal in and of itself, with assumptions being made in order to attain that goal irrespective of their realism and conceptual validity from other perspectives or aims. Individuals needed to have fixed preferences over given goods, with single-minded motivation, and with similar simplistic assumptions about the nature and role of (materially and culturally fixed) resource endowments and technology. On this basis, a perfected intellectual technology and architecture was achieved soon after the Second World War, with the duality of producer and consumer theory for the individual and general equilibrium for the economy as a whole.

In order to do this, everything else was stripped out to focus on rationality. This involved intellectual compromises at the time that were often acknowledged, both within economics and between economics and the other social sciences. At most, this scientific economics offered an account of one aspect of economic behaviour, that confined to a Weberian economic order. Systemic economic properties and the impact of the non-economic upon the economic (and vice versa) were to be studied elsewhere. In short, the marginalist revolution and its aftermath witnessed the division of the social sciences into separate disciplines, with economics appropriating the study of economic rationality, together with the presumption that its scope of analysis was to be confined to individual optimisation directed towards or even within the market.

As is already at least implicit, this outcome involved the resolution of a tension across a number of dimensions – rational/irrational; market/non-market; economic/non-economic; social/asocial; historical/ahistorical – and the division of subject matter and methods across disciplines, and so on. The strains across these aspects intensified once economics had established technical supremacy by its own standards. For, crucially, whilst the corresponding economic principles, such as utility maximisation, are in principle universal and without specificity of time, place and sphere of activity, in practice in the first instance a settlement was reached in which their scope was more or less confined to (the limited concept of) the market, to supply and demand. Once the technical apparatus had been established, however, and lay, as it continues to do, at the core of economics as a discipline, the potential boundaries attached to its scope of application are unlimited. If behaviour is to be rational, it should be rational in all circumstances. At most, there is an accepted boundary between the rational and the irrational although where it lies has no fixed parameters. Hence is created the underpinnings of economics imperialism, whether in its initial as-if-perfect market phase or in its later as-if-imperfect market phase.

In short, the process of establishing rationality within economics (in the narrow technical form of utility maximisation as if a logic of choice) severely constrained the scope of subject matter, at least until a decade or so after the Second World War. But, once established, as a core part of the discipline, subject matter was open to an expanded coverage, both within economics itself and across other social sciences, with Becker as pioneer. But, by the time that social capital comes on the scene, Becker as economics imperialist is already in the process of being superseded in deference to emphasis upon a market imperfection approach, itself a more conducive housing, both for economics imperialism in general and social capital in particular.

3.3   DEPARTING NEO-LIBERALISM?

The relationship between social capital and economics will be taken up again in Chapter 8. In major part, it is indicative of the much bigger story being played out around the rise of social capital across the social sciences more generally, for which Robert Putnam is universally acknowledged as the leading figure, reputed in the 1990s to be the single most cited author across the social sciences. His initial work on Italy, suggesting that differences in social capital between north and south had persisted from the twelfth century, thus explaining differential development, had been undertaken by him for at least a decade before he first used the term itself. It only first appears in the final chapter of his book *Making Democracy Work* (1993), and seems to have been picked up casually and opportunistically as a theoretical afterthought out of acquaintance with Coleman's contribution on how social capital allows for better school performance.

But Putnam exploded into prominence, once he moved on to pastures new in the United States, with the use of social capital to emphasise the role of television and the loss of associational life in civil society as the source of the country's economic and social decline.[12] Whether for Italy or the United States, Putnam's work has been subject to what can only be described as a deluge of criticism, on methodological, theoretical and empirical grounds (see Chapter 8). Disregarding these criticisms for the moment, there are six elements of his approach that are of significance for the continuing evolution of social capital.

First, despite the nostalgia for a putative associational and civil life of the past and explicit acknowledgement of debt to Coleman, there is little or no reference to the rational choice origins of social capital, and even less to the alternative root (and route) offered by Bourdieu. This was essential in order to offer some appeal within an intellectual environment that was moving away from neo-liberalism and rational choice, and to appear progressive in relation to it, while nonetheless hardly breaking with its emphasis on the virtues of capitalism – though it was explicitly posed in these terms much more rarely than in those of liberal democracy (Blakeley 2002).

In short, Putnam's break with rational choice is definite but limited. Second, this does itself involve a minimalist scope of analytical framework. In a sense, personal history aside and reflecting origins within his Italian work, it is otherwise more or less arbitrary what variable should form the focus for promoting the social capital hypothesis. For Putnam, associational life was most favoured, although, for example, for Coleman it had been family and neighbourhood. The addition of television as a significant factor neatly combined an explanation for the failure of civic involvement as well as appealing to the values and activities of the past in reaction against the (not so) new (albeit without reference to the substance of television programming and its commercialism in light both of its corporate source of provision and customers for revenue).

Third, the minimal scope of social capital has been complemented or accommodated through its structural confinement within civil society, equally narrowly defined. This has the effect of constructing social theory on the basis of a structural division between civil society and everything else, and isolating civil society for scrutiny of its impact within itself and upon other structures, most notably the state and the economy. The results, and limitations, are evident from Figure 2.3. Quite apart from whether it is appropriate, however natural (or fetishised), to structure understanding of society in this way – an alternative, for example, being an emphasis upon class and other relations and how they are expressed through these structures – state and economy might be thought to be more important determinants of civil society than vice versa (as A and/or B variables within the diagram).[13]

Fourth, there is heavy reliance upon an empiricist methodology, US pragmatism if you like, especially in the form of finding loose or statistically grounded relations between variables – television and decline for example. This is in part a consequence of the continuing influence of the rational choice origins of Putnam's social capital, in that this empiricism takes its categories of analysis (not least social capital and civil society) as unproblematic and universal in scope across time and place. There is little or no attention to the shifting meaning of the categories of analysis other than in the problems that this poses in measuring them or describing them for quantitative or (narrow) qualitative analysis, respectively. Just as civil society is civil society, so politics is politics, religion is religion, and so on.

Fifth, as previously argued in Chapter 2, this all involves a reductionism to social capital as explanatory variable. This takes the form of homogenisation of the diverse under the social capital umbrella, and the use of social capital as residual explanatory variable where it is not posed as prime mover. In this way, the potential is created for the unlimited scope of application of social capital. As Mohan and Mohan put it:[14]

> Given these significant conceptual problems, one wonders why social capital has become so popular over the past decade … scholars are interested in it because it apparently offers the power to explain residual variance in models of several kinds of activity. (2002, p.200)

Last, and neatly reflecting the nature of the limited break with neo-liberalism, is the overwhelmingly positive associations attached to social capital. If laissez-faire involves leaving everything to the market, social capital suggests that the market does need to be complemented by a healthy civil society (as is accepted, as remarked above, by neo-liberalism). Whilst the possibility of dark, negative, tellingly perverse social capital is accepted, it is generally overlooked altogether or only acknowledged in passing as the abnormal. The self-interested, indeed atomised and selfish, individual of rational choice theory is allowed to evolve a little into a person with greater sociability and benevolence. If these can be consolidated into social capital within civil society, then market and non-market neatly complement one another in furnishing more effective outcomes. The nature of the individual constituted by social capital theory is, accordingly, remarkably thin, being deprived of the formative influences of class, gender, race, and so on (unless these themselves be seen as social capital). By the same token, the analytical structure connecting the formation of the individual to the formation of social structures and outcomes is equally shallow. For it exactly parallels the previous approach of neo-liberalism, market versus non-market, but with the difference that for neo-liberalism an almost totally negative take is implicitly adopted on the social capital that is not spontaneous, in which it is associated with corruption and nepotism at the expense of the efficacy of the market.

These matters will be taken up in Chapter 9 in the context of how social capital has informed policy debates. For the moment, it is appropriate to observe that the Putnamesque stamp on social capital was decisive in precluding from social theory those variables that were previously associated not only with civil society itself but also with the state and the economy (understood as capitalism). These include power, conflict, class, gender, race and so on. As covered in Chapter 4, this has allowed the more recent social capital literature to gather an ever greater momentum, by the simple expedient of bringing back in what was left out in the earlier literature. One effect has been to build upon Putnam by criticising him and others for these omissions and adding all and sundry to the social capital juggernaut. Another effect has been to allow social capital to absorb all criticism by adding another variable or three rather than prompting fundamental reconsideration of the underlying approach and its continuing methodology and methods.

3.4   SOCIAL CAPITAL AS PLOUGHMAN'S LUNCH

In addition, having provided the platform on which to expand the universe of social capital in the future, Putnam also allowed for a particular reflection on the historical origins of social capital, an exercise in which he is wont to engage casually himself. This is less concerned with highlighting the embarrassing rational choice origins of the term than with a preoccupation with its use prior to Coleman (and the neglected Bourdieu). An academic micro-industry has emerged tracing out who used social capital when, but, it should be emphasised, confining itself to the Putnamesque meaning of the term, as opposed to other meanings that are even more disturbing for the social capitalists than the rational choice connotations (see the next section).

The corresponding literature has stretched back to highlight the work of, and presumed precedent set by, Lyda Hanifan, in particular.[15] His focus was on rural school community centres, and he defined social capital as 'those *tangible* substances [that] count for most in the daily lives of people' (Hanifan 1916, p.130, emphasis added). But, by far the most accomplished contribution in this vein of putatively retracing the origins of social capital has been made by Farr (2004). He has brought to the fore the use of social capital by John Dewey at the beginning of the twentieth century, implicitly accusing earlier fans of Hanifan of oversight. He has also highlighted how social capital was then used differently in many respects from how it is used today. He cites, for example, a definition of social capital in a book by Mary Austin that was commissioned by the YWCA and published in 1918:[16]

> Social capital is the measure of group potentiality. It grows out of the capacity of men to combine. Ten men socially combined can do more than ten men working separately. This extra potentiality is the Social Capital of that group. But its value depends on the vitality of the spiritual organization of the group. Men are said to be spiritually organized when they are held together by some alikeness of aim of spirit. (Farr 2007, p.57)

With metaphorical emphasis on production (by men), married to spirit, Austin is shown to deplore the neglect of the potential of both social capital and, paradoxically, women by industrial managers in promotion of the US war effort. In this vein, so the search can go on for pioneers in the world of social capital and contributors would sparkle if doing better than Farr (but see below for a broader search of alternative uses).

In debate with Farr (2004 and 2007), however, I take an entirely different approach (Fine 2007e). His view is that social capital must have an intellectual history; let's discover it. Mine is that social capital does not have an intellectual history at all (beyond the last 20 years or so), although such a history can be and has been invented in light of those 20 years. In other words, the history of social capital is a fairy tale, pure invention. Significantly, for example, the librarian Forsman (2005) deploys the analogy of social capital as a conceptual Sleeping Beauty. Indeed, not only has the late-twentieth-century kiss awakened the princess, it has had the same effect on what were otherwise relatively obscure social scientists of the past, including Hanifan. Those precursors of social capital had hardly been heard of, let alone referenced, before social capital became popular. Far from signifying the source of social capital, they are themselves its ex post invention – Hospers (2006, p.723), for example, raising the profile through obituary of another social capital 'pioneer', Jane

Jacobs, 'an early, maybe the first, evolutionary urban economist and modern inventor of the concept of "social capital"'.

In setting aside social capital as a concept with historical origins of its own, three arguments are of importance. First, as already seen, the volume and influence of the literature over the past two decades have been as extraordinary as their scarcity before that. This, then, is not to suggest that there is no intellectual history or context to social capital, only that this must be used to explain its *absence* in the past, not to trace its presence from there. And this must be set against its explosive contemporary growth, explanations for which have already been offered in terms of the intellectual climate and dynamic of the last 20 years.

Second, then, why is use of social capital so minimal in the past (especially when present-day proponents tend to argue that it was in there all the time, occasionally in name but more often in principle)? In part, this is explained by the oxymoronic character of social capital. If *social* capital is distinctive, there must be some capital that is not social. The vast majority of social theory, however, especially when we delve further into the past, tends to see (economic) capital in its social and historical context, as attached to capitalism. So there will be an aversion to adopting a term that at least implicitly regards the economic as constituted by a capital that is *not* social. By the same token, there will be an aversion to attaching the notion of social *capital* to something that is non-economic, especially once the economic is associated with capitalism and its market/non-market distinctions. The exception to this has been mainstream economics, but this has traditionally interpreted capital as being derived from a physicalist interpretation, often absenting social relations altogether in light of its methodological individualism.

Third, as is evident from the 'search and find' intellectual history of social capital (see the next paragraph), this conundrum has not entirely deterred its use in the past. Nonetheless, as Farr has accepted in his debates with me, those uses that do not conform to the present perspective of social capitalists have simply been overlooked. If we only look for an invented ploughman's lunch of cheese, pickle and bread, that is what we will be liable to find. Yet there have been prominent and recent uses of the term 'social capital' that have been totally overlooked in its history and continuing use. This is especially true, for example, of O'Connor's (1973) *Fiscal Crisis of the State*, once a standard contribution to the political economy of the welfare state, in which social capital essentially serves to represent state expenditures for social reproduction and, as such, is both an economic *and* a social category, presumed functional for both capital accumulation and working-class acquiescence.

But, in addition, whilst researching the place of social capital within the discipline of history at the end of 2006 (see Chapter 5), I made a JSTOR search on 'social capital' at www.jstor.org. This has the advantage over the BIDS searches undertaken previously (see previous chapter) of allowing the user to specify history journals alone, the object of the exercise. It has the disadvantage of restricted availability: journals are subject to a variable moving wall of a few years, access being denied to those from more recent years; the most recent history journal reference on social capital was from 2004. The JSTOR search, though, is more comprehensive, covering the presence of the term anywhere in the text of the journals, and not just in key words, for example.

The JSTOR search through the social capital literature brings to light for the first time, if not surprisingly, other more refined, interesting and significant marriages of the social with capital, and ones that are appropriately teased out by historians. There has been a missing history of the history of social capital. For historians, and others, have been concerned with the social as *economic* capital, not as its antithesis – not least because differing social forms of economic capital are attached to what are often major processes of historical change. Leaving aside references to social capital in which 'capital' is used in the sense of 'capital city', the usage that is most common and least remarkable (other than in being overlooked in intellectual histories) is in the sense of economic infrastructure, especially but not exclusively transport. Such social capital is reasonably deemed in historical studies to be a key element in economic development. And it is but a short step from social capital as physical or economic infrastructure to its more general position as social and economic infrastructure, incorporating education for example.

Strikingly, then, Dubé et al. (1957, pp.1–2) suggest, in examining Canada's economic prospects, that '[s]ocial capital is taken to include schools and universities, churches and related buildings, hospitals, roads and streets, airports, sewer and water systems, and other buildings and installations appertaining to public institutions and departments of government', with some agonising over arbitrary boundaries in constructing statistical series and the presence or not of a direct or indirect profit motive (social capital as social or business services). But they ultimately settle on a definition that is essentially the opposite of its current location within civil society: 'assets for which society as a whole, through the medium of *governments and other public institutions*, desires to assume a direct and continuing responsibility' (p.3, emphasis added). Inevitably, then, these considerations attach social capital to the role of the state, public expenditure and nationalised industries – the opposite of its use today.[17] Indeed, McDougall (1966) sees social capital as state capital; Zobler (1962) sees it as being any economic capital other than physical capital; Simon (1983) argues that social capital in the form of roads is a major factor in reducing malnutrition; and Nast (2000) sees social capital as infrastructure, as the means of combating racial disadvantage by rectifying unequal provision.

On a different tack, social capital, as is entirely reasonable, has appeared in the history literature as the total or aggregate of *economic* capital. But, in general, such usage has been far from mundane because it has been endowed with an analytical content that goes far beyond adding up over individual capitals, and this is so in a variety of ways. In general, there is the presumption that the whole is more than or at least different from the sum of the individual parts. To a large extent, stepping outside the social capital literature, historical or otherwise, this is a matter of economic theory or political economy, one with a systemic or holistic bent. It concerns the workings of the economy as a whole, and the place of the social capital, or capital as a whole, within those workings. This is most obvious in the case of Marxist political economy, and of Marx himself, in addressing the laws of motion of capitalism, such as the tendency of the rate of profit to be equalised and to fall (see Fine and Saad-Filho 2004 for an overview).[18] More generally, it is indicative of social capital in this sense that it has properties that are different from, or independent of, the individual components out of which it is constituted. By the same token, social capital once considered in aggregate, systemically, can be broken down again into its separate components in ways that differ from how it was made up out of individual capitals. Thus, themes that have occurred across the history literature with explicit reference to social capital include its national and international distribution, ownership and control, its monopolisation, and its impact upon the prospects for inducing productivity increase through spillovers, diffusion or whatever. These and other themes around the total, or social, capital are so well worn as to be obvious ports of call for occasional reference to them in the past as social capital.[19]

Another strand of the history literature lies somewhere askew of the infrastructure and total capital approaches. For the idea of social capital can be attached to the claims of society and not just to the individuals who own it. For all forms of revolutionary socialism, this is an incentive to highlight the exploitation of those who work by those who do not, merely by virtue of (collective) ownership (or not) of a portion of the social capital. As quoted by Kelso from the French cooperative labour movement of the 1870s:

> The social capital or the instruments of production, which is the same thing, should not be appropriated either by individuals or groups of individuals; but it should, by virtue of the principles of solidarity so resolutely asserted nowadays, be the *impersonal, indivisible, and inalienable property of the masses of workers*, considered either by trades, or by department, city, canton, or commune. (1936, p.179)

Such considerations, in the context of solidarity over risk of injury in South Wales coalmining, lead Bloor explicitly to reject social capital:

> Resemblance to theorists' social capital and policy-makers' empowering partnerships is only a superficial one, that the improvements in pit safety stemmed from a collective impulse that owed more to class consciousness than to civic engagement, and that miners sought to improve safety in self-conscious opposition to owners and managers rather than in partnership. (2002, p.92)

Thus,

> the Fed and the South Wales miners were not engaging in civic effort, rather they were engaging in a process of transforma-tive conscientization ... Only if the coalowners and managers [and government officials] are excluded from South Wales civic society can the collective health behaviour of the miners be linked positively with contemporary analyses of social capital.

Or, as Smith and Kulynych (2002a, p.169) put it more generally, 'for Putnam to conceptualize ... [working-class] solidarity as a form of social capital makes a mockery of ... aspirations that working-class solidarity can help birth a new world not plagued by capitalist economic, political and social relations'.[20]

And, at the opposite extreme politically to critique of social capital as capitalism is the critique of the latter's destructive implications for the ancient regime. As described by Wilson of early-nineteenth-century Action Française:

> The Jew was here the ideal symbol of the evils of urban capitalism and of its disruptive mutability ... However, if certain aspects of capitalist society were repudiated by the Action Française, notably any features that threatened to alter the social hierarchy, capitalism, as such was staunchly defended ... on the contention that man was not an individual but an heir, the inheritor of a social capital. (1976, p.146)

Similar sentiments, but in favour of a reformed capitalism, are to be found in Catterall's (1993) study of the interwar labour movement in the United Kingdom, especially once married to nonconformist socialism, and its corresponding use of social capital:

> This objective, of a better society in which all God's children will be able to live fulfilled lives without the blights of poverty, unemployment or poor housing and education, provided a moral vision of the purpose of socialism. The emphasis was thus on the better distribution of social capital. (p.683)

Once attached to the capital of society, social capital for the labour movement, and especially for nonconformist socialists, took on responsibilities of its own as well as requiring responsibility of individuals. Social capital must be put to the public and individual good through moderating the excesses of private ownership, even to the point of abolishing it.

Of course, milder stances can be adopted, as reported in Elwitt's study of education and the social question in late-nineteenth-century France. Elwitt quotes a commentator on Comte:

> The spiritual power, supported by a powerful public opinion, would then excommunicate the squanderer of social capital. Corporations will boycott him. These sanctions constitute sufficient force to prevent the industrial and financial patriciate from becoming a parasitic, corrupting, and tyrannical plutocracy. (1982, p.59)

This is an appeal to social capital to show its human face. As Elwitt suggests: 'the summons to the rich held the hope that they would appear with generous purses'. The good news/bad news nature of social capital is more pervasive and less overt for Smith in his account of the Tonypandy community in 1910:

> Effluence poured into the river from works and houses, so that in the summer the high, rich smell of decayed matter and slaughtered meat was pungent indeed. Nevertheless the prevailing grimness of the environment was countered, in turn, by the very social capital which had brought it into forced being. Here a whirligig of sounds, smells and sights caught up a population barely a generation (and often not that) away from the land. Packaged foods and ready-made goods were consumer luxuries that made shops seductive enticers to debt as well as welcome centres of social intercourse. (1980, p.172)

Thus a truly social and antisocial capital!

But when it comes to those who still retain their attachment to the land, and traditional forms of ownership, social capital takes on a meaning that is incompatible with capitalist ownership, social or otherwise. For, as Fischbach observes:

> In colonial settings such as India, this sometimes came into conflict with local 'units of thought' about land usage that understood land as social capital and not merely a tool for rational exploitation. The British honed their colonial land polices in regions such as India, Australia, Fiji, British Honduras, Egypt – and, in the case of Transjordan, neighbouring Palestine. (2001, p.536)

Thus, land as social capital is economic by departing from the principles of private ownership and use (see also Logan and Mengisteab 1993 for Africa).

Exactly the opposite is primarily the case in the most obvious collective and hence social form of ownership of capital, that attached to finance. As Bryer perceptively reveals in his study of the emergence of limited liability in the United Kingdom in the 1850s, this is not primarily a matter of exploitation, squander, effluent, access to land or whirligig, nor even of naked self-interest as was recognised by those in pursuit of, and opposed to, these. For:

> As William Entwhistle, a banker representing the Manchester Commercial Association, and strident opponent of change, neatly put it, the choice on offer was between whether 'we deal, and ought to deal, with men as individuals and not with an

abstraction called capital, which we are thus called upon to recognise as possessing a separate and independent existence' ... this distinction between a world fit for *individual* capitalists and a world fit for *social* capital, was the axis on which the debate turned, a debate over, and choice between, different theories of political economy. (1997, p.44)

In short, limited liability needed acceptance of social capital both in practice and in principle and, for Bryer, this is itself best expressed by Marx, for whom:

> With unlimited liability capital could not free itself from the idiosyncrasies of its owner and conform to the law of social capital, to be employed to earn the risk-adjusted general rate of profit. From the point of view of social capital, an 'equal return for equal capital' was of a higher moral order than the responsibility of individual capitalists for their debts. (p.49)

Thus, with limited liability, we have social capital without risk of loss of other assets contingent upon collective performance, something anticipated in the *commenda* of mediaeval Mediterranean trade, although Udovitch (1962, p.198) sees this as a reason for asserting that 'in the *commenda* there is no social capital formed' even though profits and risks are shared by investors and their agents.

Yet it is the stock exchange that is social capital par excellence. You share simply by putting up money to buy. Barsky and DeLong (1990, p.268) view it 'as a social capital allocation mechanism'. This is hardly controversial although, from Keynes and after if not before, there have been different views than theirs over its efficacy in anticipating and generating the swings of the twentieth century in response to bull and bear markets. Does social capital in this form generate sufficient investment, allocate it efficiently, and temper rather than generate economic crises? Posing such questions, let alone answering them, is not to be found in the modern social capital literature despite the money-like properties of social capital in some respects, and its application to the recently highly prominent world of microfinance and Grameen banking (Chapter 4). Indeed, I do not know of even a single study of social capital, in this sense, that critically engages with that legendary network of associates known as yuppies, who drive the financial system or at least its inflated rewards.[21]

3.5   CONCLUDING REMARKS

One of the most remarkable examples of the McDonaldisation of social theory through social capital comes from my own experience. At the end of the 1990s, I had done my best to access everything written on social capital in preparing my book. I came across the World Bank website on social capital (see Fine 2001a, Chapter 9, and Chapter 6 of the present volume for a fuller account) and found it had its own annotated bibliography of hundreds of items compiled, interestingly, at the University of Michigan under the leadership of Professors Lindon Robison (Department of Agricultural Economics) and Marcelo Siles (Institute for Public Policy and Social Research). They are, to put it mildly, at the extreme end of rational choice (economics) and economics imperialism. They had done the work under a $27,000 contract from the World Bank. To my dismay, I soon realised that they had included a majority of entries that I had failed to acknowledge and, even more astonishing, these appeared in many cases to have preceded what I had taken to be the emergence of social capital over the previous decade. To my continuing amazement, it turned out that E.P. Thompson and Barrington Moore had been social capitalists. All was explained when at last I came across an abstract that confessed that the author being abstracted had not himself used the term but he could be interpreted as if he had! Everything could be, nay had to be, forced through the social capital mincer in view of its otherwise unfortunate absence from the literature.

Social science has long recognised the mutual interaction of, and tensions between, economic and social relations without ever having felt the need to collapse them into the notion of social capital. For the record, remarkably close to the earlier quote from Austin is an even earlier indication from Marx that he anticipated it all, if with a rather different audience in mind than the YWCA. It is to be found in the *German Ideology* of 1845/6:

> It follows ... that a certain mode of production, or industrial stage, is always combined with a certain mode of co-operation, or social stage, and this mode of cooperation is itself a productive force.[22]

Yet social capital is at best the second most prominent concept emerging to rapid prominence in the 1990s. It is heavily trumped by 'globalisation', which, nonetheless, shares many of the characteristics hypothesised above, not least that its substantive concerns if not its terminology have long been recognised by social science. Equally, though, there are some aspects that distinguish globalisation from social capital and which, in addition, explain why the two have extremely rarely been utilised in tandem. It has addressed the economy (with finance and, to a lesser degree, culture as key metaphors), the state (and whether its powers wither away or not), and issues of power, conflict and the systemic. To do so, it has broken with postmodernism, neo-liberalism and economics imperialism in ways that go far beyond the tame search for collective self-help that is attached to social capital. If the latter has a conceptual history, it can only be invented, for it begins with the last decade of the twentieth century, reflecting peculiar material and intellectual circumstances. Whether social capital has a conceptual future remains to be seen, but it is hardly a welcome prospect other than to social capitalists themselves.

4
The BBI Syndrome

4.1 INTRODUCTION

As already revealed in earlier chapters, with the capacity to range over social theory, what constitutes social capital has expanded without limit alongside its preferred as well as its marginal domains of application. The *manner* in which this has happened has been to incorporate within the definition of social capital any variables that might otherwise be thought either to condition it or to be its underlying source. This creates a rolling momentum that even the metaphor of snowball, and certainly not that of a rolling stone, fails to capture, as each of these only moves in one direction at a time, and social capital gathers moss and all other scattered debris into its accommodating embrace. The result has been to render social capital definitionally chaotic, degrading the concepts that it incorporates – not least because of the conflation of cause and consequence. This glosses over the capacity for social capital to be both positive and negative, universalising across different situations. And, as revealed in Chapter 9, social capital fails to deliver on its exaggerated promises with regard to policy relevance, apart from offering a highly prominent rhetoric along the lines of creating and/or using more (positive) social capital to smooth rather than to determine, let alone enhance, the policy process.

But it is not only the scattered debris of social theory that has been incorporated by social capital. As a result of its ultimate origins in civil society and the hidden, even discarded, figure of the (rational) individual, it initially necessarily set aside the major and traditional variables of social theory. Whether by personal disposition, changing intellectual climate (against neo-liberalism), partial response to criticism, or the sheer unavoidable weight of presence in specific case study, major variables could not be set aside fully and indefinitely. In other words, there has also been a strong and irresistible *motivation* for expanding the definitional scope of social capital to correct for the absence of the decisive and, let's be honest, the obvious. Given the broad and broadening definitions of social capital, the inclusion within its scope of the all-embracing relational – distinctions by class, gender and race, for example – cannot be overlooked. As a result, their glaring absence in defining social capital in the first instance becomes apparent. Yet there is a simple remedy. Far from starting over with these variables to the fore, the solution is to bring back in what has necessarily been left out in order to get social capital going in the first place. This has now become commonplace within the literature across a wide range of variables, so that it warrants an acronym, BBI, 'bringing back in'. Section 4.2 discusses some general aspects of BBI by social capital, although specific instances are unavoidable.

In Section 4.3, the process of BBI gender is focused upon, a previously omitted factor that has possibly reappeared more strongly than most others. This is then followed by consideration of a couple of other variables that have been reintroduced, race and community. Across each of these, as also with gender, the presence tends to remain limited, often unconscious or unquestioning in terms of its wider implications and, not surprisingly, the manner of reintroduction can be both token and generally degrading of the rich literature and understanding that had previously been forged. This follows from the attempt to fit the variables into social capital, thereby offering a degrading by the degraded. Social capital tends to detract from rather than to add to whatever it incorporates. This is particularly brought home by the main focus of Section 4.4, the BBI of 'context'. Here, it is shown that the literature does acknowledge that the universal claims of social capital are, indeed, shallow since it has different effects in different circumstances. The consequence, as already mentioned above and addressed in Chapter 9, is to preclude policy implications – it all depends upon everything else – but the response of social capital as such is simply to add context as a variable, thereby degrading the meaning of context itself to the presence or not of other variables.

This is illustrative of the wonderfully flexible response of social capital to any criticism. In case of omitted variables, no problem, add them. It is like punching a pillow, or a cross between a pillow and a flabby balloon, since there is some, but little, reshaping of the literature as it evolves. Nor is it without irony. For the reintroduction of context breathes memories of bringing Bourdieu back in (BBBI). As demonstrated in the concluding remarks, this is a Bourdieu who is degraded too, with limited attention being paid to the analytical richness deployed in his (partially flawed) understanding of the contextual reproduction of social stratification.

4.2   SOCIAL CAPITAL AS BLACK HOLE

The previous chapters have brushed a broad picture, with the occasional detail, of the nature and dynamic of social capital. In brief, it has become a surrogate for social relations/interaction and, as such, has evolved a gargantuan scope of application, become chaotic in definition and theory, and has degraded the social theory with which it comes into contact and absorbs. Its diversity of scope and content reflects its serving as a universal category of analysis, necessarily homogenising over diversity and extinguishing complexity across time, place and circumstance. Further, in practice, social capital has incorporated a core content that has shifted away from Bourdieu through Coleman to Putnam, at the expense of marginalising more radical, even some conventional, perspectives.

These features of social capital have not gone unnoticed in the literature. Indeed, they have allowed it to flourish, as a typical response has been to focus on one or more of the aspects of social capital or to add one or more of those that have been omitted. The latter is almost inevitable in any considered account, especially case studies, where specificities involve either qualifying the role of social capital in light of conditioning variables or redefining it to incorporate them. The result is the BBI of variables that have previously been disregarded, despite what has previously been their prominence within social theory. It involves the paradox that attempts to address the deficiencies of social capital have the effect of worsening the chaotic definitional conundrums, and so on.

At the grand level, this situation is in part graphically summarised by Montgomery (2000, p.228), for whom 'social capital remains a black hole in the astronomy of social science'. But, at least as a starting point, it should be added that 'civil society [is] the sea in which social capital swims' (Heffron 2000, p.483). And, as observed by Edwards and Foley (2001), this is a big ocean which conceals at least three monsters – socialisation, public or quasi-public functions, and representation and contestation other than through the state. Accordingly, Inkeles astutely comments that,

> [c]oming on the intellectual scene only after material capital and human capital had staked their claims, social capital is a residual category. It gets what is left over. But the situation is not that bad, because there is a great deal left over. (2000, p.246)

This places demands upon social capital to address, to BBI, the big stuff. Thus, Radcliffe (2004) argues that social capital is dead unless it brings back in the appropriate elements with which to address the geography of development, civil society and inequality. Mohan and Mohan (2002) suggest that a geography of social capital would need to filter the discipline's concerns – with demography, location, uneven development, institutions, context, process, and so on – through the concept. Johnston and Percy-Smith (2003, p.332) seek to resolve the chaos and confusion that surrounds social capital by closing with the suggestion that there be 'a re-engagement with historical context, structural considerations, path dependency and the role of the state at the local and national level'. Keating (2001, p.217) points to the need to untangle the relationships between 'culture, institutions, social relations and leadership' in addressing local regional development, and so the same would apply to social capital. And Chandhoke (2001), starting from the dark side of social capital, suggests that both civil society and social capital are sites of struggle over the democratic nature of the state, not just a complement or substitute for it. Accordingly, specific attention needs to be paid in depth to gender, class, race, and so on.

And dynamics means BBI social processes, the mechanisms by which social capital is attached to outcomes (Keele 2005). Interestingly, such an imperative has been raised in contributions that are individualistic in outlook, precisely because attention is focused on how the individual is translated into, or reproduces, the social. Thus, for Rothstein and Stolle,[1] political institutions and embeddedness are essential for addressing the creation and diversity of social capital. Indeed,

> [g]enerally, the struggle to distinguish the 'good, the bad and the ugly' in the world of social interactions underlines the lack of theoretical parameters that define a micro-theory of social capital. In sum, so far we know that the use of membership in voluntary associations as a *measurement* of social capital should be handled with caution [in explaining why one interaction should lead to another]; and that its use as a *producer* of social capital is misplaced. (2002, p.6)

However, 'we argue for a methodological individualism which emphasizes that it is necessary to account for the motives, intentions and beliefs that makes the individuals act in a certain way'. It follows that 'institutional explanations must be combined with an explanation of the *social mechanisms* that induce individuals to act in accordance with the demands of the institutions and therewith reproduce them' (p.14).[2] The issue of the how of social capital is also addressed by Torsvik (2000, p.453) through game theory; he observes that 'the machinery of social capital resembles a black box'. He draws attention to two different mechanisms that might deliver the goods – the 'trust' that derives, for example, from repeated prisoner dilemma games with punishment for opportunism, and pro-social moral principles that may or may not be induced from self-interested behaviour.[3]

But this is just one amongst many ways of explaining individual and social action. Stone (2001) argues that social capital as trust does not really move beyond the micro-level to get to grips with civic capacity, for which what is required is initiative and innovation in new, difficult and conflictual circumstances rather than in mundane repetitive daily life. In addressing the environment, Pretty and Ward (2001) extend social capital to range over trust, reciprocity, exchange, common rules, norms, sanctions, connectedness, networks and groups, the latter making up the local, internal, external, vertical and horizontal – with three phases of development from 'reactive-dependence' through 'realization-independence' to 'awareness-independence'. Myant and Smith (2006, p.168) point to the limitations of social capital as an approach to regional development, especially in transition economies, unless it addresses 'the importance of actors playing active roles, initiating ideas, reaching compromises and forming coalitions that enabled them to exploit complementary assets'. Krishna (2002b), in a study of participation in 69 village communities in India, stresses the need to disaggregate into glue and 'gear',[4] structure (such as caste) and action respectively, with the need for a capable agency for the latter, in part dependent upon personal attributes. In an entirely different context, Murphy echoes Krishna in attaching social capital to the presence of an agency to deploy it:

> a firm's capacity for innovation is related not only to the quality of the social structures available to it ... but that innovation is also driven by the social capabilities or competences of the agents managing change within the enterprise. (2002, p.614)

So it is recognised that, 'it is imperative that we more closely examine and better elucidate the cognitive processes that enable individuals to trust outside narrow groups' (p.615). And in the context of violence, Goodhand et al. conclude of social capital that

> the concept has value in providing a unifying interdisciplinary discourse, which may counterbalance the overemphasis ... on the economic functions of violence at the expense of social analysis. However, the critical factor is the interaction between social, economic and political processes, rather than notions of social capital divorced from the wider context. Rather than focusing on engineering social capital, external agencies need to focus on understanding better the preconditions for social capital formation ... This requires as a starting point a rigorous analysis of political and economic processes. (2000, p.405)

As is apparent, social capital is either being forced or is flowing naturally onto the terrain of individual *and* social action. For Thompson (2003, p.7), approaching social capital through networks involves 'conduct', itself comprised of 'attributes, rules, conventions, habits, routines, standards, and "qualities" of networks'. Inevitably, social capital is subject to social construction (embedded within but not determined by its milieu); assemblages of diverse components; discourse as formative of but not determining linguistic practices; relations; self-reflecting practices, and so on. Significantly, Tuan et al. (2005), in investigating social capital as structural (networks) and cognitive (beliefs), seeks to validate the concept through asking interviewees how they themselves respond to the notion. If it is in, and of, use would not agents themselves be conscious of it? Such self-referential validation of social capital is extremely rare, despite, or possibly because of, doubts about the transferability of its diverse substance between diverse contexts. Precisely because the different elements in the social capital portfolio have different effects and in different ways, agents themselves are not liable to see them as common elements of the same thing.

There is, for example, a distinction to be made between emotional and instrumental supports and connections. Schmid (2002), following Sen, sees a norm of behaviour as being based on commitment and/or sympathy as distinct from self-interest. Consequently, both emotions and motives become a form of capital. This has implications for (national) trust surveys, since responses may reflect feelings as opposed to assessments. Whilst each may or may not affect action, they will do so in different ways, also in part dependent upon the radius or scope of trust. In case of the return of a wallet left in a taxi, for example, this may not reflect honesty but levels of confidence in whether the police will pass it on if it is handed in.

So from the elements of grand theory down to the motives and emotions of individuals, there is no apparent limit to what has been, or may be, brought back in by social capital. Here are some more examples, with key words in bold, chosen for being representative of the literature and the process of BBI. Cattell (2001) finds social capital alongside **social exclusion** useful in explaining well-being and health, not least for a tower block resident who had been thrown out of home at the age of eleven.[5] This is because **deprivation** can serve both as a source of despair and of motivation for the action and empathy that underpins social capital. La Ferrara (2002) puts forward a model of group membership, including potential for excludability, in which benefits from group membership increase with level of wealth and, testing it against rural Tanzanian data, finds that greater **inequality** means less social capital in the form of group membership.[6] Brinton (2000) distinguishes personal and institutional social capital, the latter provided by Japanese schools that can serve as a conduit for screening entry into the labour market, in part as a form of **social control**.

Schafft and Brown (2003, p.331) tartly observe that 'despite the occasional protestations from theorists that social capital theory *can* meaningfully account for **power** ... in practice this is seldom, if ever, the case'. Similarly, Bowles and Gintis (2002, p. F419) suggest that social capital is popular with those on the right for correcting market imperfections and with those on the left for accepting that the market is not enough. They want something more than self-interested behaviour, especially **reciprocity**, but also **shame**, over and above punishment, and **honour**. They prefer 'community governance' as a term in place of 'social capital'. This is primarily because of the problems of making explicit contracts, even where **conflicts of interest** are limited, but these are worse the greater is the **inequality** and **privilege** that also serve to undermine the possibility of community governance. Drawing on a 1998 survey of 39,211 visitors to National Geographic website, Wellman et al. (2001) show that the Internet has an ambiguous effect on social capital, depending upon 'community commitment' and whether it is connecting or **alienating** (see Chapter 9 for further discussion of the Internet).

And all of this, and more, can be wrapped up in the appeal to **culture**. For Kliksberg, seeking to mobilise both for **development** and **poverty** alleviation, sees culture as being a component of social capital: 'Culture extends across all the dimensions of the social capital of a society, underlying the basic components of social capital such as mutual confidence, responsible civic behaviour, and degree of associativeness' (1999, p.88).

In Kliksberg's first case study, however, association, mutual confidence and civic behaviour arise as follows:

> In 1971, several hundred poor people invaded some publicly-owned land on the outskirts of Lima. They were joined by thousands of slum-dwellers from that city. The government stepped in to expel them, but finally agreed to let them settle on an extensive sandy wasteland. (p.89)

Of his second, he writes:

> Underlying the [Venezuelan cooperative] Markets is a conception of life which, according to the actors involved, gives priority to solidarity, personal and group responsibility, transparency in relations, the creation of mutual confidence, personal initiative, and a readiness for hard work. (p.92)

Indeed, as recorded by a participant in the cooperative, '[t]he large numbers of hours spent on meetings might be seen as a loss of productivity, but in fact they are the main means for achieving the dedication, enthusiasm and commitment of the workers in the organization' (p.93).

Whether such labour is appropriately deemed to be a source of social capital, it certainly is not (economic) capital and might even be thought to be its antithesis! For Campbell, writing of social capital in Africa,

> the usefulness of the concept is limited by insufficient attention to differences of culture, history, and politics between western and non-western societies ... In effect, the term operates as a metaphor rather than an analytical construct. Many writers using the concept of social capital tend to *assume* its existence (i.e. as a value or norm, as something that inheres in particular social actions or institutions, as a pre-requisite for specific social and economic transformations), and/or they see it as conceptually equivalent to solidarity, participation, co-operation or trust. Few studies define the term with sufficient clarity that might

allow social capital to be observed or measured, with the result that research findings are contradictory and policy analysis is confused. (2003, p.161)

There is a need to distinguish the cultural and structural forms of social capital, its historical dimensions, and 'analysis needs to *demonstrate* and measure the manner in which social action is deployed within and across institutions, localities, social groups and socio-economic activities' (p.162).

There are two tensions that arise for social capital in BBI, in relation to which it is worth highlighting differences with economics imperialism – which, equally, initially excludes as the basis for restoring (within a weakened, degraded and degrading framework). In the case of economics imperialism, though, the result of reducing everything to optimising individuals is to provide a limited but universal theory that explains everything in BBI on the basis of a universal (axiomatic deductive) methodology and technical apparatus (organised around production and utility functions, equilibrium and efficiency).

By contrast, for social capital, BBI has, on the one hand, been extraordinarily catholic across methodologies, techniques and conceptual apparatuses. These cannot be reconciled any more than can the definitional chaos involved. And, on the other hand, there is a parallel tension in the universal claims of social capital as a concept and, yet, its highly contextual specificity from one case to another, not least as different variables differentially benefit from BBI.

4.3 BBI GENDER ON THE DARK SIDE

In the recent social capital literature, there have been a substantial number of contributions, paradoxically from a cumulative point of view, arguing for the need to BBI gender. How many articles do you need deploring the absence of gender before it is accepted that gender has, indeed, been brought back in? Unfortunately, in other areas of study over the period since gender studies have risen to prominence more generally, there is an accepted sequence of progress through three stages: pointing out the omission of gender; BBI on the basis of existing theory; and rejecting that theory as inadequate in light of its failing to be thoroughly reconstructed to take account of gender-blind (or male-dominated) origins. Social capital and gender seem to have stalled, perhaps inevitably, as will be seen at the second stage.

This might be explained by the extent to which the literature is replete with familiar tensions and varieties of responses once social capital considers gender. The simplest and most unsatisfactory is to neglect gender altogether, to treat a male-populated and -dominated world as if it were natural, and not demanding of notice, let alone interrogation. This is true, for example, of the following example of social capital, which has been cited so often – from Coleman (1988) to Halpern (2005) – that it has become a cliché. This concerns the community of trusting traders that make up diamond dealers in New York, and elsewhere, who rely upon one another not to cheat over the quality and quantity of these valuable commodities. Yet no mention is made of exclusion from this community by religion or gender, for example, or of the advantages of tax evasion and avoidance, and no account is ever given of the current and historical circumstances that allow the community of traders to be reproduced (and which sustain the diamond price itself). For the market is attached to the longest-standing international cartel, organised by de Beers and its predecessors, without which the diamond price would simply collapse. The cartel grew out of the control gained over the Kimberley mine from the 1870s onwards, and has equally long been attached to the crudest forms of colonial and post-colonial exploitation of labour. Take all this away and away go the trusting traders too. Further, as DeFilippis suggests of the Jewish community that controls the New York diamond market:[7]

> Aside from the complete denial of exploitation that takes place *within* ethnic enclave economies, the problem with this, and every other enclave like it, is that it completely closes off the market, to anyone who is not part of the ethnic group creating the enclave. A brilliant, hard-working, innovative Irish Catholic immigrant (for instance) who wanted to enter the diamond trade in New York would have an exceptionally difficult time doing so. (2001, p.792)

Presumably, DeFilippis has in mind an Irish Catholic *female* immigrant. The committed social capitalist might respond that bonding capital within the male traders has to be complemented by bridging with women, the Irish, Catholics, and so on; and, further, the state should enact linking legislation to ensure equal opportunity. But this is bordering on the ridiculous, leading to preconditions for such changes that would render the world itself an entirely different place.

A second response to gender and social capital is to acknowledge that women are different, but to perceive their role or situation as given, often stereotyped in light of the role of the family as a site of social capital and as an antithesis and alternative to the market or economy. Continuing the theme of traders, for Fafchamps and Minten, the more agricultural traders in Madagascar know and interact with one another, the better they do. They do specify a mechanism of sorts:

> a reduction in the high transaction costs typical in agricultural commodity markets ... social capital enables traders to deal with one another in a more trusting manner, allowing them to grant and receive credit, exchange price information, and economize on quality inspection. (2002, p.152)

But there is an enormous degree of fungibility presumed here – from familial or other relations, through trust, to credit, price and quality, quite apart from the uncritical acceptance of beneficial effects. Why should the association not be for price-fixing and the creation of entry barriers?

Further, though, they simply report without comment from their detailed survey of 850 traders (729 in a second round) that '[o]n average, Malagasy traders are thirty-seven years old, male, and married with three children' (p.127). But, leaving aside age and number of children, why is the fact that the typical Malagasy trader is male (68 per cent) so much taken for granted that it warrants no further investigation, with one comment by way of exception?

> Other variables have little effect on the development of social capital ... The gender of the trader shows a negative sign in all regressions, but it is significant in only one. Women may be less successful than men in developing social capital in Madagascar because they have to spend more time on household chores and childrearing. (p.144)

No doubt,[8] but here the entire broader context of gender relations is simply set aside, necessarily undermining policy conclusions, which are inevitably designed to reduce (the 68 per cent male) trader transaction costs.[9]

Not surprisingly, then, in view of these two responses, Lowndes (2004, p.47), noting the absence of gender in Putnam's study of Italy, concludes: 'In short, "a disciplining discourse" has grown up around the social capital concept that renders women's citizenship "invisible".' And, where they *are* visible, they are liable to be transparent or superficial in the sense of not being substantively situated. So the absence of gender cannot be rectified by adding women and stirring, as the weaknesses of social capital at the micro-level (50 per cent?) are revealed. For Lowndes, there are compelling questions around whether women have the same amounts and types of social capital and whether what they do have has the same impact as for men. Her conclusion is hardly surprising: there *are* differences, especially in moving from community action to formal politics, but these depend upon context (see below).

Third, then, the tensions between social capital and gender have been negotiated by taking gender as a starting point and, inevitably, to a greater or lesser extent and in different ways, highlighting the subordination of women, in which social capital necessarily plays an ambiguous role. This is marked in the women-as-traders literature. For, as reported by Kusakabe et al. in their study of female micro-vendors in Phnom Penh, those with more (associational) social capital do prosper. But this comes at the expense of accepting gender subordination. In conclusion, they write:[10]

> Creating association itself even if it is a women's association does not in itself make the members challenge the existing unequal gender relations. Even though collective action might foster social capital, it does not necessarily lead to higher awareness of women's subordination. It can even work for the opposite. With the effort to be integrated into the mainstream society and economy, members can opt for acting and thinking that conforms to a [sic] dominant gender norms and identity. (2001, p.35)

Similarly, Mayoux, in the context of microfinance in Cameroon, points to rosy views of household, kinship and community, 'the uncritical treatment of relations within households, families and kin groups' (2001, p.450).[11] Indeed,

> men's social capital within communities frequently serves to reinforce gender subordination in relation to access to community resources and markets as well as within the household ... This meant in effect that women's savings were being recycled as low-interest loans to men. (p.454)

Further, there is the need to address 'power relations between women themselves', which leads to exclusion of the poorest and most disadvantaged women and 'increased inequalities within communities and within groups because of the emphasis on group repayment'. Also in the context of microfinance, Rankin (2002, p.3), points to 'the instrumental role of associational life and collective norms and values in *producing* and *maintaining* existing gender (and other social) hierarchies'. In this sense, social capital is complicit in putatively locating corresponding inequalities in a zone of activity outside of formal politics, potentially consolidating hierarchies along the lines of class, caste and gender.[12]

All this has begun to put social capital in the much wider context of the restructuring both of gender relations and the broader economic and social reproduction to which they are attached. For women traders in Tajikistan for example, Kanji (2002) suggests that neo-liberalism has undermined both economic and other opportunities for women and their social capital. It is, therefore, something of an irony that social capital should be seen as the instrument through which women traders should enhance their financial circumstances, not least as those engaged in trade would prefer secure employment.[13] In any case, any positive results out of the creation of social capital have to be set against the intensified burden across formal (cash payments) and informal (domestic) care and the like that remain women's responsibilities.

So Molyneux (2002, p.172) sees the gains of the women's movement as having been compromised by the neo-liberal Washington consensus (see Chapter 6). Whilst social capital is indicative of a new paradigm, it offers a less critical assessment of the role of women within civil society than the notions of social cohesion and inclusion, which it has displaced. For, '[s]ocial capital is arguably weaker, both as a conceptual construct and as a policy instrument, than either of these alternative conceptual clusters' (p.174). This is because social capital is conducive to a loss of the traditions associated with anti-authoritarian forms of struggle, and views civil society from a perspective outside the broader context of development, inequality and politics. And gender studies and social capital primarily adopt parallel tracks, especially within the World Bank, which has organisationally separate units for the two topics – with the major exception of microfinance (see below):

Thus, the social capital of bowling clubs and sewing groups in the United States is clearly not the social capital of the poor in Latin

America ... [and] can only be adequately grasped in relation to specific political and social formations and development strategies, both local and global. (p.170)

Much of the preceding discussion has focused upon gender and social capital in the context of development, where, to some extent, the idea of improving the lot of women through social capital has rationalised neglecting to tackle continuing structured inequalities. In particular, the discovery of social capital as something that can enhance the economic and social lives of women (so that being female can even be akin to a form of social capital) either ignores the downside of oppression by gender or locates it at most as a qualification. Correctives to this way of thinking, for micro-credit and Grameen banking studies, have been more or less overlooked by the social capital juggernaut, with Ito (2003) for example offering an outstanding critique of how social capital focuses on the horizontal benefits of microfinance at the expense of vertical hierarchies and powers, and takes the credit for any positive benefits from micro-credit, irrespective of what the causes may be. For developed countries, however, there is more of a presumption that gender inequalities will be found and that they are unacceptable in and through social capital. Thus, Brynin and Schupp (2000) find that the level of education of a (marriage) partner brings advantages of social capital, but more so for men than for women. For Warr (2006), in a study of voluntary work in children's schools, social capital is found to be gendered in the context of class and disadvantage, whether in getting by or getting ahead, with 'art and craft' required by the disadvantaged by contrast with the easy availability of options for those who are more privileged.

Yet it is in paid work that the weakness of social capital as a remedy to gender inequalities is at its most obvious, even though some, such as Timberlake (2005, p.34), viewing social capital as a commodity to which men and women have unequal access at work, project that, in this respect, 'untold benefits and rewards may be generated once workplaces are democratized and equalized'. Others are less sanguine.[14] For Livingston, for example,

[c]ontrary to conventional wisdom, women who use network-based job searches are less likely to obtain formal sector employment than women who find work without network assistance. Conversely, using network-based job searches increases the likelihood that men will find work in the formal sector. Since

employment in the formal sector is correlated with wages, as well as nonwage benefits, this suggests that using networks in the job search has markedly different effects on the overall economic well-being of male and female Mexican immigrants in the US. (2006, p.43)

And Morokvasic (2004) points out that social capital in migration can be disastrous for women subject to (sex) trafficking.

At the top end of the labour market, Valentine and Fleischman (2003) suggest that women lawyers are liable to do better where tolerance for diversity and corporate goals are in place (treating these as a form of social capital) since they militate against traditional gender outlooks. For Perna (2005, p.277), '[t]he analyses reveal that the contribution of family ties to tenure status and academic rank is different for women than for men'.[15] Collin et al. (2007) show that career progress in Swedish auditors is gendered through social capital, and the same applies to the careers of athletics coaches in the United States (Sagas and Cunningham 2004). And the potentially gender-neutral Internet does not compensate for female disadvantage in creating working links for scientists (Miller et al. 2006).

Significantly, and unsurprisingly in view of its origins and dynamic, the literature incorporating gender has tended to see social capital as a source of gender inequality or as a potential way of compensating for it (although gender is more or less confined to a male/female dualism, with a focus on women). Otherwise, to a large extent, the structured inequalities experienced by women remain unexamined, although addressing these absences can be pushed to the limits within a social capital framework. This is especially so of the volume edited by O'Neill and Gidengil (2006), in which the major benefit of social capital is somewhat inconsistently seen, in that 'it signals a *rediscovery* of the importance of social relationships and interconnectedness ... a direction that many feminist researchers have been advocating for some time' (Gidengil and O'Neill 2006, p.379). In conclusion, they point to two questions that have been addressed: 'What can a gendered analysis tell us about social capital? And what can social capital theory tell us about gender and politics?' They conclude that 'the findings reveal the extent to which women disproportionately bear the costs of social capital creation, while deriving fewer benefits' (p.380), leading them to question how social capital is measured, whether it has, indeed, been declining and is beneficial (as opposed to being 'a hindrance that holds women back'), and where the boundaries of politics lie. They close:

The goal is ultimately to improve upon the usefulness of social capital as a conceptual tool; it should be inclusive in scope, specific in definition, and yet sufficiently flexible to accommodate variation in the sources, development, and effects of social capital in both private and public spheres.

Whilst the specific goals are laudable, there is little reason to believe that social capital can fulfil this agenda either conceptually or strategically. It is instructive to substitute the equally universal, if deterministic, notion of patriarchy into the preceding quotation. Arguably, it would perform better in all respects!

As Adkins has suggested, in a rare contribution explicitly rejecting social capital from a gendered perspective,

[it] has provoked much concern for feminist theorists ... because the concept appears to reinstate many troubling assumptions about women and gender which for the past thirty years or more feminist social scientists have sought to excavate, problematize and go beyond. Thus, on the part of feminists, we see strong critiques of and attempts to rethink the social capital concept. But do these critiques really go beyond the social capital paradigm? (2005, p.195)

Her answer is no, for the result has been to 'fall into ... a "correctionist" mode of thinking, where there is an emphasis on correcting and modifying existing socio-theoretical discourses to include the interests of women'. In short, BBI gender to social capital is indicative of the degradation of feminist scholarship, additional correctives for which are only liable to degrade further as other elements of economic and social life also need to be incorporated on unsound foundations.

4.4   SOCIAL CAPITAL IN CONTEXT – OR VICE VERSA?

In previous sections, attention has been focused upon the BBI of what has been omitted from social capital in establishing itself as a category of universal application. Section 4.2 pitched this at a general level, and Section 4.3 addressed the BBI of gender. Not surprisingly, the BBI of other major variables of significance across the social sciences is also to be found in the literature, not least in explicitly noting their absence or in the less conscious and dull compulsion of needing to take them into account by virtue of the particular case study involved.

Thus Navarro (2002, p.427), in criticising Putnam, observes that social capital replaces the language of race, class and gender, leading to a 'remarkable absence of *power* and *politics*'. And Muntaner et al. report:

> In social epidemiology, more specifically, social capital presents a model of the social determinants of health that excludes any analysis of structural inequalities (e.g., class, gender, or racial/ ethnic relations) in favor of a horizontal view of social relations based on distributive inequalities in income. As a consequence, political movements based on class, race/ethnicity, or gender are also ignored as explanations for reducing social inequalities in health. (2001, p.213)

In case of BBI race (and the distinct category of ethnicity), then, the literature has offered two separate, if occasionally overlapping, strands.[16] One is to find at least a residual if not a determining role for *racism*, with a need to address the corresponding issues of power, conflict, culture and the role of the state – BBI on a grand and wide scale. Thus, Crozier and Davies (2006), noting the relative absence of gender and ethnicity in social capital (and family) studies, conclude that the extended family, community and religion cannot necessarily compensate for the deleterious effects of institutional racism on educational achievement, whatever the motivation to succeed.[17] James (2000) finds, after correcting for human capital, that in financial services blacks experience a slower rate of promotion than whites, but that this is due not so much to social capital (closeness to colleagues), of which they do have less, but to the fact that this leads to less psychosocial support in career advice and advancement. Cross (2003) suggests that the legacy of slavery should have offered considerable bonding capital for Afro-Americans as a basis for integration, but Arriaza (2003) finds that this legacy creates tensions in the role of black teachers – how both to engage with the disadvantaged and incorporate them into an oppressing culture. For Hays (2002), charitable provision of housing is better at building social capital amongst providers than for beneficiaries, furnishing 'an organization overwhelmingly governed by white, college educated persons making over $75,000 a year' (pp.265–6). And McGhee (2003, pp.376–7), in the context of social capital as community cohesion in Bradford, points to 'the relative de-emphasis of material deprivation and socio-economic margin-alization ... [and] the criminalization of young male British–Asian "rioters"' and the corresponding 'criminal justice system which is perceived by the Asian community in Bradford (and not without foundation) as not offering them equal treatment' (p.401).

Not surprisingly, the vast majority of the social capital literature steers clear of racism as a starting point (and other elements irreducibly attached to power, oppression and conflict) and emphasises the diversity and complexity of outcomes whenever race and ethnicity are involved. Anderson and Paskeviciute (2006) study the impact of linguistic and ethnic diversity on civic participation across a large sample of countries, and conclude there are no uniform effects as such. This is hardly surprising since the associational life of ethnic minorities may be either defensive and introverted or engaging, and may or may not lead to greater political participation (see special issue of *Journal of Ethnic and Migration Studies*, vol.30, no.3, 2004).

As is apparent, the nature, incidence and impact of social capital, in the presence of race or otherwise, depends upon the 'community' to which it is attached and how that community is located and interpreted.[18] Through the prism of social capital, community becomes, at least potentially, a positive resource in developing the local economy (Kay 2005), although the promise far exceeds the action. As Kilpatrick et al., vigorous promoters of the relationship between social capital and lifelong learning, put it:

Social capital is an appropriate analytical framework for diagnosing the strengths and weaknesses of the social assets of a community ... and identifying aspects where intervention, for example, by community development practitioners, could usefully build community capacity to manage change and develop. (2003, p.431)

But, as McClenaghan suggests in concluding her response,

[t]he challenge ... is not, therefore, to ignore or obscure economic and power relations under a blanket concept of the social as capital but to identify ... the economic and political discourses constituting the social field in which community development action takes place ... and [shift] system imperatives and practices in the interests of economic and social justice and equity.[19] (2003, p.438)

Where does this lead social capital and the community? In the extreme, social capital has displaced community,[20] which has itself been a highly contested notion but one with long-standing traditions of critical scholarship. These are liable to be lost by the shift in terminology. To guarantee otherwise, Onyx (2005, p.4) puts forward the idea that the study of social capital and community must involve their dark sides, including power, political economy, inequality and exploitation, conflict, bonding and bridging, and wider structural economic and political forces operating at the state (provincial), national and global levels. In similar vein, Forrest and Kearns review social capital in light of neighbourhood literature:

> The current fashionable search for evidence of, and measures to enhance, the stock of social capital in a neighbourhood needs therefore to have a sensitivity to the different forms of social capital that may exist with different purposes. Coping with social problems is not the same thing as overcoming them and renewing neighbourhoods ... will not necessarily reform society. (2001, p.2141)

To contribute analytically, social capital must 'set out to situate the neighbourhood within more general debates about social cohesion ... and to illustrate how contested and complex these discourses are'.[21] Following Morrow (1999), Forrest and Kearns refer to '"*deficit* theory syndrome" – something lacking in individuals or communities' (p.2141, emphasis added), and they finish with an appeal 'to embed conceptions of social capital in a more general exploration of human, cultural and economic capital, all within a wider audit of neighbourhood resources and dynamics' (p.2142).[22]

From race to community, then, social capital tends to be subject to a deluge of traditional variables once it embarks upon BBI one or other of what has been omitted. The preferred approach to such challenges is to situate them within a partially disaggregated framework of bonding, bridging and linking social capital, with its negative versions thrown in for good measure, and otherwise to stress context as a conditioning factor. The remaining purpose of this section is to illustrate how and just how much this has been done in terms of the BBI context itself, selectively drawing upon the wealth of case studies and the analytical framework laid out in Chapter 2. But, as will be seen, context is as difficult to pin down as social capital itself.

The most obvious way in which to interpret context is as the presence of conditioning variables which are external to social capital but which affect its impact by their presence (variables A and B in Figure 2.3); although it is important to recall that A and B are subject to capture by social capital in its own definition. Thus, Polèse and Shearmur (2006) argue that social capital is a factor in local regeneration, but that many other preconditions are also essential, leading them to conclude that '[t]he proposition that geography and exogenous forces can overwhelm even the best-conceived local economic development strategies should now be uncontroversial' (p.43). Similarly, for rural redevelopment, social capital is insufficiently sensitive to the complexity of micro-politics (McAreavey 2006), and Morrison (2003) suggests that impoverished European neighbourhoods may be further impoverished by 'inward looking initiatives', as opposed to those that address wider social integration.

For neighbourhoods, Saegert et al. (2002) point out that physical environment is important to the incidence of crime and that social capital within one location may deter crime by merely displacing it elsewhere. Significantly, Leeder (1998, pp.3–4) notes that Coleman's (1990) example of neighbourhood safety built on social capital between families in Jerusalem (in contrast to Detroit) depends upon neglect of 'how many Israeli soldiers, armed to the teeth, were needed to achieve this level of social capital within fortress Jerusalem … at the expense of the rest of society'.[23]

In the case of economic performance, Engstrand and Stam (2002) find that social capital can be associated with either impeding or promoting the process of sector restructuring, in part depending on location (Sweden versus the Netherlands, for example) and sector (shipbuilding versus electronics). Not surprisingly, Bresnen et al. (2005) suggest that in construction team-working cannot build social capital, because of the casual (sub-)contractual nature of the business, just as Bakker et al. (2006) conclude that social capital as trust is less important for corporate knowledge sharing than longevity of team-working. The presence of the state leads to ambiguous results for social capital. It needs to be there for conservation projects to be effective (Peterson et al. 2006), but it may crowd out altruistic and cooperative behaviour amongst local businesses keen to preserve their symbolic identity as independent of the state (Phillipson et al. 2006). On the other hand, Marger (2001) finds that successful business migrants to Canada with pre-migration human capital show 'a minimal reliance on social capital in establishing and operating their firms', in contrast to the importance they attach to state support (p.439). And, similarly, for Chinese immigrant entrepreneurs in Toronto, Ooka (2001) finds that ethnic firm linkages and employment do not raise business income.

Thus the impact of social capital depends upon context, in the sense of what other variables interact with it. This is so to such an extent that social capital can be positive in one instance and negative in another, or even both simultaneously, for different processes and connections. In the case of urban regeneration, Bull and Jones (2006), comparing Bristol and Naples, find that more social capital is not necessarily better, given contextual complexity, conflicts and corruption. For sustainable local community development, Newman and Dale (2005) believe that excessive bonding social capital can lead to enforcement of social norms that hinder innovative change (although bridging capital can do otherwise). Fyfe and Milligan (2003, p.408), in the context of voluntary work, argue that 'high levels of social capital ... may be divisive, exclusionary restrict individual freedoms ... [and] would simply favour those who are already powerful and articulate, and who already enjoy a greater capacity to engage'. Chase (2002) finds that donor funding of local infrastructure in Armenia has a negative effect on the completion of non-funded projects – social capital for some at the expense of others. Cleaver (2005) suggests of Tanzania that social capital involves inclusion and exclusion, with inequality, power and conflict where there is inclusion, and the need for material resources, especially for the poorest of the excluded. Mitchell and LaGory (2002) show that children and employment mitigate stress in impoverished communities, but that social capital in the form of interpersonal networks raises stress levels due to a network of obligations in helping others in 'getting by', with social capital allowing user costs for health services to be paid through financial solidarity among the poor (Aye et al. 2002). By the same token, Jacobs and Kemp (2002) discover that the social capital amongst Bangladeshi traders means they have no need to keep records, precluding economic calculation on the basis of these. And Field (2003, p.71) explores 'A Walk on the Dark Side' of social capital by targeting how it reinforces inequality and supports antisocial behaviour.

As should already be apparent, context also involves attention to detail and complexity. This can include the disaggregation of social capital into its multifarious elements. Thus, Saxton and Benson (2005) show that the different dimensions of social capital have different impacts on the growth of the not-for-profit sectors of the economy. For Ferguson (2006), in a case study of Mexico, children's educational performance is affected by social capital, but successful supportive intervention needs to be specific to individual families and children. Warde and Tampubolon (2002) find that social capital in leisure consumption is rendered chaotic in light of the different types of friendships and networks involved. Dinovitzer (2006) studies five different types of social capital, each having different effects, not always positive, on Jewish lawyers' careers. And for Flap and Völker (2001), different types of network have different content and give rise to different levels of job satisfaction. They conclude, quoting Podolny and Baron (1997, p.674), that 'the network structure that is most conducive to maximize access to information and other resources is not the structure most conducive to social identity, and vice versa', indicating the tensions not only across the diversity of social capitals but also in what social capital can be used for.

This is all compounded by acknowledging context in terms of social capital as a process. Bankston and Zhou, then, in a study of academic achievement by family structure and ethnicity, emphasise social capital as a conditioned process, and the limitations or tautology of analyses in case such conditions and processes are excluded or included respectively. They conclude, 'it is difficult to judge on purely theoretical and a priori grounds just what aspects of social groups and social settings qualify as capital and as liabilities' (2002, p.312). And also:

> If networks and norms are not identical but are two steps in a process, with what degree of confidence can the existence of the first step assure us of the existence of the second? Do closed networks lead to effective norms sometimes, most times, or only under the proper conditions? (p.290)

Similarly, John finds that social capital is not necessarily good for school performance for those from lower socio-economic backgrounds, and hence that 'social capital is thus not a simple good, nor has universal benefit – much depends on the context … Rather than being an independent factor, the impact of social capital is intimately bound up with the processes that generate inequalities in societies' (2005, p.652).

With social capital as a conditioned, diverse, heterogeneous, and complex process, Staber, in addressing regional clusters, observes 'the neglect of the situational context', concluding that 'acontextual studies can lead to analytical error and flawed conclusions concerning the performance outcomes of social capital' (2007, p.505). He points to five contextual effects: the impact of social capital may only prevail over a limited range; the effect may differ at different levels of development; it may change sign; it may change direction of causation; and it is conditional on the presence of other variables. Hence analytical remedy is sought through

> (1) thick description of the research setting; (2) a context-sensitive sampling plan; (3) a focus on processes and events; (4) attention to co-evolutionary processes at multiple levels; and (5) attention to the social mechanisms that link actions at multiple levels. (p.513)

This is to push context as far as it can go without explicitly adding culture as an element in its own right, subject to varieties of inter-pretation across time, place and application.

Thus, in a study of career progression and mentoring through *guanxi* networks in China, Bozionelos and Wang suggest that,

> in contrast to the Anglo-Saxon context, interpersonal relationships in the Chinese cultural context cannot exist in instrumental form only; as the establishment of expressive elements is a pre-requisite for the development of instrumental aspects in a relationship within the Chinese cultural environment. (2006, p.1541)

For Norchi (2000) traditional knowledge of the Onge people (from the Indian Nicobar and Andaman Islands) is social capital that must be kept intact as multinational pharmaceutical companies seek to exploit knowledge-derived products. Chapter 2 has already indicated that, for some, imaginary social capital (derived from, not obstructed by, television) is as potentially significant as the real thing. And the same might be said of religious capital, as knowledge of its rituals and traditions allow clergy to bond with one another, potentially at the expense of the laity, with seminaries providing both instruction and interpersonal attachments (Finke and Dougherty 2002).

But what of other 'religions', new and old? For the cultures and practices attached to the Internet have recently prompted the emergence of a rapidly growing literature. Is Internet use alienating and isolating and at the expense of social capital? Or is it not only conducive to the formation and use of social capital but even social capital as network itself? Significantly, the role of the welfare state, that old religion of social democracy, occupies an analytical place similar to that occupied by the Internet. For the culture and practices attached to the welfare state are of importance in conditioning both the presence and the influence of social capital. Do they create, undermine or work in tandem with it?[24]

All this, however, is intended to push towards a deeper understanding of the relationship between social capital and culture (as context), one in which culture is endowed with specific meaning. Thus, in a comparison of Istanbul and Moscow, Secor and O'Loughlin (2005, p.80) demonstrate 'how social capital is constructed within and through particular historical and local conjunctures', with those lower socio-economic groups that are less engaged in civic activity being more trustful of government in both cities. This is hardly surprising given that such engagement may expose those involved to the nature of government (or even induce an oppositional response to it).[25] But trust in fellow citizens is more associated with civic activity in Istanbul and less so in Moscow. Silverman (2002, p.164) examines the interaction between race and religion and, in looking for mechanisms of racial reconciliation in Mississippi, finds that 'all forms of social capital are not alike, and the degree to which various forms of social capital are compatible is structured by local history and context', with mobilisation on the basis of race incorporating 'historical baggage' and the alternative basis of faith limiting the scope of what can be addressed. Marjoribanks and Mboya (2001) find that South African youth's self-concept depends upon familial human and social capital, but equally on parenting style. Style is of importance to youth, as highlighted by the study of Lovell (2002), which explores how to get drug addicts to be more socially responsible in needle behaviour through social capital. But different people have different roles in the drug scene, from the reformed evangelist through to the user–dealer. With addicts' role playing potentially to the fore, substance abuse can have different meanings to abusers, depending upon familial and cultural background (p.816). Lovell concludes (p.819): 'Fundamental social conditions ... define social space and shape the circumstances of risk taking that drug researchers should now target, alongside the individual-level characteristics already examined in published studies.' And Kreuter and Lezin accept that 'failure to take social and political context into account is a major barrier to the effective evaluation of community-based health promotion' (2002, p.251). They conclude that there are different ways of knowing, and different interpretations of 'reality' ... an epidemiologist, an anthropologist, a health educator, and a layperson are likely to view a given problem through different lenses. More importantly, each is quite likely to detect a glimpse of reality that others may miss. All ... need to seriously explore how their various views of reality can be combined to give us new knowledge.

In postmodern words and worlds, social capital is socially constructed even if it is rarely deconstructed.

4.5   BBBI BY WAY OF CONCLUDING REMARKS

The purpose of this chapter has been to chart the necessarily chaotic fashion in which social capital, as a universal category of analysis that is of general application, has inevitably been forced to bring back in what has been left out. It has incorporated missing and conditioning variables (as important as gender, race and class), complexity and diversity, heterogeneity, culture and, ultimately, context. To some extent the last serves as a symbol of the tensions involved – the more we examine social capital, the more we find it depends upon context, however broadly and deeply it is defined. But the more we appeal to context, the more social capital loses its appeal as a universal category. Consider carefully the extent to which the case studies covered in this chapter are addressing the same analytical category, social capital, in anything other than name. Often it is even apparent that the conclusions drawn do not depend upon social capital at all. Social capital merely serves as a diversion in identifying underlying and more important causes.[26]

The strategy of BBI missing elements is exemplified by Simon Szreter (2002a and b). He seeks to rescue social capital from criticism by BBI class, power, politics, ideology, mass unemployment, globalisation, inequality, hierarchy, the state and history, alongside a whole array of other analytical fragments.[27] Continuing weaknesses within British society are perceived to arise out of 'a surplus of bonding social capital, only, among the comfortably-off, and a deficiency of bridging and linking social capital'; thus Szreter poses the problems to be resolved by New Labour. As he puts it, with a stunning clarity:

It is implicit in this reading of social capital theory that there is an optimal dynamic balance of bonding, bridging, and linking social capital, which simultaneously facilitates democratic governance, economic efficiency and widely-dispersed human welfare, capabilities and functioning. (2002b, p.580)

It is a moot point whether this reading is able to BBI the critical elements of social theory associated with power, conflict, hierarchy, and so on.[28]

This observation is brought home by one further element characteristic of the more recent social capital literature, BBI Bourdieu or BBBI. Not surprisingly, in light of some of the other BBIs, Bourdieu is now making a small but significant comeback. This has induced Szreter (2002b, pp.616–17) to accuse me of inconsistency in observing both the omission of Bourdieu and the subsequent claim of BBBI. In doing so, he does himself miss the point that this is not the restoration of the status quo ante. The vast majority of current social capital studies continue to overlook Bourdieu even if restoring context and other elements that had been taken out of his pioneering studies. Further, those that appeal to Bourdieu explicitly often do so only partially and with distortion.

Indeed, those who do genuinely restore Bourdieu to social capital studies are not only the exception, they also tend unavoidably to be highly critical of the vast bulk of other studies. Thus, Campbell and McLean (2002, p.645) distance themselves from studies that, 'frequently draw on survey items which superficially match Putnam's "laundry list" of networks and norms', preferring research that focuses on 'the forms taken by social capital in various contexts, and [research] into the mechanisms underlying the link between social capital and health', thereby appealing to Bourdieu and concepts both of social capital and social identity. They conclude that social capital has neglected race, class and gender, and that it is better seen as a material and symbolic source of inequality. In other words, though this is not explicitly stated by Campbell and McLean, social capital needs to be sensitive to the nature and incidence of racism and other forms of oppression.[29]

In short, Bourdieu's use of social capital involves class, elites, power, hierarchy, conflict and how these are reproduced. In its early founding phase, Bourdieu's social capital did benefit from some attention, especially from those engaging in cultural studies. But the rapid expansion of social capital, and the shift of its core to a Coleman–Putnam axis, quickly marginalised the substantive content of social capital from the perspective of Bourdieu. And the different capitals to which Bourdieu and others have pointed have tended to be rounded up into a single social capital, homogeneous in name but heterogeneous in content. Paradoxically, as indicated in Chapter 3, Bourdieu was sidelined during social capital's meteoric rise, but he is now being brought back in on a piecemeal basis as an incoherent fixing device for context for the unduly abstract social capital, so diverse and contingent is its scope of application. Significantly, Bourdieu's other types of capital, and his emphasis on class, conflict, power, and so on, remain notable for their absence other than occasionally as a token ex post addition of context. The point, as emphasised, is that whilst Bourdieu can be brought back in, this does not mean you get Bourdieu back by doing so, as is evident from the attempt by Svendsen and Svendsen (2003 and 2004) to construct a social capital with 'Bourdieuconomics' that moulds him in a market imperfection direction, entirely compatible with mainstream economics. By contrast, for Bourdieu, context is intimately related to practice and, as such, is highly specific in constructed material and cultural content and meaning – a somewhat inconsistent position that undermines the generality of his own use of terms such as social capital (see below), let alone that of others.

There is, then, much to commend in Bourdieu's approach to social capital, as discussed in Chapter 3. First, he sees it as complemented by, not including, cultural and symbolic capital. Second, despite its huge range of application, social and other forms of capital are seen as contextually specific, in the richest sense. And, third, as emphasised, Bourdieu is focused upon questions of class, power, conflict and the reproduction of hierarchy and oppression as opposed to positive-sum, collective self-help.

Despite these qualities, though, there is a triple buffer protecting social capital from the impact of BBBI. The first is to ignore him altogether. The second is to bring him back in on a piecemeal and/or false basis. And the third is that, despite, or even because of, more favourable elements in Bourdieu's notion of (social) capital, there are still the continuing weaknesses of his own approach, even if social capital gets past the other two buffers. As Swartz (1997, p.6) suggests, he is attempting a general theory of his own in which power comes to the fore: 'For Bourdieu power is not a separate domain of study but stands at the heart of all social life.' For '[t]he exercise and reproduction of class-based power and privilege is a core substantive and unifying concern' (p.7). Indeed, '[i]t is his ambition to create a science, applicable to all types of societies, of the social and cultural reproduction of power relations among individuals and groups'. In this, crucial for Swartz is that Bourdieu rejects 'the subjectivist and objectivist forms of knowledge and the substantialist view of reality that he believes pervades them ... his concepts shift in emphasis and scope depending on the opposing viewpoints they address' (p.5). Thus, whilst Bourdieu is seen as applying material interests to all activities, economic and cultural, these are seen as being practical and dispositional rather than as narrowly goal-oriented, and also as being defined by positions in the social hierarchy. This is to allow for a distancing from Marxism in an effort to avoid reduction of culture to the economic, even though culture is nonetheless tied to material interests (p.72). As a result, Bourdieu's notion of capital is universal and designed to express all forms of power (p.73).

This all leads, first and foremost, to a limited understanding in Bourdieu of *economic* capital, not least as attached to capitalism. If this were there, for example, then it would be impossible for other capitals to range so freely historically across contexts where capital has yet to develop its modern forms and play an influential role on the symbolic, cultural and social. For, once capital as such is pinned down, it is necessary to have distinguished between capitalism and its economics, and that of other historical periods where it does not prevail, as well as between the world of capital within capitalism and its own non-economic counterparts. As Swartz puts it (p.80), 'Bourdieu's concept of capital does not permit him to distinguish capitalist from noncapitalist social relations'. This is true both of economic capital across different historical periods and of the different types of non-economic capital within a given society. These concepts remain general until they are complemented by the notions of habitus and field, invented by Bourdieu in order to allow for specificity in the role of different capitals, both within and across different societies. This is all put precisely in Némedi's account of Bourdieu:

> The Algerian experience was very important in the formation of Bourdieu's social theory. The recently published fragments of an autobiography and L. Addi's analysis of Bourdieu's anthropological theory allow a more detailed evaluation of the contribution of Kabyle ethnology to the Bourdieusian conceptualization of the society. The concepts of habitus and social capital both have their origin in the analysis of Kabyle peasant economy while they are central to the examination of the reproduction of modern French society. In this way, Bourdieu *reduces* the differences of modern

and archaic society. This difference was constitutive of classical social theory. Bourdieu's social theory shares the '*timelessness*' of much modern social theory, including that of [Talcott] Parsons. (2005, p.35, emphasis added)

The timelessness of Bourdieu is something shared not only with Parsons but also with Coleman and Putnam, even if with a very different analytical content.

Further, it is precisely the peculiar nature of 'economic' capital, and its attachment to capitalism, that has inspired social theory to comprehend the special relationship between the economic and the non-economic, ranging over Weber's Protestant ethic and rationality and order, Polanyi's embeddedness and double movement, anthropology's gift versus commodity, and so on. Despite his emphasis on context, Bourdieu's notion of capital floats too freely across history as an embodiment of power, thereby failing to identify the structures, processes and relations to which capital and capitalism are attached as opposed to non-capitalist societies.

There is, however, an exception that proves the rule of the absence of an economics of capital in Bourdieu. It is a feature of (economic) capital on which he heavily relies. This is the fluidity that it enjoys, its capacity, even its necessity, of changing from one form to another – value as market exchange relations. Specifically, for Bourdieu, if not exactly as if a price relationship, each capital is money-like in the sense of being exchangeable to a greater or lesser degree into another type. As the qualitative and quantitative natures of such relations are so diverse and variable, with the exception of money capital itself, it makes little sense to treat the cultural, symbolic and social as if they were capital even within a capitalist society – they are not value relations in the economic sense, from the perspective of almost all economic theories other than the most reductionist. Significantly, Swartz (1997, p.8) acknowledges of Bourdieu: 'He conceptualizes culture as a form of capital with specific laws of accumulation, exchange, and exercise ... These are not tidy, well-delimited theoretical arguments but orienting themes that overlap and interpenetrate.'

The weakness and timelessness of Bourdieu's economics, his notion of capital, are an attraction for social capitalists, who are less concerned to incorporate power, class, hierarchy and conflict, other than, at most, as context to case study. This also courts the risk of taking the economic not only as given, but as non-social, as opposed to the non-economic. By contrast, for Marxist political economy, for example, (economic) capital is profoundly social with definite relations, structures, forms, processes and laws of development of its own, as well as with profound implications for corresponding impact upon the cultural, symbolic and social (as non-economic). This is not a matter of reducing these to the economic but of not reducing the economic to the asocial. Of this, of course, Bourdieu is not deeply guilty, if only because of his insistence upon class, power, conflict, and so on, and context, even if he does not draw heavily upon a political economy of capitalism. If the social capital literature had confined itself to Bourdieu-type analyses, there would be something, but only little, about which to complain, and we would have received a bag of disparate case studies with nothing to connect them to one another other than a common and peculiar terminology. Such was the situation before Coleman trumped Bourdieu, after which the common terminology is taken to suggest that the different case studies share something substantive in common – the social as represented by social capital.

5
Social Capital versus Social History[1]

In his contribution, 'Do Social Historians Need Social Capital?', Dario Gaggio (2004) correctly observes that historians have ignored the academic, and more general, bandwagon that has accompanied the meteoric rise of this concept from the mid 1990s to a position of extraordinary prominence across the social sciences. Implicitly at least, Gaggio offers good reasons why the attractions of social capital should have been disdained by historians. It is because for him, drawing upon the work of Bourdieu, there is only one version of the concept that is acceptable. This involves him in a radical critique of Putnam, who, departing from Bourdieu's approach, takes rational choice sociologist James Coleman as his source of social capital. As a result, the bulk of the literature that Putnam has inspired is dismissed as methodologically eclectic, seeking a third way out of the individualistic orgy of the 1980s, negligent of political economy, unduly reifying the separation between civil and political society, and insensitive to the salience of context. Gaggio entirely approves my own critique and deconstruction of social capital on these grounds but, at the last breath, comes to an opposite strategic conclusion. Whereas my position is uncompromisingly to reject social capital in all its forms and applications, he encourages historians to participate in its use in order to drive out its erroneous manifestations.

The purpose of this chapter is to challenge Gaggio's stance in the specific context of history and historians. I seek to explain in full why social capital should have been neglected by historians, rather than, as with Gaggio, leaving this explained implicitly, partially and, to some extent, erroneously. For, if social capital is so bad, why has it been taken up by other disciplines, unless we are to privilege the intellectual acumen of historians? And what underpins such beneficial conceptual discrimination on their part? Essentially, history's position depends upon the evolving features of social capital itself as well as the intellectual environment of the late twentieth century in which it has prospered. Again, reaction against individualism aside, Gaggio offers little attention to the more general analytical trends at work that have inspired social capital, on the one hand, and historians on the other. By coupling these with the specificity of social capital itself, I fully support Gaggio's exhortation for historians to engage with social capital, but by way of critical rejection and the offering of alternatives, drawing upon their own expertise and their situation in relation to the social sciences. My starting point in the next section, though, is to provide some background to the story of how social capital came to be the way it is and my own preparations, only conscious in part, for this chapter.

This means revisiting some ground covered earlier concerning economics imperialism, but setting it within the context of history. In this way it can be shown why social capital, for very different reasons, is found in neither of the two broadly parallel fields (and methods) within the discipline. For economic history, at least to the extent that it succumbs to the unsubtle charms of mainstream economics, it is because the new institutional economics has provided an alternative catch-all for the non-economic, and that field got there first. And for social history, the sensitivity to historical change, and traditional and richer ways of understanding it, have not been conducive to the deployment of social capital in anything other than a casual fashion, just as for economic history, if for different reasons. Accordingly, Section 5.3 finds that the limited presence of social capital within history is something of a scattergun affair, sporadic and unsystematic. The same is so, as suggested in Section 5.4, of the application of social capital to the contemporary historical processes of transition and development (see Chapter 6 also for the latter). The final section argues that, as for other disciplines, there is an alternative strategy that historians might adopt in relation to social capital. This is neither to accept nor to ignore it, but to engage with it through active critical dismissal – or risk the penalty of being besieged or overwhelmed by it.

5.2 THE HISTORICAL DOG THAT DID NOT BARK

As outlined in Chapter 3, in 2006 I made a JSTOR literature search, covering the period up to 2004, to investigate the usage of the term 'social capital' in the discipline of history. The exercise confirmed the relative absence of social capital from the history journals. Whilst the JSTOR search threw up 292 items, only 161 of these were articles, with many book reviews and front and back pieces (such as advertisements) making up the numbers. Only 19 items scored for 'social capital' in title or abstract, over half of these from the special double issue on social capital of the *Journal of Interdisciplinary History* (see below). Many of the items arose from area publications, such as the *Journal of Southern African Studies*, or publications only *related* to history, such as *Economic Geography*, which were, nonetheless, classified in the JSTOR archives as history journals. Further, social capital's 'relevance ranking' in the articles (an artefact of the search engine provided as a service to readers) proved to be extremely low. One element in relevance is the number of times the term appears and, in the articles covered, this soon degenerated into one or two alone, frequently as a term in a cited reference only. By way of contrast, general JSTOR searches in history journals for 'postmodernism' and 'globalisation' returned 3,430 and 1,558 items respectively, and 'consumption' scored 216 hits even on the narrower search by title or abstract.

The absence of social capital from history is confirmed by a useful, and independent, study of the concept's birth and growth by Forsman (2005), a librarian offering a bibliographic study for social capital of some quantitative and qualitative sophistication. She divides the diffusion of social capital across the social sciences into three waves: the first to economics and sociology; the second to education and medicine; and the third to business and psychology. History is notable for its absence but, as seen in Chapter 3, where it *does* make a presence, it offers insight, even if only as the exception that proves the rule. In the past, prior to the period covered by the Forsman study, historians used the term 'social capital' in an entirely different way – as the systemic or aggregate properties of capital, an economic category within capitalism, as opposed to some aspect of civil society floating free of the economy.

As a result of its gargantuan appetite, and not surprisingly, social capital has been applied to historical case studies of great diversity. By analogy, we can find it in history as easily as, if not more easily than, we can find money, commodities and exchange more generally (and social capital is often seen as a precondition for these to be present). But, as already indicated, historians themselves have not sought out and deployed social capital in this way. Why is this? A full answer will only emerge subsequently, but, with respect to social capital as gourmand, historians of today are liable to view the functionalist/structuralist/deterministic underpinnings of the social capital juggernaut with considerable distaste, as have social theorists more generally in the past – to the extent that its history as a concept has had to be invented in order that it could be discovered (Chapter 3).

One reason why social capital and history should not mix is because of the distance between social capital and the economic, the previously preferred arena for historians (with the economic understood here as infrastructural or systemic economic properties). For the vast bulk of the social capital literature, other than within the discipline of economics itself, the economic does not figure at all. Where it does, it sits unexamined in the background, at most, or it is the object favourably enhanced by the presence of social capital as a cure-all for growth, poverty alleviation, and such things. Significantly, this does imply a breach with the purest commitment to laissez-faire. Markets work imperfectly in the absence of social capital or, putting it more positively, markets work better in its presence. But, crucially, and reflecting its middle-range character, such putative economic benefits are presumed, and are not based on any actual economic analysis. However the economy performs, and whichever economy it is, it does better if supported by social capital.

This has placed social capital in a particular relationship with mainstream economics (see Chapter 8). It has meant that the concept has been treated with suspicion, since, from an orthodox perspective, a capital should be a stock purposively built up by deliberate investment and underpinning a return. However, this in part physicalist interpretation of capital has also been the basis for broaching (social) capital as those (productive) resources that depart from this simple formula. Whilst natural, physical, human (and, more generally, personal) and financial capital serve as the core in resource allocation, efficiency and equilibrium, social capital stands for anything else not private or tangible that might contribute to economic performance. Social capital neatly falls within the realm of this economic framing of the rationale for the non-market or non-economic.

There are, though, three important aspects of the incorporation of social capital into economics. First, as argued in Fine and Milonakis (2009) and Milonakis and Fine (2009), the highest priority within an orthodoxy that excludes alternatives to an unprecedented degree is its commitment to its technical apparatus of production and utility functions and, to a high if lesser extent, its commitment to its technical architecture of optimisation, efficiency and equilibrium. As a result, social capital is treated, and often appears formally, as an element in a production or utility function, as if a material input or consumption good respectively. Alternatively it is presumed to reduce transaction costs or to smooth the operation of the market. Second, mainstream economics purports to assess theory against the evidence through econometrics. This has rendered social capital a particularly attractive avenue for investigation, as its many dimensions and corresponding data sets, generally available or case-study constructed, fit readily into professional practices.

Third, social capital has emerged across the social sciences just as economics imperialism, or the colonisation of the other disciplines, has entered a new phase, corresponding to the shift away from Becker's economic approach, reducing the social to the narrowly conceived economic rationality in as-if-perfect market conditions. By contrast, the market imperfections approach to economics has opened up the social as never before, both in scope and palatability, to the other social sciences. Not only is the market no longer seen as primarily perfect, but the non-market or social is also seen as significant as the endogenised response to those imperfections. To put it in the vernacular, institutions, customs, history, culture and, of course, social capital now matter to economic performance, and economists can prove it by mathematics, and especially through game theory!

This new phase of economics imperialism has spawned a range of new fields in and around economics, or developments within them: the new economic sociology, the new institutional economics, the new political economy, the new economic geography, the new financial economics, the new development economics, the new welfare economics, and so on. These have offered corresponding incursions into the other social sciences. But the nature and extent of the impact of economics imperialism across the social sciences is uneven, reflecting both the continuing dynamic of colonised disciplines and, in particular, the acceptability of the methods and content of mainstream economics. For, whilst the new phase of economics imperialism does accept the salience of the non-economic, it continues to rely upon the technical apparatus and architecture of the methodological individualism associated with economic rationality.

All this is pertinent to the general reception of the new economics imperialism within history, and of social capital in particular. The discipline became marked by a division between 'economic' and 'social' history, whose origins derive from the earlier assault of mainstream economics upon history in the first phase of economics imperialism, giving rise to the cliometric revolution or aptly named new economic history (Lamoreaux 1998). Inevitably, social history has either steered away from the economic altogether (on which see below), or has deployed an entirely different basis for its economics in its understanding of capital, capitalism, class, power, institutions, and so on.

With the new phase of economics imperialism, however, cliometrics has itself gone through a corresponding reform and has advanced on its own terms to give rise to what can be dubbed the 'newer economic history' (Fine 2003a, Fine and Milonakis 2003 and 2009 and Milonakis and Fine 2007, 2009 and forthcoming). This purports to accept the criticisms of the new economic history for its neglect of institutions, culture, and so on, and to re-engage with social history on these terms. Some time after this initiative had been launched, one of its originators, Peter Temin (1997), felt it appropriate to suggest to the readers of the *Journal of Economic History* that it is 'Kosher to Talk about Culture' as a force of economic history. He made explicit reference to Putnam and to social capital, seeing it as a force for industrialisation and as a reason why 'historians need to make these connections themselves to get through the plethora of information and communicate with economists' (p.282, see also p.272). Indeed, in a claim only a little less modest than Putnam's, that social capital is the key to differential development between the north and south of Italy over the best part of a millennium (see below), Temin argues 'that the particular form of social capital I call Anglo-Saxon culture was uniquely suited to the progress of industrialization over the past two centuries' (p.268).

This is very big history on a very wide scale, and there are good reasons why the corresponding overtures to social historians will and should have failed in light of the continuing antipathy to mainstream economics, even in its market imperfections version. Most telling in Temin's casual use, apart from its exaggerated claims, is the limited extent to which social capital has been used by *economic* as opposed, paradoxically, to social historians (see below). If, indeed, Temin and his culture are the historical handmaidens of mainstream economics, social capital should have been adopted within (the newer) economic history itself at an early stage and used extensively (even by Temin himself), just as it has been across the other social sciences. Why has this not been the case?

The simple and compelling answer is that an equally flexible and all-encompassing category was already in place within the new(er) economic history prior to the emergence of the social capital juggernaut. This was the idea of institutions and its corresponding attachment to the new institutional economics (see Hadiz 2004 for a critique of the new institutionalism and social capital as a component part in the context of decentralisation in Indonesia). And, just as the single figure of Putnam more than any other has symbolised social capital, so institutions as the residual explanatory factor for economic history have been associated with Douglass North. As a leading figure in founding the new economic history, he subsequently refined his analysis to incorporate property relations, followed by institutions. Significantly, these are defined as the formal or informal arrangements through which society governs itself and the economy, either more or less efficiently, through customary behaviour and ideological beliefs. There is an exact analytical correspondence with social capital. North's treatment of institutions in this way attained its analytical pinnacle and point of reference for the new institutional economics and economic history with the publication of *Institutions, Institutional Change and Economic Performance* in 1990.

Thus, just as social history has had scant regard for social capital, especially in light of the direction it has taken, so economic history has had no need for it. In the case of economic history, this is an accident of the division of the discipline into these two camps, the evolution of the new(er) economic history around the trajectory taken by Douglass North, and the new institutional economics more generally. In the case of social history, the more palatable version of social capital for social historians associated with Bourdieu was already in decline by the mid 1990s as the concept took off (see previous chapter). At most, social capital for social historians occasionally retained that link whilst discarding (or being squeezed out of) the uses that had equally occasionally arisen on an entirely different basis in the past, as social and economic infrastructure or systemic *economic* properties (see Chapter 3). Social capital might prove more attractive to social historians by bringing Bourdieu back in, but this cannot fix context so easily as for other disciplines and topics that see BBBI as simply confined to path-dependence, initial conditions or presence and/or strength of contingent variables (as opposed to historically situated meaning).

5.3   FROM SOCIAL CAPITAL TO HISTORY

It is evident that social capital can, in principle, address almost any topic and, especially, do so across a wide range of methodologies and within, and across, disciplinary boundaries. This does not, however, mean that its presence has been universal and uniform across the social sciences, as has already been illustrated by its marginal importance to history, which is far from being alone in its relative lack of interest. In part, this unevenness is explained by the substantive evolution of the content of social capital as a concept. For, whilst it has incorporated any consideration in principle, it has proved at least partially selective in practice in terms of subject matter, disciplines, content and methodology.

Indeed, insofar as social capital has exhibited a number of no-go areas (such as the state, class, conflict and power), despite these being at the heart of social interaction, it is liable to prove unattractive to historians, since the salience of these factors is integral to their understanding and, unavoidably, to major historical change itself, as opposed to short-term positive-sum improvements. Not surprisingly, even on its own preferred terrain of civil society, there are grander approaches, which are familiar to, and deployed by, historians, than that offered by social capital, although these have been almost if not completely neglected by the social capital literature. One of these, the gift relationship, a supposed antithesis to commodity relations, derives primarily from anthropology (see Fine 2002a and Lapavitsas 2003 for critical overviews). Whatever the validity of the distinction as an analytical starting point, the opposition between gift and commodity is at least as rich as social versus other types of capital as a means of approaching the historical as a relationship between the economic (or the market) and the non-economic.

Thus, on just one occasion, Bestor (1999, p.39) refers to social capital in passing in her study of fifteenth-century Florentine marriage: 'The groom's ornaments magnified the bride, transforming her into an iconic symbol of the material and social capital she brought to her marriage.' But this is embedded within a contribution that is firmly composed, and entitled, around such marriage transactions as reflecting a (Maussian) gift. Similarly, Cooper's (1995) study of wedding gift exchange in twentieth-century Niger prefers 'gift' to 'social capital', the latter again appearing just once (p.138): 'The giving of the gifts continues to create not only material wealth but also (and perhaps more importantly) social capital: the recognition of worth and value, social personhood, dependency and patronage.' Benedict (1996, p.61), on the other hand, in studying seventeenth-century Montpellier, again refers to social capital only once, in a table concerned with its contribution to dowry, but finds no need to mention gift. Basically either concept can be freely, even extensively, deployed by historians, but it is hardly surprising if social capital is pushed into second place. Elsewhere, if only in passing, the history literature has brought gift and social capital together, with the latter in a subordinate position, by reference to Chinese *guanxi* (Kipnis 1996 and Yang 1989; see also Chapter 9).

A second alternative to social capital which is of appeal to historians is the analytical framework posed by Polanyi, and the interaction between the commercial and the traditional. Once again, despite its potential affinities with the subject matter and the strength of this tradition, Polanyi has been studiously ignored by the social capital literature, although Granovetter and embeddedness has had some, predominantly indirect, presence through appeal to networks. Interestingly, in the broader critical literature on social capital, Craig and Porter (2005) and Robison (2004) have explicitly seen it both as an impoverished contribution relative to Polanyi and as a way of promoting some form of compromise between neo-liberalism and Third Wayism (see Chapter 9). As Craig and Porter put it (pp.257–8), in part referring to social capital, such concepts 'are hardly substitutes for the engines of social contest and embedding Polanyi described ... Thus, a Polanyian perspective also encourages the prising apart of these consensual domains and rationales, to see whose interests, contests and voices are being smothered'. And, for Robison, social capital is simply the technocratic and neo-liberal reflection of Polanyi's double movement in the era of globalisation under US hegemony. In a JSTOR history search on Polanyi, the score is at least double that of social capital, indicating where the discipline's preference lies! But, possibly, the greatest put-down for social capital in this respect comes from Granovetter. As a modern pioneer, he is the least sophisticated proponent of embeddedness, confessing to having drafted his classic contribution (1985) without any thought of Polanyi; but he also describes how he sought unsuc-cessfully to push Putnam to be more refined when the latter first mooted the use of social capital (Krippner et al. 2004). If social capital lies to the other side of Granovetter in the understanding of the relationship between the economic and the social, it is hardly surprising it has had little appeal to social historians.

This all provides the context within which to review in more detail, if selectively, the impact of social capital on the discipline of history. The obvious starting point is the special double issue of *Journal of Interdisciplinary History*, reprinted as Rotberg (ed.) (2001) and, presumably, there must have been some social capital, as it were, in putting this together, not least with Putnam contributing as an author. At the time of its publication, I wrote as follows:

It is edited by Rotberg ... in an introductory essay entitled 'Social Capital and Political Culture in Africa, America, Australasia, and Europe' that, together with the chronological span of the articles, indicates the putative geographical as well as historical scope of the notion. (Fine 2001a, p.83)

Two footnotes are added, one to the effect that 'Almazán (1999) ['The Aztec States-Society: Roots of Civil Society and Social Capital'] addresses social capital in 15th and early 16th century Aztec society but only uses the term in the title to his paper!', and the other observing that, '[r]ather than taking opportunity here as well as elsewhere to address critiques, Gamm and Putnam (1999) ['The Growth of Voluntary Associations in America, 1840–1940'] is primarily a descriptive and statistical account of associational activity in the United States'.

This all points to features that remain characteristic of the literature incorporating social capital into history. The range of topics is more or less unlimited, reference to the term is casual, and Putnam proceeds apparently oblivious of devastating and mounting criticism, much of it from historians or those dealing in historical topics. His account of Italy borders on the ridiculous and is readily undermined on its own terms (associational activity in the south caught up with that of the north within a decade of his own study), his use of social capital is itself an afterthought, and its transposition to the United States is dependent upon analytical and empirical acrobatics (Fine 2001a, ch.6). Over the past decade, the critical literature on Putnam has reached deluge proportions, his work often being taken as the critical point of departure for the typical article, due to his erroneous methodology, his limited understanding of social capital itself, as well as of civil society, his misunderstanding or omission of relevant variables, their interaction in ways that negate his approach, and so on (see Chapter 8). More specifically, if selectively, contributions to McLean et al. (2002) show how Putnam has only partially understood and also misrepresented de Tocqueville; Edwards et al. (2001) question his limited interpretation of the nature of civil society; and Boggs (2001 and 2002) finds his understanding of politics to be a 'fantasy' (see Chapter 8). Arneil (2006) demonstrates his rosy, uncritical view of US civil society in the past (racist, sexist and religiously conservative and intolerant).

Whilst some of the articles in the special issue do fully embrace social capital, others can be perceived to be offering criticisms of this sort, pointing to what social capital cannot do as much as what it can. Much more significant for our purpose, however, is that the double special issue is the exception that proves the rule. Presumably, this should have been the launching pad for social capital within history. If so, it has failed miserably, with no further special issues (which are common across the other social sciences) and limited numbers of contributions that do fully embrace the notion as opposed to casually mentioning it in passing.

In this vein, contributions from within history have tended to fall on either side of the discipline in economic or social orientation, flirting with the new institutional economics and its analytical foundations in offering an alternative in line with the new economics imperialism, or doing likewise with the cultural without economic content respectively. Some fall across the divide, as social capital is a recipe for eclecticism, and the motivation and origins for contributions in using, or referring to, social capital are idiosyncratic and not always transparent. What follows is a cursory overview, drawing predominantly upon the JSTOR search introduced above.

On the economic side of the divide, Allen and Reed (2006) construct duelling from 1500 to 1900 as a 'screening device', a means of demonstrating commitment to, and gaining, patronage, a way of overcoming informational imperfections with regard to loyalty to the crown. Carp (2001) points positively to social capital as constituting the bonds between firefighters in the eighteenth-century United States, not least in Charleston and the south more generally, as a consequence of the firefighters' defence of private property and their connections with local politicians. This allowed them to take a lead in the fight for independence from Britain, and even to start fires in order to prevent property from falling into British hands. But one cannot help but wonder about the implications for slavery and racism, see McNamee and Miller 2004, p.76 on contemporary New York, and the exclusive employment practices involved. For, citing Waldinger (1995, p.557), 'social connections utilized by white ethnics in the construction trades and the fire and police unions of New York effectively kept racial minorities out'. Carmona and Simpson (1999) deploy social capital in their account of the rise and fall of sharecropping in Catalonia, but essentially rely upon the moral hazard, opportunism and principal-agent discourse of the new information-theoretic approach to economics. This has itself been prominent in new literature on sharecropping, offered as an alternative to analyses based on class and power (and, it would appear, to sharecroppers' own self-perception). As Carmona and Simpson put it, 'contemporaries often considered the contract synonymous with "exploitation" and "impoverishment", terms frequently found in the more traditional literature on sharecropping' (p.290). Contracting is also perceived to have been difficult across scattered Australian gold mines at the end of the nineteenth century, resulting in less social capital by which to come to amicable agreements and, hence, more costly litigation in the courts (Khan 2000). In an early application in this vein, Majewski et al. (1993) deploy the notion of social capital, referencing Coleman, to explain the laying of plank roads in New York for public use as a reflection of the ability of community spirit to overcome the problem of free riders. Unfortunately for them, despite being published contemporaneously with Putnam on Italy, they do not seem to have been able to project a metaphorical absence of planks to present-day US civil society and to have shared in Putnam's social capital glory.

Not surprisingly, moving towards the other side of the divide from the economic, social historians have referenced social capital when dealing with gender and marriage. For Brightman (1996), social capital facilitates foraging and hunting in primitive societies, but offers more in terms of standard anthropological concerns with taboo and gender politics. In Kapteijn's (1995) study of northern Somali, with reference to gifts, bridewealth and reciprocity, women are social capital for their men, and children for their mothers, relations that tend to be undermined by commercialisation and the state. Pouwels (2002) sees marriage as the social capital by which merchants could integrate themselves into local society and promote their business along the African east coast prior to 1800.

In an unwitting anticipation of a rapidly growing literature on the connection between (lack of) social capital and crime (or any other deviancy), McIntosh suddenly imports the idea into her response in a debate on the controlling of misbehaviour across the medieval–early modern divide. Social capital accumulates with the formation of the nation-state, again anticipating social capital as modernisation. She wishes to incorporate religion and social factors. To do so, she draws 'upon the powerful concept of "social capital"'. Her analytical opportunism, freely referencing Bourdieu, Coleman and Putnam as an unproblematic troika of sources, is scarcely concealed:

> Regardless of whether one prefers a definition drawn from
> sociology/political science or a more anthropologically focused

usage, social capital is produced by interactions between people, either informally or through more structured associations ... Because social capital serves to link individuals and groups, operating both laterally and vertically, it is an important explanatory tool when examining the development of a participatory nation-state. (1998, p.294)

And, also, one that controls 'misbehaviour'. Significantly, as Gaggio (2004, p.509) also recognises, her contribution to the special issue of the *Journal of Interdisciplinary History* is one that emphasises the positive gains and role of women in medieval and early modern England, as opposed to their exclusion and oppression (McIntosh 1999).

Other more sophisticated uses of social capital are explicit about their ties to Bourdieu-type interpretations and uses of the concept. Shetler (1995) focuses on an object as limited as a Kiroba text of popular history as a form of social capital in Tanzania, since it depicts a constellation of networks and social relations that can inform and sustain those who draw upon it. Pellow (1991) perceives the powers and legitimacy of chiefs as representing their shifting social capital in response to shifting circumstances in turn-of-the-last-century Accra, not least in being contingent upon British patronage. Smith (1995) allows for intersection between race, ethnicity and gender, as colour of skin as social capital allows for a better marriage in Guatemala. Franklin (2002) has inspired a number of studies of the way in which Afro-Americans have used their social and other capital to promote community education and other advances, although the social capital of racism is equally important in the history of 'exclusion'. MacHardy (1992 and 1999) does deploy the entire repertoire of Bourdieu's capitals to address dissent amongst Protestant nobles in sixteenth- and seventeenth-century Habsburg. The same is so of Schoenbrun's (1996) account of gendered relations around the east African Great Lakes before the fifteenth century. Without explicit reference to Bourdieu, Muldrew (2001, p.111) rounds up 'the social capital of display' as a feature of early modern England, both in and of itself, and in acts of generosity: '[silver] plate was also an important item in gift exchange'. But such social capital is perceived to have been under threat from money or moneyed capital, for 'the hoarding of money, and the advantage it gave one person to do what they wanted, were always seen as a threat to trust, sociability and the circulation of social capital upon which early modern exchange depended' (p.119). Literature on the modern period sends this antithesis between social capital and money into reverse, with the one serving to support the other in light of the need for trust of the borrower on the part of the lender. Interestingly, this theme within the newer economic history and the newer financial economics has been muted as far as social capital is concerned, except when it comes to Grameen banking and the like, for the new institutional economics suffices for the purpose. Yet, for van Leeuwen at least, such money allowed an entrée into higher status:

> Poor relief was a many-sided litmus test: vis-à-vis one's peers, apropos subordinate members of society, and, in fact, toward God and one's own conscience. In another respect too, charity could be useful; the nouveaux riches, economically successful but socially inferior, could exchange money or time for social capital. (1994, p.596)

But the poor themselves are perceived to have had less honourable motives, displaying 'an intuitive knowledge of the value of what sociologists and anthropologists call social capital', creating norms of mutual support, 'not solely [as] a form of spreading risks over time' but also as a means of accessing information on support from others (p.603). In short, as far as social capital is concerned, '[t]he virtual certainty that an investment would pay off in the future naturally increased the willingness to invest'.

This is to return to social capital and economic history, or even economic and social history proper. And, in this vein, by a long way, by far the most accomplished use of social capital in history is to be found in Ogilvie's (2003) book on women in early modern Germany and the role of guilds. Her starting point is social networks, and these are used to frame the creation and significance of social capital (which only really appears in her book after page 340). Networks only become social capital through closure, by restricting membership as well as allowing it (p.341), whether by gender, ethnicity, religion or whatever. Just as inclusion can benefit those who are members, so exclusion can harm those who are not. She concludes: 'social networks generate social capital, which not only facilitates collective action but also sustains commonly shared norms ... these norms not only penalized women in each generation, but perpetuated and entrenched themselves, penalizing future generations' (p.352). Ogilvie seems, however, to go further in her article (2004), recognising that guilds achieved or lost power not as a function of whether their social capital offered efficient institutional solutions to market failures, but as a function of whether it endowed them with a powerful bargaining position within the local institutional and political framework. (p.329)

In other words, 'social capital', and she herself uses inverted commas, is a consequence of the social networks of power, and not the more or less effective correction of market imperfections, as would be proposed by economic theory and its extrapolation to history. With this approach and its application, I have no complaints. But it is far from clear what light is shed by appealing to social capital, nor that it is open to generalisation from one case study to another.[2]

5.4   THE PRESENT AS HISTORY

Whilst there has been a significant degree of application of social capital to historical topics, if predominantly by non-historians, the vast weight of the literature has focused upon contemporary topics. Nonetheless, in this respect, there are two broad areas of application in which historians might take more than a passing interest, in view of concern for major socio-economic change. First and foremost is development, for which there is an extensive social capital literature, pioneered by the World Bank (see Chapter 6). It is difficult to believe that historians could take this literature seriously as a contribution to the history of the present.

Second, from humble beginnings, social capital has mushroomed in its application to transition economies. The World Bank sponsored a social capital initiative to explain ill health in Russia by distribution of social capital – this modest aim to be set against the drama of mortality rates having risen over the country's transition, unprecedented for a relatively developed economy. In this vein, absence of social capital at all or of the right type has been seen as the cause of malaise within transitional societies. The inevitable conclusion is that successful transition depends on creating the right type of social capital, and/or that social capital is seen as amelioration of some for the negative excesses of an otherwise unexplained transition. For Korosteleva, Eastern Europe is subject to hierarchical social capital (*blat*):

the shadow societies of vertical networks [are] based on blat ... rendering the official 'democratic' settings inefficient and often invalid. Such a system is also a good method of keeping discontent under control by diverting the grievances and dissatisfaction to informal infrastructures that can deal with specific concerns more efficiently. (2006, p.186)

It all becomes a matter of, 'How can a society break through to the "virtuous circle" that produces positive social capital?' (p.187). Significantly, then, the bulk of this literature has regressed to the modernisation framework, taking some sort of ideal western market (and social capital) democracy as its goal. Whether in the form of secure property rights (free from state interference and continuing oligarchies), political participation through a well-functioning electoral system, or a vibrant civil society, social capital offers an analytical and policy panacea. Yet even the social capital literature itself, mercifully, has recognised that social capital has become unduly homogenised over a highly diverse set of transitional societies, for which individual histories and continuing context are of decisive importance.[3] As the most comprehensive and sophisticated review of the literature puts it (Mihaylova 2004, p.136): 'The use of the term can be pseudoscientific and lead to poor quality research ... problems with its definition, operationalization and measurement, as well as with determining its sources, forms and consequences.' But there is still seen to be scope for continued use of social capital in avoiding 'cultural essentialism, ahistoricism, functionalism, blind rational choice adherence, apolitical attitude and reductionism', if only because 'it is obvious that social capital has now firmly established itself in scholarly discourse and development practice and has a life (or many lives) of its own which cannot easily be dismissed'.

More generally, the issue is not about what sort of social capital is needed, and what sort of effects this will have in transition but, in the first instance, about what sort of transition is desirable – even if inevitably this is to some form of capitalism. The latter serves as an ideal against which to describe divergence (inadequate social capital or of the wrong type) and as the basis on which to advise a target for transitional convergence. But, for Uslaner and Badescu,

> the bumpy transition to democracy in Central and Eastern Europe challenged three of the core tenets of social capital theory. First, democratic regimes should stimulate participation ... Second, democratic regimes should breed trust in others ... Third, civic engagement leads to more trust. (2003, p.219)

It may be that with such conundrums in mind, historians of transition have been protected against the Putnam phenomenon by previous experience of Fukuyama (2002, p.34), who quickly jumped onto the social capital bandwagon himself, perceiving it as bountiful in developing countries, but as not corresponding to modern political and economic organisations, and hence as an obstacle to development. This is because for Fukuyama (1999, p.3), familial 'groups have a narrow radius of trust', and also, '[t]he economic function of social capital is to reduce the transaction costs associated with formal coordination mechanisms like hierarchies, bureaucratic rules, and the like' (p.4). So, for him, globalisation is the antidote, having become the bearer of social capital to developing countries, creating the functional new and destroying the old (Fukuyama 2001). Does (modern) social capital also bring the end of history, and a recognisable euthanasia of the historian?[4]

5.5   THERE IS NO ALTERNATIVE?

In this light, whatever the inducements for historians to address the contemporary, social capital is unlikely to appeal as conduit. And this is no more than the condensation of the deficiencies of social capital from the perspective of historians as laid out above, something explaining its absence in their deliberations over the past decade. Will this continue to be the case? Across the profession, there are three potential directions, and these are not mutually exclusive. One is for social capital to gather strength and prosper, contingent in part upon how it evolves. BBBI apart, its evolution is most likely to be confined to the newer/newest economic history, as it opportunistically complements or displaces institutions.[5] The second direction, at the opposite extreme, is for historians to continue in the main to ignore social capital, although, as and when it does prosper on or across the discipline's boundaries, it will prove both irksome and potentially a Trojan Horse for the previous outcome. Significantly, the recent book on civil society edited by Hall and Trentmann (2005) fails to address the social capital phenomenon. When I asked why, I was told that social capital was not to be taken seriously. At the very least, historians can hardly be expected to take seriously the claim by social capitalists that they are BBI civil society or civilising economists. For whatever the validity of the claim that civil society is absent across other social sciences, this is laughable as far as (social) history and historians are concerned.

Nevertheless, the third direction, and the one I favour, is for historians to engage fully and uncompromisingly critically with social capital by exposing its legion deficiencies and offering constructive alternatives that reject it rather than proposing new, improved versions. Here, of course, I depart from Gaggio. Although, as already observed, there is considerable overlap between the two of us over the poverty of the bulk of the social capital literature as it is, there are also differences. His stance is one of acknowledging the limitations of social capital and of putting these right in individual case study. His own study (Gaggio 2004 and 2007) of the Italian gold jewellery industry is exemplary, and one of the most rewarding and sophisticated amongst those that cling to social capital despite acknowledging its legion deficiencies. Although, from my own perspective,[6] he relies insufficiently critically upon the industrial district/clusters paradigm for the sources of success, he does so through recognising that Putnam fetishises civil society and associational life as a source of economic success without regard to other causes and consequences (not least the organising power of politics, whether through socialism or fascism, pp.35–6). He charts the passage of a particular local entrepreneur, Carlo Balzano, from social capital to fraud and embezzlement (p.49), and, indeed, as has been revealed on a grander scale in many countries, it is far from clear whether the two differ. And, in perceiving an industrial district as a form of social capital,[7] he breaks with Granovetter in viewing social networks as cultural and political, 'not as static structures but as historical processes forged in conflict', with the capacity of actors 'to reflect on their own lives and embed economic action in, or disembed it from, other realms of action' (p.324).

I do agree, then, with Gaggio himself as illustration, that the presence of social capital is sufficiently fluid conceptually that it can take on any mantle, including excellent critical and constructive analysis. But to rely upon this alone is to take an unduly narrow view of the intellectual dynamic of social capital, for the following reasons. First, Gaggio takes insufficient account of the collective weight of the critical deficiencies of social capital that have been exposed here and which explain the historian's reluctance to engage. Its capacity to absorb each and every variable has provided it with the separate but related property of being more or less immune to criticism. As argued in Chapter 2, this often takes the form of pointing to an anomaly in light of an omitted variable, itself often related to a specific context. So criticism, acknowledged in a piecemeal fashion, is readily perceived as seeking the addition of an otherwise missing variable or method, so that the remedy, within the loose bounds previously indicated, is to incorporate what is otherwise absent and move forward. On the other hand, where criticism is offensive to the core values of social capital, it is usually simply ignored, especially in relation to the points already elaborated. This is so much so that those contributions that do acknowledge criticism do so selectively, for the purpose of supporting their own particular contributions, adding to the collectively chaotic but all-encompassing nature of social capital. In this respect, at least, if not by extent of criticism, Gaggio conforms to a typical article – BBBI and proceeding on this basis to promote social capital amongst historians.

Second, then, this means that individual contributions, however scathing and reconstructive, will be deployed to legitimise social capital and not to move it from its current trajectory. The dead weight of continuing hackademics is too great. Third, and most important, Gaggio takes no account of the broader intellectual environment that has spawned social capital. For, as laid out in Chapter 1, social capital thrived in that intellectual context peculiar to the 1990s in which there was a dual reaction against the extremes both of neo-liberalism and postmodernism. Like its counterpart, globalisation, but as its complement and opposite in many respects, social capital has rejected the idea that markets work perfectly and embraced the idea of getting real about how people go about their (daily) lives (Fine 2004a). The global, though, is notable for its absence from the world of social capital (Schuurman 2003), with the exception of a recently burgeoning literature on global management (see Chapter 7). Social capital is more about communities accepting the world as it is and bettering themselves on this basis.

Thus, whilst globalisation and social capital parallel one another in seeking to come to terms with the nature of contemporary capitalism and extend their insights into the past, they otherwise differ considerably in content and direction (although each is equally promiscuous, if selective, in range of application, method and impact). For globalisation has been won away from the neo-liberal agenda that the market is benevolently triumphant over the state. Instead, globalisation has been situated systemically, as a matter of power and conflict, where the role of the state remains significant, and context by time and place is paramount (as neatly captured by the notion of glocalisation). By contrast, social capital has compromised with neo-liberalism, is middle-range at the expense of the systemic (with roots in methodological individualism), and is most uncomfortable if not self-destructive about BBI power, conflict, and so on, and, most significantly, the contextual. In this light, it would appear that historians do not have the choice of accepting social capital and then simply reforming it with the removal of a wart or seven.

On the whole, history's disregard for social capital is a reflection of its own positive qualities. But it is precisely because of these that it should critically engage with social capital, shedding light on the methodological and theoretical lessons that can be gleaned historically for understanding the past as well as contemporary capitalism. The point is not only to halt social capital in its tracks and send it back to where it has come from, but also to offer alternatives to social science, currently as open as it has ever been, in the dual retreat from postmodernism and neo-liberalism. Otherwise, there is the prospect of a creeping, if not a rapid, march of social capital across the newer/newest economic history, and a corresponding reduction in the scope and influence of a genuine economic and social history.

6
Social Capital is Dead: Long Live Whatever Comes Next[1]

6.1 INTRODUCTION

In September 2006, a panel chaired by Angus Deaton published a major evaluation of the World Bank's research, covering the period from 1998 to 2005. As well as the report itself, 20 or more background papers were commissioned from assessors across the various topics that were felt to represent the Bank's work (Deaton et al. 2006). The Deaton assessment was extremely damning, one major criticism being that poor-quality research and questionable results had been promoted whenever it suited the Bank's position. Just to pick out one of many statements to this effect:

> the panel has substantial criticisms of the way that this research was used to proselytize on behalf of Bank policy, often without expressing appropriate scepticism. Internal research that was favorable to Bank positions was given greater prominence, and unfavorable research ignored ... balance was lost in favor of advocacy ... there was a serious failure of the checks and balances that should separate advocacy and research. (p.6)

The report goes on to perceive this as deriving from an internal institutionalised system of commissioning and delivering research within the Bank that needs to be reformed, not least with regard to the incentives offered to individual researchers and the independence of the research process from the needs of advocacy.

Despite its trenchant and welcome criticisms, the Deaton report is also extremely limited in certain respects. First, its own assessment of quality is more or less entirely based on the criterion of what would be publishable in a mainstream economics journal (with some deference towards taking into account development and policy implications). Second, then, this means a failure to get to grips with interdisciplinary and heterodox approaches, especially those derived from developments studies. Third, there is also a notable absence of any explicit and fully specified concept of development against which the contributions to research might be assessed. Fourth, the criticisms offered by Deaton have been made many times before and, to some extent, in much greater depth and breadth. These earlier contributions are not simply overlooked by the report, but there is a failure to address why the Bank is so unresponsive to what are often devastating critiques of the quality of its research and other practices (other than to suggest different incentives for researchers and their greater independence). Fifth, and possibly most surprising of all given the report's conclusions, there is little or no reference to the apparently dramatic changes in the Bank's own research and policy ethos over the period covered by the report's assessment. In particular, this period witnessed the apparent demise of the Washington Consensus and the rise of the post-Washington Consensus, coupled with the Comprehensive Development Framework and Poverty Reduction Strategy Papers (PRSPs). No consideration is given to these shifts, even though they are generally acknowledged to have been the leading elements in the evolution of the Bank's advocacy and scholarship (if not of its policy) over the previous decade.

In my previous book (Fine 2001a), I devoted two chapters and more to social capital at the World Bank. I carefully distinguish between the roles played by scholarship, rhetoric and policy in practice, arguing that these are not unrelated, but that they are not necessarily mutually consistent, and that the relationship between them varies over time and topic (and, it should be added, place). Social capital has primarily played a legitimising role for the Bank in rhetoric and scholarship with very limited impact upon policy (and, as with other areas of research, a particular and usually peculiar relationship to reality is implicit in the vision and sources of development that it offers). In an extremely prominent and heavily promoted fashion, social capital was being used to legitimise the shift from the Washington to the post-Washington Consensus, with the design of incorporating both the non-economic (or civil society) and the non-economist (development studies) into the process, at the expense of the (developmental) state that had proved so effective in questioning the Washington Consensus, especially by reference to the East Asian NICs.

Yet, necessarily, as a special case of what has already been argued, Deaton seems to be blissfully unaware of these shenanigans, despite its emphasis on the gap between research and advocacy. Despite the extraordinary rise of social capital at the Bank over the last years of the millennium, the main report only mentions social capital *once*. It could not be more dismissive of the concept (p.81): 'There is much political correctness, including mindless cheerleading for cultural touchstones such as women, trees, and social capital, as in "women are an important engine of growth".' Clearly, the report has scant respect for research on social capital since it is seen as a mere 'cultural touchstone' (like women, let alone trees!). As a result, the report misses the opportunity to reflect upon how and why such a concept could be so heavily promoted within the Bank, and outside by it, in the arenas of both research and advocacy.

This is all the more unfortunate since the decline from prominence of social capital at the Bank, as will be seen, has been as rapid as was its rise. In the context of scholarship, advocacy (or rhetoric/ideology) and policy, why should it have been subject to such an experience? The last major publication from the Bank on social capital, at least as scholarship/advocacy to promote it, appeared as Grootaert and van Basterlaer (eds) (2002). Its view of social capital could not have been more different than that purveyed by Deaton. In his two-page foreword, Robert Putnam asserts that 'experts in the field are now converging toward a "lean and mean" definition of *social capital*, focused on social networks and the associated norms of reciprocity and trust' (p.xxi). It is to be suspected that this unsubstantiated (and false) view, one that classifies as experts only those who hold to Putnam's own approach, reflects both a pride in and a nice-to-be-scared horror at the conceptual monster that Putnam, more than any other, has been responsible for releasing. Putnam himself refers to 'one of the hottest concepts in social science globally ... a very far-reaching expansion – virtually an explosion' (p.xxi). So it's time to get lean and mean, in order to defend social capital against the charge of a definitional chaos that is even acknowledged, and yet consolidated, by its ardent proponents, as they shift its use to suit their own particular purposes.

But, on the second page of his foreword, at least indirectly, Putnam is unable to restrain his predilection, and that of the literature, for a plump and benevolent definition of social capital. He welcomes the correctly observed burgeoning scope of application:

> While early work had focused primarily on governance, macroeconomic rates of growth, and (in closely related work) school performance and job placement, we now are beginning to see how social capital can influence everything from infant

mortality rates to solid waste management to communal violence. (p.xxii)

Leaving aside what is both a selective and self-serving early history of work on social capital, is it surprising that its definition should career out of control when it simultaneously seeks to encompass so many aspects of economic and social life?

This chapter, then, charts the rise and fall (or benevolent but rapid neglect) of social capital at the World Bank. It does so against the background, covered in Section 6.2, of the shift from the Washington to the Post-Washington Consensus, in which social theorists at the Bank saw an opportunity to promote social capital as a lever in persuading Bank economists to take the social more seriously. The results are at best mixed, in light of close examination of Grootaert and van Basterlaer (eds) (2002). It could be argued that it was the economists that were doing the levering and welcoming social capital, as a way of legitimising their unreconstructed economics and its extension to the non-economic. As documented in Section 6.3, the World Bank's own social capitalists think otherwise and consider themselves to have successfully and strategically deployed an admittedly flawed concept in moving the Bank's economists to more progressive and rounded positions. As far as they were concerned, social capital had done its work at the Bank and attention could move on to other issues.

But Sections 6.3 and 6.4 offer a rather different interpretation of social capital's fall from prominence at the Bank. First, if the economists were moved by social capital at all, it was only to use the concept as a means to address the social with otherwise unchanged methods. Second, whilst this meant that the social capitalists had done as much as they could with the economists, it was little if not nothing of substance. Third, economists themselves had little further use for social capital, not least because, within the wider literature, it was becoming more irksome in its social content than they could accommodate.

Thus, in a brief if glittering career, social capital has had at most a peripheral impact at the Bank – primarily one that has smoothed the transition from Washington to post-Washington Consensus and sidelined attention to the developmental state. But there has also been a much wider impact of social capital in development studies, where, as unpicked in Section 6.5, it has attained the status of a 'buzzword'. This means that the impact of social capital has been, and remains, far from negligible. As suggested in the final section, the concept should be rejected in development studies, as in other applications, with the lesson to be drawn from its use at the World Bank that even apparently good intentions are perverted when attached to it.

6.2   SOCIAL CAPITAL'S IRRESISTIBLE RISE ...

It is hardly surprising that social capital should have been applied to development, especially as it has been applied to so much else. But the prominence of social capital within development has been considerably strengthened by its heavy promotion from an early stage by the World Bank. Why should this have been so? Like participation and empowerment, social capital offered a dream concept for the challenges faced by the World Bank in the 1990s, enabling it to offer a more radical rhetoric whilst retaining flexibility in policy substance. Thus, in retrospect, Porter and Lyon (2006) see social capital as having been a means of BBI culture for the World Bank and, for Watts (2006, p.36), it has been a matter of 'domesticating' the concept, although it was already pretty well domesticated ab initio once Bourdieu had been discarded in favour of Coleman and Putnam. For the previous decade had brought a growing crisis in the Bank's (and the IMF's) legitimacy, with mounting criticism of the neo-liberal conditionalities attached to loans. The Comprehensive Development Framework (CDF) and the post-Washington Consensus (PWC) were designed to restore that legitimacy (Fine et al. 2001). The rejection of the Washington Consensus at the rhetorical level was evident. Yet it is arguable whether these shifts had any impact on policy itself, as an even wider range of market-supporting interventions than under the Washington Consensus became legitimised through a rationale of correcting market and non-market imperfections (van Waeyenberge 2007).

These shifts also reflected changes that were under way within the discipline of economics in general and development economics in particular (Jomo and Fine 2006 and Fine 2008c). The old 'informal', 'classical' development economics had long given way to the 'new', with its emphasis on mathematical techniques, econometrics, the virtues of the market, and the corresponding need not to distort it through rent-seeking, corruption, and the like. But, in its reaction against neo-liberalism, mainstream economics had begun to emphasise the importance of market imperfections and the need to correct them through non-market mechanisms. This has fed through into what I have termed the 'newer' development economics, with the PWC to the fore.

In one major respect, the CDF and the PWC exhibit a marked difference from earlier ideologies emanating from the World Bank. Although completely different from one another, the Keynesian/welfarism/modernisation stance of the McNamara period and the neo-liberalism of the Washington Consensus had their own relatively simple messages on how to achieve development. In contrast, the PWC emphasises that the incidence of market and non-market imperfections is uneven and contingent in form, extent, and consequences so that not one model fits all, and everything is micro-based, not least in addressing the macro. Social capital is at core the negative, mirror image of such practices as rent-seeking, with the same analytical framework but diametrically opposed conclusions – that non-market influences can be beneficial (rather than detrimental) to the market. As such, it incorporates the non-economic in a way that is consistent with the (non-)market-imperfections approach and is sensitive in principle to differences between one application and another. I hasten to add that this does not necessarily make a policy difference; rather, it simply offers richer scope in justifying policy. After all, there are limits to using neo-liberalism as the rationale for substantial intervention. Stein (2001, pp.18–19) reasonably concludes, then: 'Unlike some people that argue that SCI [the World Bank's Social Capital Initiative] is aimed at creating a post-Washington consensus, the initiative is focused at propping up the orthodox model while disarming some of its critics' – although it might be even more reasonable to see this as the PWC itself rather than as an alternative to it.[2]

In short, social capital offered considerable leverage in the World Bank's dealings with the external world. In addition, it allowed for certain internal institutional interests to be promoted. The World Bank is dominated by economists, numerically and intellectually, and of the worst type from the perspective of the social scientists under the shadow of the Washington Consensus – who, in leaving the economy to the economists, would have to subordinate themselves to economics and to rational choice, both in approach and in being confined to a restricted range of applications. The CDF and PWC, though, offered some opportunity for non-economists to be taken seriously. Social capital was strategically chosen as a judicious concept for that purpose.

Given my own interest in social capital for other reasons, I was onto its importance for the World Bank from an early stage. I dredged through the Bank's dedicated website, http://worldbank. org/poverty/scapital, and, initially, exaggerated its importance as a way of circumventing the idea of the developmental state as an alternative to the Washington Consensus (Fine 1999a), although that the PWC would (seek to) circumvent the developmental state proved correct. But my efforts did prompt a mole within the World Bank to contact me with three gems of wisdom in terms of the reaction I was likely to receive for my criticisms. First, I would be asked to back off, as the World Bank was changing for the good. Second, none of my criticisms would be addressed. And, third, I would be offered a job of sorts to internalise, incorporate and neutralise criticism.

Sad to say, even moles can get it wrong, and the last of these never materialised. Only on one occasion, the exception that proves the rule, was there any serious attempt to engage in discussion with me from the World Bank's social capitalists. This was a seminar organised jointly by the London School of Economics and the Overseas Development Institute, specifically to provoke debate, and with Michael Woolcock as my opponent.[3] To my astonishment, he insisted as a precondition for participation that I provide him with three questions to answer, and he would reciprocate. I offered the following:

1. Discuss critically the relationship between social capital and globalisation.
2. Assess critically what is the social capital of the World Bank and other IFIs.
3. Discuss critically what social capital understands as, and adds to the understanding of, development, with what economic analyses it is consistent, and how it understands 'non-social', especially economic, capital, and capitalism.

These were indicative of a wish to explore the relationship between social capital and globalisation, economic development, and the practices of the World Bank itself. I do not have a record of Woolcock's questions but one was to ask what I would say to a South African nurse asking me how I would deal with HIV/AIDS,[4] and another was why I did not publish in respectable journals. The latter is ironic in view of the World Bank's total exclusion of my work (in spite of its adopted role as a 'Knowledge Bank') from its social capital website (including its extensive annotated bibliography on social capital) and from its overall website altogether (other than once for a legitimising exercise[5]). In the event, while I did answer his questions, he totally ignored mine, preferring to offer a tangential discourse on some obscure management framework before departing to overview the implementation of the World Bank's social capital toolkit household survey for Albania. With social capital surveys having been widely adopted across developed and developing countries, whatever the intentions of the World Bank's social capitalists in shifting internal dialogue and practice, the external impact has been considerable in this respect at least.

Otherwise, two other skirmishes mark my dealings with the World Bank social capitalists. One was also with Michael Woolcock, through email exchange, in which he chose to voice his own views through an anonymous third party, to the effect that '[w]hat makes social capital most useful is its neutrality; a neutrality that you cannot get in discussions about participation, discrimination, exclusion, etc., which I consider manifestations of social capital'. And, the anonymous commentator continues:

> Ben Fine seems to be in a real minority here. While many people are still undecided about the value-added of social capital (which I can understand), Ben Fine seems to be the only one who thinks even considering social capital is actually destructive or distracting.

As will be seen, the presumed virtues of retaining a 'neutral' concept of social capital lay in its putative capacity to engage and shift economists at the Bank. The issue is how that neutrality was going to be coloured in at the Bank itself and with what effects.

This exchange with Woolcock took place around my commentary on the social capital contribution to the draft for comment for the World Development Report (WDR) for 2000/1 on poverty (ultimately World Bank 2001). I had pointed to my usual criticisms of social capital, suggesting in unduly compromising fashion that at most social capital should serve as an investigative category and that it otherwise offers no causal analytical purchase in and of itself. To drive this home, literally in terms of their draft, I observed that although the section discussing social capital *preceded* those on gender, discrimination, stratification, fragmentation, conflict and institutions, none of these then cared to draw upon social capital at all, scarcely even to mention it, and so they could do without it altogether. In the final version, this embarrassing oversight was resolved by the simple expedient of changing the order, so that social capital was located *after* the others (as if these other issues were brought to fruition through social capital!).

Nonetheless, this WDR symbolised the high point of social capital at the World Bank. In addition, though, the leading position played by non-economists in its rise was at least in the beginnings of being eclipsed, as is evidenced by the collection of Grootaert and van Bastelaer (eds) (2002) that appeared soon afterwards. Initially, observe, possibly echoing Putnam's expert appeal for the lean and mean, Grootaert and van Bastelaer advise against too great a level of fungibility in definition. For:

> There could be a temptation to extend the concept of social capital too broadly, turning it into a catch-all category designed to capture any asset that does not fall under the conventional categories of natural, physical, and human capital. A concept that encompasses too much is at risk of explaining nothing. The challenge for research, therefore, is to give meaningful and pragmatic content to the rich notion of social capital in each context and to define and measure suitable indicators. (2002, p.5)

Apart from indicating the narrow basis on which the contextual is to be constructed – judicious selection of variables from one case study to another – a genuine problem is identified. If social capital encompasses everything, over and above the unquestioned traditional (economists') categories of capital, it becomes an empty residual explanatory factor and is, thereby, rendered tautological – the 'missing link', to recall Grootaert's (1997) subsequently regretted phrase.

Yet, despite good intentions to avoid circular reasoning, and corresponding definitions, Grootaert and van Bastelaer still tend to fall victim to such simple charms. Social capital is 'rich' because it can be anything beyond the traditional categories of capital, but not all of its wealth will always be present in all circumstances. So social capital still serves as a residual explanatory factor but, like God or the devil, moves in mysterious and diverse ways, for good or for evil, from one context to another. Definitionally, the lean and mean also proves elusive. In a table, detailing the use of social capital across the book's chapters and entitled 'Classification of chapters by scope, forms and channels of social capital', Grootaert and van Bastelaer range over micro, meso and macro, and informational, collective action, structural and cognitive. That pretty well covers all social theory in broad terms! Throughout the volume, there is also appeal to other categories of social capital – the bridging, bonding, linking, vertical, horizontal and dark side. This all reflects a futile attempt to impose some general classificatory order over a category that is free to roam wherever its users care to take it – as if religions could be classified according to their icons, canons, and standard practices, such as frequency of worship.

In this light, not surprisingly, tautology is never far removed from the contributions' conclusions. Collier's chapter (2002), which opens the collection, is an outstanding if deeply depressing example of the economist's art of speculative or make-believe theorising. It begins with the insight that social capital as social interaction is variable according to composition and structure. A marriage is composed of the same two people whereas a singles bar is subject to shifting personnel. From here, it is a short step to including social capital as an input in a production function, one that varies as social interactions accommodate externalities, or not, through teaching, copying, trusting, pooling, and so on. Ultimately, we are led to the following 'implication for a pro-poor policy' (p.39): 'The distributional consequences of different mechanisms suggest that public policy should focus on promoting mechanisms that are distributionally most progressive and attempt to redress the regressive aspects of the other mechanisms.' I remain uncertain over whether this means we are in favour or not of marriage and/or singles bars.[6] Less speculatively, other chapters in the volume find that the presence of social capital, however understood or measured, has an ambiguous effect depending upon the presence or absence of other factors (or context). This is so for Gugerty and Kremer (2002) on donors' attempts to build social capital through their programmes in Kenya; for Krishna and Uphoff (2002) on watershed management in Rajasthan; for Pargal et al. (2002) on waste management in Dhaka; and for Bebbington and Carroll (2002) on federations of the rural poor in the Andes. What do these have in common, contextually, apart from the common foisting of social capital upon them?

For, in each case, the reason for the ambiguous effect of social capital is different, although, not surprisingly, there is some emphasis on the necessary presence of grass-root participation and its attachment to higher-level decision making and other factors. Essentially, this is equivalent to the conclusion that for social capital to be effective, some further factors X must be present. In a sense, this view is confirmed by the more upbeat case studies. For Isham and Kähkönen, for example, in their study of community-based water projects in central Java:

> Our results indicate that in villages with high levels of social capital – particularly in villages with active village groups and associations – household participation in design is likely to be high and monitoring mechanisms are more likely to be in place … Donors may want to avoid investing in community-based piped water systems in villages with low levels of social capital. (2002, p.185)

Now, what results of this sort mean is either tautology – participation is high where it is high if associational activity or the like is sufficiently close to water provision – or that some other form of association and its associated activity gives rise to spin-off effects to water. This latter option is precisely where social capital is at its most fungible – or should that be vulnerable? For, why and how should one set of social interactions be transferable to another? Such is the enigma that has been widely noted in various ways as surrounding social capital, especially in pointing to lack of attention to how social capital is created and how it has its effects, quite apart from its differentiation by context.

The same issue arises in slightly different ways in other papers in the collection. Knack's (2002) exercise in growth and poverty accounting, which utilises a variety of social capital variables, is highly questionable on its own terms. In any case, as Temple has concluded:

> What can a policy-maker in Mexico or Turkey actually do, confronted with the evidence from the World Values Survey that they govern a low-trust society? Standard recommendations, such as attempting to eliminate corruption and improve the legal system, are nothing new, and make good sense quite independently of any emphasis on social capital. (2001, p.92)

But, whatever the validity of the empirical conclusions and their policy implications, the point being emphasised here is that social capital depends for its explanatory purchase upon its *generation* as some sort of resource in one activity or context and its *use* in another.

This point is unwittingly confirmed by Collier's contribution from within mainstream neoclassical economics. It is based entirely on the idea of social capital as arising, purposefully or otherwise, in the context of asymmetry of information between contracting parties, with more positive outcomes potentially being built out of cumulative individual interactions, especially where this results in the market allocating resources more efficiently. The problem with this is that nothing new can ever arise, as has been recognised more generally in the neo-Austrian critique of neoclassical economics. So social capital in this perspective lacks a place for innovation and entrepreneurship, even within its chosen framework of methodological individualism. Collier's account is remarkably defective in that it fails to explain fungibility between one activity and another, and the ability of individuals to go beyond the circular limits of their literally received knowledge or experience; it is not completely generalisable. Thus, for example, on the one hand, social capital arises out of copying and pooling of information on the basis of individual interactions (p.26); this can only replicate what already exists. On the other hand, a choir generates trust amongst its participants, 'trust is the output, which is durable', even if the choir is disbanded (p.24). Albeit on narrow terms, choir-generated trust becomes a resource that can be put to use in novel, non-choir, applications – but what, how and why? By the same token, game theory can only lead to outcomes that are preordained by the game itself. It cannot break out of them, let alone bring about 'development', however that might be specified as a process of unchartered change.[7]

This raises a further aspect of the general fungibility of social capital: that it can be negative as well as positive, as has now been occasionally, sometimes reluctantly, accepted. This is hardly surprising since, in its analytical framework, social capital is isomorphic to rent-seeking and corruption. Such is implicitly recognised in the conclusion of Gugerty and Kremer (2002, p.232):[8] 'Where programs try to impose collective decision-making on what is more naturally an individual household activity, such as agricultural production, they may promote rent seeking as much as social capital.' To be provocative, it is not clear what is different between rent-seeking and social capital, except you downplay the one you do not favour. For social capitalists, the dark side of the force may or may not arise, depending upon context. This is formalised in the (World Bank) account of Woolcock and Narayan (2000).[9] They consider that the state and social capital can complement or substitute for one another. They posit a two-dimensional framework, with (dys)functional states on one axis and bridging capital on the other, giving rise to four quadrants: social and economic well-being for + +; coping for – +; conflict for – –; and exclusion and latent conflict for + –. This reduces the world to a two-dimensional map of states across time and place!

However, the idea that social capital is positive or negative depending upon context is unacceptable in anything other than an idealised world in which win–win cooperative games present themselves as enduring outcomes. However, and however much, social capital incorporates social relations and processes, it is, thereby, 'embedded', to use the vernacular of the new economic sociology, in matters of exclusion and inclusion, power, conflict, exploitation, oppression, hierarchy and conflict. Not surprisingly, these are notable for their absence from the social capital literature as a whole; they are generally present only in the more tempered and neutral terms of vertical or bridging relations through hierarchies and/or with the state.

Such criticism is most apposite. For Grootaert and van Bastelaer reveal the logic of their position on social capital by reference to that standard-bearer of a physicalist (and individualistic) interpretation of capital, Robinson Crusoe (2000, p.5):[10] 'Although every other form of capital has a potential productive impact in a typical Robinson Crusoe economy, social capital doesn't (at least until Friday emerges from the sea).' Yet such disregard for the meaning of the social and of capital runs much deeper, as a result of the universal application of social capital across so many contexts. The result is to homogenise the understanding of variables, like trust, across different societies and instances, as if each of the multidimensional aspects of social capital (from friends and family to confidence in government and moral values) always had the same meaning and significance, even leaving aside the omission of other critical elements such as power, class and conflict.

The result often takes the form of one of two extremes. At one extreme, precisely because it can be anything and is in vogue, social capital can be used to legitimise and promote an analysis of something else, by association with itself. This is so even though the analysis makes no use of social capital at all, except in a title, an abstract, a keyword – the term can be entirely absent from the substantive text itself. The volume provides an exemplary illustration in the contribution of Bates and Yackovlev (2002) on ethnicity and violence in Africa. Their opening paragraph suggests, 'ethnic groups promote the forces of modernization: phrased more fashionably, they constitute a form of social capital' (p.310). They close their chapter without ever mentioning the term again, although when they veer towards stating the obvious the influence of social capital is marked (p.331): 'The most desirable institutions would be those that weaken the prospects of winner-take-all outcomes and assuage minorities' fear of permanent political exclusion, thereby countering the logic that leads political violence to replace political protests in ethnically diverse settings.'

At the other extreme, contributors fall over themselves to mention social capital at every possibly opportunity, not least because it is anything that everybody does together, and it can be minutely categorised as bonding, bridging, linking, horizontal, vertical, dark, and so on. Coletta and Cullen's contribution, again a study of ethnic conflict, provides an example. Writing about Cambodia, they suggest:

> Violent conflict often shapes social capital in favor of bonding relationships and a survival orientation in the emergency period, postconflict market penetration may easily reverse this pattern and lead to more outward-focussed, bridging social capital in the medium-to longer-term transition. (2002, p.292)

Turning to Rwanda, and neatly combining economic and social analysis in a way that once again borders on tautology, they write (p.299): 'This perverse manipulation of social capital made possible the mass recruitment of Hutu ... Tutsi elimination would benefit Hutu who participated in killings by decreasing number of competitors for land, homes, cattle, and other possessions.' Lest this be insufficiently clear, Putnam and Goss (2002, pp.11–12) cut through the gobbledygook to get to the point: 'In other words, bonding without bridging equals Bosnia.' As will be seen elsewhere in this book, more bridging and less bonding is a recipe for curing all ills. It is where social capital, in the hands of economists and the like at the World Bank, leads us.

It almost goes against my better judgement to have covered the volume edited by Grootaert and van Bastelaer in this book in some detail, in part because much of the text offered here was already available as a result of an earlier review article (Fine 2003c). But, at this later stage, Grootaert and van Bastelaer's volume now appears in many respects as both the high and the end point of social capital at the World Bank, and it needs to be understood as such. So the rationale for addressing the volume again lies first in indicating where social capital had got to at the World Bank by the turn of the millennium. It was offered as standard fare with uncritical application across multifarious topics. Second, though, the contributions did reflect a particular orientation across the vast social capital literature, one with a strong contribution from mainstream economists, with little or no residual influence from the more radical or cultural content that might be derived from Bourdieu and his followers.

Third, though, the volume is of some importance when we place it in the context both of what was about to occur at the World Bank with regard to social capital and more generally. For, as detailed in earlier chapters, the broader literature was at least in part in the process of BBI all those omitted factors that were previously traditional within social theory, if not mainstream economics. This was not beyond the capacity of the economists, but it could only be done on an extremely limited and unsatisfactory basis. Now, suppose you were a social theorist at the World Bank, seeking to civilise the economists to take the social seriously and in an acceptable way through the medium of social capital. The volume of Grootaert and van Bastelaer will definitely now appear to be the best you can hope to achieve, with the possibility that this achievement will be sacrificed if it is pushed too far or if social capital itself becomes too closely associated with more radical or more unfamiliar modes of thought than could be countenanced by World Bank economists.

6.3   ... AND FALL

In short, the situation seems to have arisen in which social capital could go no further at the World Bank other than as a mundane application in which the Bank's social capitalists were complicit with its own economists. The latter had made use of the concept in their own way in response to the prompting of non-economists. There was even the danger that the latter would lose ownership of the concept at the Bank, the more it influenced, or was appropriated by, the economists. The evolution of social capital outside the Bank, as the BBI process strengthened, was also not particularly conducive to continuing engagement by its economists. So the situation arose in which neither World Bank economists nor non-economists had much to gain by continuing commitment to social capital. It was more or less peremptorily dropped by both sides of the economist/non-economist divide, but with one exception. The non-economists, possibly with a twinge of conscience, felt obliged to explain why they had promoted social capital in the first place and to justify having done so.

One bizarre consequence of this was that the lack of engagement with criticism of the concept of social capital by the World Bank's social capitalists was dramatically reversed in 2002, with publications accruing in 2004, but in the most sudden, peculiar and token of ways. This followed from the overt notice that was given to the effect that social capital was about to be abandoned by the very social capitalists who had promoted it within the Bank – although residual affection has persisted to some extent across its erstwhile proponents, especially Bebbington (2004, 2007 and 2008).[11] As already observed, until the article by Bebbington et al. (BGOW) appeared (2004),[12] the World Bank capitalists had simply failed to respond to criticism at all. By contrast, publications in 2004 offered a watershed in which scarcely a page could not go by without my being referenced: 13 times in 7 pages in Bebbington (2004) and, in Bebbington et al. (2004), I am cited ten times in an article that contains a hundred other references. Yet, as already indicated, the social capital website, and the Bank's overall website more generally, have effectively persisted in failing to acknowledge *any* of my work at all.

Did this mean that, at last, a proper debate would ensue? – unfortunately not. Bebbington (2004) himself in his first two pages explains the poor results of a debate that had not in fact taken place in terms of its tone, anger, acrimony, fiddling whilst Rome burns, general antipathy to the World Bank, preaching to the converted, undue passion and indignation, and lack of modesty, reflexivity, self-criticism and creativity. Later he offers lofty advice on problem framing, interdisciplinarity and middle-range theory. But, much more important than all of this non-engagement with the substance of social capital is that its critics have simply been breathtakingly undermined by the total acceptance by the World Bank social capitalists of more or less all of the criticisms of them. This assessment is confirmed by Knorringa and van Staveren when they suggest that Bebbington and the World Bank collaborators

> by and large seem to agree with the critiques of methodological individualism, instrumentalism, and lack of attention to power and social structures … [and] attribute these shortcomings to the ideological framework to which they are bound, that of the Washington Consensus driven by the World Bank, favouring markets over states, individuals over groups, and ignoring issues of power. (2007, p.2)

So there's nothing to debate, since the following criticisms, in summary form, now seem to be have been both recognised and accepted at a level of 99 per cent or more.

Social capital:

- is totally chaotic in definition, method and theory;
- is indiscriminately deployed across applications and can be more or less anything, in principle if not in practice;
- is parasitic on, and crudely simplifying of, other social theory;
- misunderstands both social and capital;
- is complicit with mainstream economics, 'economics imperialism' and rational choice theory;
- neglects the economic, power, conflict, the state, gender, race, class, ethnicity, global, context, etc.;
- is self-help raised from individual to community level;
- has discarded Bourdieu but is bringing him back in piecemeal, alongside other omitted factors;
- induces hack academia ('hackademia') in publication, research and funding;
- fails to address criticism other than incorporating it as another factor;
- is Third Wayism as weak response to neo-liberalism;
- has been heavily promoted by the World Bank as a rhetorical device associated with the shift from the Washington to the post-Washington Consensus;
- is a peculiar end-of-millennium product of the retreat from the dual extremes of postmodernism and neo-liberalism.

In short, I have spent the last ten years or so offering these criticisms in print and by word of mouth, even exaggerating in order to solicit response and get a debate. Now, we know why there was none other than, usually in private, an apology for being guilty (though to a lesser degree than charged) and a plea to be excused on grounds of pursuit of other worthy ulterior motives. This claim to virtue, however, overlooks the broader picture of legitimising an inadequate concept by participating with it. As a critic of social capital, I have been accused of many things and motives, not least by Bebbington (2004), from anger to Marxism; but a casual reading of my book (Fine 2001a) indicates that my primary concern is with the degradation of scholarship that has been attached to social capital in general, at the World Bank in particular. Failure to debate with critics and then agreeing with them is but a sideshow in all of this, and Bebbington points to a worthy motive of his own for promoting social capital, and on a grand scale. This is nothing less than that social capital should serve as 'a language mobilized for struggles *within the Bank*'. Indeed, 'the social capital discussion ... was a real *battlefield of knowledge* inside the Bank' (p.346, emphases added). With this, and on the wider terrain of 'social and cultural dimensions of development ... it may be nearing the end of its useful life' (p.348). So debate on social capital can now at most be an obituary and the slate wiped clean as we build bridging social capital around future intellectual endeavours (p.349).

Yet, the purported short life of social capital as practised by its World Bank proponents cannot be so readily exonerated, quite apart from the monster that it has in part spawned in the real battlefield of knowledge *outside* the Bank. Bebbington (2004) offers little other than assertion on these inner struggles, but the BGOW article (Bebbington et al. 2004) offers a fuller account, equally remarkable for accepting criticisms of social capital and again, to emphasise, referencing me fulsomely, where previously there had been total lack of engagement. Still, at the time of its writing, BGOW's article was unique in some respects for revealing inner workings and dissent within the World Bank, and I recommend everyone to read it for this reason – and also, if to put it harshly, as an exercise in virtuous self-delusion. For a start, BGOW run the paradox of beginning with a *general* appeal to *critical* discourse theory, but concluding *in particular* in favour of establishment, World Bank, postures as an example of it in practice! Critical discourse means uncritical discourse.

One way in which they do this is by drawing upon case studies purporting to show the positive role played by the World Bank and social capital. This is echoed in Bebbington (2004) and Bebbington et al. (2006). Leaving aside the issue of how this represents a victory in the internal battle for knowledge, these studies are notable for lack of independent evaluation, and for one of the cases examined, one of BGOW is not only the authority cited for a favourable outcome but was also the project manager! Is it possible that, far from social capital promoting the projects, the latter are being used to promote the discourse of social capital in a token exercise or three, and as part of a broader rhetorical strategy of legitimising the Bank? There is already a tradition of social capital being imposed ex post on research already undertaken, starting with Putnam himself (1993).[13] Why not construct projects anew to demonstrate its powers? Yet, notably absent from BGOW's account is any acknowledgement of examples of the negative impact of social capital in Bank projects (for examples, see Fine 2001a on coal-mining in India and the ludicrous application of social capital to Russia's health and welfare crisis; see also Chapter 9 below for the limited purchase of social capital on policy, irrespective of its impact where applied).

In short, a more rounded, independent assessment of case studies is needed to make an overall judgement, something Bebbington only looks for in the future. But the wider (critical) social capital literature is already questioning not only whether there is much by way of policy conclusions that can be drawn from social capital (other than that if it's there, it may help, depending on context and what has been left out of consideration) and whether it serves more as an instrument of central authority parading as decentralised participation. Hewison, for example, observes the rhetorical shift to the PWC, but sees little or no effect in practice upon social policy in Thailand, specifically with regard to social safety nets, following the Asian crisis. There was a continuing neglect, if not denial, of the class basis of policies, a feature of the Bank's literature on Thailand more generally. However, on the basis of interviews with Bank employees:

> The World Bank's analysis of the social impact of the crisis in Thailand placed considerable emphasis on social capital. Initially, much of this discussion had little empirical or theoretical underpinning. In fact, Bank consultants and officers used 'social capital' in contradictory ways, with little understanding of the theory embodied in the concept. (2002, p.7)

Ultimately, though, social capital was used to suggest that the impact of the crisis would be moderated by the high levels of social capital amongst the poor.

Even more important than impact on social policy is the bigger omitted picture of a huge and continuing shift within the Bank from public- to private-sector support in infrastructure and other lending. Even if social capital is on balance favourable to a given project or two, this effect is dominated by overall portfolio effects that will subordinate the social to the private (and profitable), despite, or even as a result of, the current Bank rethink on privatisation for example (Bayliss and Fine 2007). Thus, whilst social capital is a highly significant marker in the passage from the Washington to the post-Washington Consensus, policy has been little transformed by the process, even where social capital is explicitly incorporated. Fox and Gershman (2000, p.408) note the neglect of gender and ethnicity across a selection of World Bank development projects around social capital. Further, 'most of the case studies found that project managers either ignored or were hostile to existing forms of pro-poor social capital' (p.413).[14] And the case studies in the Grootaert and van Bastelaer volume can scarcely conceal the link between social capital and privatisation. For Pargal et al.:[15]

> The most important policy implication of our work is that the introduction of public–private partnerships or self-help schemes is more likely to be successful in neighbourhoods in which the level of social capital is high. Social capital proxies or determinants can thus be used as predictors of success when targeting neighbourhoods for different social or public good-oriented interventions. (2002, p.205)

So social capital is about community self-help to support the World Bank to privatise.[16] Social capitalists have addressed neither this nor the potential of continuing privatisation to destroy the social capital that they seek to build up in the odd project here and there (Champlin 1999). Nor have they paid any attention to the patterns of lending and conditionalities that have accompanied loans in the shift to PRSPs. Rhetoric to the contrary, these have tightened by comparison with the practices of the Washington Consensus (see van Waeyenberge 2007 for an outstanding and detailed account of tightening aid allocation in practice). Whilst, rightly or wrongly, Bebbington (2004, p.348) is dismissive of the virtues of grand narratives, and regrets that social capital has become one, there is a yawning gap between an isolated case study demonstrating the virtues of social capital and the generalities of grand narrative. And it is a gap that, as far as the World Bank is concerned, is heavily filled out by (private and privatised) business as usual, irrespective of, or even masked by, the rhetoric of social capital.

6.4   STRATEGIC WEAKNESSES ARE TACTICAL STRENGTHS?

These are my own assertions on the relationship between the scholarship, rhetoric and policy practice of the World Bank. There is no need to justify them here as they were already laid out fully and clearly in my earlier book and other publications on social capital and the World Bank. But the point is that they are not even considered in the Panglossian view of the forward march of social capital within the Bank. Instead, absolute reliance is placed upon the idea that discourse has an effect within the Bank; but some things cannot be changed so easily, or at all, and so intellectual compromises must be made. Unbeknownst to outsiders, compromises are accepted strategically in deference to the economists, only to be won back surreptitiously through the Trojan horse of social capital. As already indicated, the now admitted list of conceptual concessions involved is astonishing, from economic alternatives through structures of class, ethnicity, gender, power, political economy, sensitivity to time and place and so on.[17] This is in order to be able to engage with Bank economists who, by BGOW's own account, would appear to have accepted the stalking horse with little or no cost, not least with Olson prevailing over Fox,[18] the quantitative over the qualitative,[19] and Collier over social capital.[20]

As an internal strategy, there seems to have been no way for social capitalists within the Bank to recognise failure, nor opportunism on the part of opponents (and themselves), let alone for them to push their strategy to the point of, or beyond, being disciplined themselves by the Bank. Was there a chance of World Bank social capitalists protesting, even resigning en masse, in solidarity with Stiglitz, Kanbur and others who were essentially disciplined by the Bank for not conforming to its perspectives? It seems not. There were those who did challenge the Bank from within at the highest level and on the grounds of economics and policy. Did their fate possibly serve as a warning on ambition to social capitalists, and a protective cover for them, rather than being seized as the opportunity for alliances to be forged? Instead of fiddling at the margins in order that the social and themselves be taken seriously by the Bank's economists, would it not have been better if they themselves had taken the economy and the chief economist, Joe Stiglitz, seriously? Their promotion of social capital hardly warrants the notion of the Bank as a 'battlefield of knowledge', and social capital victories might better be interpreted as at most Pyrrhic, in minor skirmishes, especially taking a longer view of the Bank's economics from before the Washington Consensus. This is the light in which to set Bebbington's (2004, p.347) parody of opponents as not offering alternatives but simply making calls to bring in Marxian political economy and class.[21] I would have remained critical, but I would have been more respectful if the social capitalists had at least promoted the economics that was, rhetorically, hegemonic at the time of their strategising, and remains so, and which provided them with the space to prosper – the post-Washington Consensus.

For one thing I did get wrong, at least initially (Fine 1999a), was to exaggerate the likely impact of social capital within the

Bank. I saw it as the World Bank's way of outflanking notions of the developmental state as an alternative to the CDF/PWC in the enforced legitimising retreat from the Washington Consensus. That, in the event, it was not necessary for social capital to play a major role in this respect reflects the unexpected extent of compromise (abject surrender?) made by the social capitalists on the economy! Thus, I was *more* optimistic than BGOW on what could be achieved by inner conflict. Social capital did not even serve in place of the despised developmental state approach, so low has its profile been within the economics of the Bank. It is the height of irony that Bebbington (2007) should be seeing social capital as providing the micro-foundations for the developmental state (when its use was potentially to circumvent it).[22] In a later publication (2008, p.278), he concludes that 'the issues to which the concept draws attention seem central for any understanding of the micro-politics through which a more developmental state is produced'. This may or may not be so (and it becomes more of a tautology the wider the concept of social capital is cast) but what is overlooked are the issues from which social capital draws *away* attention!

BGOW, however, by perverse way of compensation, are more upbeat on what has been achieved and claim that this is the consequence of their strategy of promoting social capital within the Bank, which privileges them as inner participants both to assess success and to dismiss critics unaware of their wider and inner purpose. But here, on their potentially strongest ground, they are at their weakest. First, social critics are homogenised and misrepresented, not least as relying upon deterministic analysis by inclination or for want of access to inner Bank discourse. I, for example, am perceived to 'reify' social capital. But even a casual reading of my earlier book not only reveals a refusal to be deterministic, but also offers a more than full anticipation of the points made by BGOW, despite their inner privilege. These are:

1. The rhetoric, scholarship and policy of the Bank are carefully distinguished. They are not mutually determining or consistent with one another, although they do each have an effect on one another and more broadly. They do shift, individually and in relation to one another and in response to external factors and inner struggles, and the relations between them are different not only over time but over topic. This is all illustrated by reference not only to social capital but also, by way of contrast, to trade, privatisation and education.

2. Non-economists within the Bank have traditionally not been taken seriously despite their efforts to the contrary. This is closely documented through reference to the work of Cernea.
3. The strategy of being taken seriously focused on social capital and had some success in light of the shift to the Comprehensive Development Framework and the post-Washington Consensus.
4. This all entailed a compromise with economists within the Bank, reinforcing the degradation of scholarship associated with the broader rise of social capital in the 1990s.

Second, if BGOW enjoyed superior knowledge of the practices of World Bank economists and how to overcome them, they offer little account of this and of why social capital should succeed. Surely, if they had put as much effort into strategy as into social capital itself, they would have addressed the six points that Broad (2006 and 2007) has now revealed in her own study of the practices of Bank economists, tying them to Bank requirements. These are concerned with hiring (orthodox, Anglo-Saxon trained economists with golden pay levels to discourage dissent); promotion, which provides incentives for 'paradigm maintenance', especially in the enforced input from research to operations;[23] tougher reviewing of publications that offer dissent; internal marginalisation of those individuals who do dissent; manipulation of data to the point of falsehood; and external projection of those who do conform to paradigm maintenance. Our social capitalists offer no evidence on how they were planning to overcome these practices or whether they succeeded, nor even that they were aware of them.

What is unusual in their account, especially in Bebbington et al. (2004), is the information and honesty they provide about the internal workings of the World Bank with regard to social capital. This began with Putnam's invitation to be involved, as a way of kick-starting the social capital enterprise, and continued with the attempts to engage the economists (success), but not to be dominated by them (failure). Not surprisingly, this is not entirely the take of the paper's authors. Rather, they see themselves as the unrecognised, strategically compromising and so reviled, heroes of a hidden internal battle to civilise the World Bank's economists, and so bring the progressively social to the intellectual and policy practices of the World Bank.

In this respect, for them, criticism of social capital has missed the point of its inner significance in shifting the Bank's thinking, and hence its policy. Of course, this leaves aside both the other influences on the thinking and practice of the World Bank and the broader impact of the promotion of social capital in development thinking and practice elsewhere. Essentially, at least in retrospective self-justification, these authors are asking us to devolve our intellectual responsibilities to them in order that they can promote their own positions within the World Bank around a concept that they themselves admit to be flawed. The parallels with the 'never mind the arguments, just do it' stance on privatisation are striking. And the situation is ironic! For whatever the impact of social capital on the design and implementation of particular World Bank *projects*, the strategy of the organisation in practice has been to shift as much of its finance as possible from the public to the private sector. This is so despite a World Bank rethink on privatisation adjudging it to have been previously too premature a gamble (Bayliss and Fine 2007).

Polemics aside, the account of Bebbington et al. (2004) is a striking illustration of how strategic thinking within the World Bank is forced, individually and institutionally, to conform to the Bank's shifting needs and practices, and how limited is the scope to buck its requirements. Such is the case on a grander scale for the resignations of Stiglitz, Kanbur, and others. But where professional recruitment and careerism prove insufficient to serve the World Bank's scholarship, rhetoric and policy, the delusion of internal influence and reform incorporates those who offer a little more by way of free thinking and altruistic motivation. This is not to say that the scholarship, rhetoric and policy of the World Bank are predetermined in and of themselves and in relation to one another. But they are embedded, to coin a phrase, in an institution and its practices that are heavily constrained and can be perverse in attaching intentions to outcomes. The reduction of the impact of social capital to the activities of a few scholars within the World Bank is at best partial and at worst misleading.

It is, then, with a cry that is more plaintive than ironic that, a decade after social capital was brought to the Bank in pursuit of civilising its economists, one of its leading proponents should feel compelled to complain 'that development is about a lot more than economics, and that, accordingly, economics should not have (as it currently does at the Bank) a near-monopoly on determining the content and validity of development research' (Rao and Woolcock 2007). This is in response to the Deaton report, 'An Evaluation of World Bank Research, 1998–2005'. They also complain that given that about one in 20 of designated research staff are non-economists, 'perhaps one of the twenty [research] evaluators [used by the report] could have been a sociologist or anthropologist?' At the least, this would appear to be a confession of abject failure on the part of the social capitalists in getting themselves taken seriously. At the most, it displays an institutional disregard for them and, having served their purpose, they are being dumped rather than themselves dumping social capital.

6.5   DECONSTRUCTING THE BUZZ[24]

As is apparent, in defending their use of social capital whilst accepting its deficiencies, the social capitalists at the World Bank have appealed to the discursive impact of the concept to justify its use. This suggests that the concept needs to be critically deconstructed more fully and more carefully. In discussing consumer culture, I have argued that it can be characterised by six Cs (Fine 2002a and 2005a), although this can now be extended by a further two. Whilst I hesitate to extrapolate from consumer culture to social capital as a buzzword, doing so does offer some insight. The first C is Constructed. Social capital has been constructed through a combination of academic and, to a much lesser extent, developmental practices that have mutually reinforced one another but to the exclusion of others, especially where critical (myself) or inconvenient (Bourdieu, power, class, state, and so on). Of course, World Bank social capitalists consciously accepted, and even promoted, such construction in deference to the need to incorporate World Bank economists, who would otherwise have refused to engage. The issue, though, is whether this was too high a price to pay in terms of what then came to be constructed, and how it came to be used, both within the Bank itself and, which is arguably more important, outside as well.

Second, social capital is Contextual, like all concepts, in the more general sense of itself being a specific product of the material and intellectual circumstances that mark the turn of the millennium. This aspect of social capital is brought out by Putnam's foisting it, as an afterthought, upon his study of regional disparities in Italy from the twelfth century onwards. He then exports it to the twentieth-century United States as the way of understanding the decline of bowling clubs and the rise of television, prior to finding an entrée into the World Bank, where, as argued, it eased the transition from the Washington to the Post-Washington Consensus, explicitly and as a direct reflection in the case of scholarship and rhetoric. But in terms of policy, its impact has been negligible, other than in the negative sense of diverting attention from what was or was not changing. And the relationship between social capital and the reality that it purports to represent is also contextually limited, in view of the factors that it has overlooked or even omitted. The context at the Bank allowed this to happen, and for social capital to be accepted and promoted as a legitimate and legitimised concept. As the contemporary phlogiston of social theory, social capital deployed and created a context as a means of legitimating itself and legitimising a much broader approach to development and the social more generally.

Third, social capital is Chaotic, not least in its multifarious uses and meanings. Far from this resulting in its dismissal from the intellectual arena, this appears to have promoted its use. It has been subject to hundreds of measures, or elements that make up a measure, so much so that it has been felt necessary to re-aggregate into intermediate categories such as linking, bonding and bridging. These all mutually contradict one another across traditional social variables (such as class, gender, ethnicity) quite apart from the conundrum of its perverse, dark or negative side (the mafia and the like).

Fourth, social capital is Construed; that is, it is not simply passively received as a well-defined and given concept, but is reinterpreted and worked upon by those who engage with it. One aspect of that reworking, for example, especially at the World Bank, has been to disassociate social capital both from Bourdieu (too radical) and from Coleman (too reactionary). How social capital was worked by economists at the World Bank was arguably more or less indistinguishable from what it would have been in the absence of the worthy motives emanating from those that introduced them to it from the broader perspective of social theory.

Fifth, social capital is the product of Contradictory pressures, as it seeks to accommodate both material and intellectual developments. How can the World Bank legitimise itself while pretty much continuing business as usual? How can the economy be ignored when we are deploying social *capital*? And how can we set aside power and conflict when we are addressing *social* capital? How can economists address the social, through the medium of social capital, whilst ignoring so much of what social science has to offer? Ultimately, these tensions seem to have been resolved chronologically by the rapid rise and fall of social capital as it was picked up and then dropped by economists (rather than being the strategically adopted instrument of the non-economists).

Sixth, then, social capital is Contested or subject to conflict over its meaning. Among social capitalists themselves, this is resolved through chaotic compromise. Otherwise, contestation takes the form of exposing and rejecting social capital for its sore conceptual inadequacies and corresponding consequences for practice. Social capital has in part risen to prominence because it has been allowed to do so by those who have not engaged critically with it. One index of this is that my polemic in *Antipode*, according to its editors, has been one of its most accessed pieces (Fine 2002b). I suspect this reflects the racy title, the prominence of social capital, and the silent but unengaged opposition to it. By contrast, while globalisation has been shown to be equally flawed as a conceptual panacea, it has been universally addressed by its critics and won away, not only from neo-liberalism, but also from the intellectual Third Wayism characteristic of social capital.

Seventh, social capital is Collective, in that the meanings to which it is attached, and the uses to which it is put, are not simply the consequences of the accumulated acts of individual scholars and pundits. They derive from the broader scholarship, practices and other endeavours with which they are situated. As is apparent, individual scholars, even the critical, cannot buck the deadweight and momentum that attaches to social capital. Indeed, the notion has exhibited an extraordinary degree of repressive tolerance, whereby criticism – especially in the form of BBI – is absorbed on a piecemeal basis, as if strengthening the concept through rendering it in part chaotic. In other words, social capital creates a community (a ninth C?) of its own.

Last, as a result and by no means least, social capital is Closed. On the one hand, closure prevails in the world of ideas, allowing or encouraging the presence of some in favour of others. On the other hand, and by the same token, social capital incorporates certain practitioners and participants whilst precluding others. Remarkably, such seems to have been the explicit intent of the World Bank's social capitalists – to narrow down the conceptual world in order to incorporate mainstream (Bank) economists, to the exclusion of, and with disdain for, those unaware of their correspondingly higher purpose and its implications for the world's poor.

6.6   GBS, HEGEL AND ABRAHAM LINCOLN

In lieu of conclusion, let me first paraphrase George Bernard Shaw by suggesting that social capitalism is not bad because social capitalists are bad but because they are good. By their own account, BGOW had honourable motives, but these were perverted by the circumstances in which they found themselves. These are talented scholars, confessing to having misled their colleagues and the rest of the world for strategic reasons. Is this an apposite model for the putative 'Knowledge Bank', let alone for those aspiring developmentalists who can be prised away from the careerism offered by the Bank? And the opportunities that arise for reform within the Bank owe a great deal to the pressures that are generated from *outside*, by the very scholars and activists whom BGOW would dismiss as having overlooked the significance of the strategy that they had adopted!

Second, to paraphrase Hegel, in this age of reason it is possible to find a rationale for anything. By their partial appeal to the bigger picture, a chain of reasoning leads from the promotion of social capitalist(ists) in the Bank to poverty alleviation, empowerment, and the like, in a project or two, with the prospect of further gains across all of those no-go areas within the Bank. But on these, there remains limited flexibility in practice, not least where the economy and the economic are concerned, despite these being the intellectually weakest (and most important) points of the Bank's posturing. Further, BGOW and other social capitalists show limited knowledge of the economics of their Bank colleagues/opponents and of the political economy they claim they would foist upon them as an alternative, for which social capital is the putative thin end of the wedge.[25]

Third, to paraphrase Abraham Lincoln, you can fool some of the people all of the time ... but not Bank economists any of the time, for they are too foolish to be fooled. They do not understand and are hostile to the issues that the social capitalists are seeking to incorporate. Yet, far from learning this lesson, BGOW close by offering the frightening prospect of fooling the fools once more by discarding social capital and moving to the more satisfactory notions of 'empowerment and community driven development. This is already happening' (Bebbington et al. 2004, p.57). As (Bank) economists are now wont to advise us, this raises huge problems of 'credibility' in light of past experience: they have already been fooled once by their own social capitalists.[26] It also begs the question of what sort of empowerment and community development our heroic social capitalists will be allowed to foist upon Bank projects.

BGOW seem to have fooled themselves into believing that their own heavily compromised struggles within the Bank unfold to the benefit of the deserving poor on the outside, without regard to broader intellectual and ideological impact. Such compromises, not battles, are necessarily carried over into external relations and effects.[27] At the practical level, soliciting funding from Scandinavians for social capital necessarily buys them into the Bank's take upon it. But these countries' own development agencies have been far more progressive than the Bank. The result is to promote the Bank's own omissions in contexts where alternatives might have prospered (and been turned against the Bank's economists).[28] And this is only a small part of the picture of the entire social capital enterprise, whether attached to development or otherwise.

Thus, the institutional logic of promoting social capital within the Bank necessarily conformed with its promotion outside, reflecting and consolidating the rise of social capital in contexts where there was no wish nor need to omit everything, from economic alternatives through to gender, power and political economy. This is implicitly accepted by BGOW, in that the criticisms of social capital are only now being acknowledged as being essentially correct, ten years after they had adopted the term. Now that's why I perceive them as social capitalists and, unfortunately, uncritical and legitimising in many respects and, as such, a part of the Bank's own 'social capital', neither offering nor achieving anything by way of a challenge to the Bank in its economics, whether as rhetoric (advocacy), scholarship or policy. Indeed, I could forgive the Bank's social capitalists everything – their failure to have debated, their deception over their true views, their pompous declarations of virtue in relation to grounded methods, interdisciplinarity, strategic engagement with opponents, reform within constraints, and so on – if only they had once genuinely challenged the Bank's economics and economists. The failure to do so is what is most visible from outside and, by their own account, from within. If, within the World Bank, social capital represented a 'political economy of language in that institution, for those who work inside the Bank' and 'in large measure this was a language mobilized for struggles with the Bank' (Bebbington 2004, p.346), it has first and foremost been a language without vocabulary (or practice) for political economy, for struggle or for mobilisation.

Is all the foregoing criticism merely ivory tower intellectual idealism standing in the way of a more progressive World Bank and social capital movement, one that marries social analysis and policy to a reformed economic counterpart? Such is the implicit stance of many, and not just of those motivated by intellectual opportunism, as is characteristic of much social capital literature. For those who continue to use social capital have also made insightful criticisms of it and the World Bank from within their own areas of expertise. Such contributions are by now sufficiently common not to be perceived as idiosyncratic. They take the form of observing the definitional chaos, inconsistencies and weaknesses, the measurement problems in principle and in practice, and the conceptual inadequacies and omissions in the use of social capital as an approach to a particular topic or field. They then proceed not to reject social capital but to suggest that it be reconstructed on the basis of correcting these deficiencies, something that only serves to reinforce both its stature and its corresponding flaws.

This will not wash for, irrespective of the more progressive and intellectually rigorous contributions that might be made, social capital has been captured in content and momentum by a 'social capital' of its own making. It has its own bridging, bonding, leaders and networks, trust and distrust, values and a legitimising dark side, and so on, that guarantee that it will endure until it serves out its role as a passing fad or is broken from outside. To reject social capital actively now, in development studies and more generally, will serve to hasten the processes of both shedding social capital and replacing it with more grounded and rounded alternatives.

7
Management Studies Goes
to McDonald's[1]

7.1 INTRODUCTION

In her outstanding empirical account of the rise of social capital from the perspective of the sociology of knowledge, Forsman (2005) finds that business and organisation studies, alongside psychology, come along in the third-wave of literature. This conforms to my own casual assessment. I remember very well sitting on the back porch of a suburban Melbourne house at the end of 1999, having for the first time come across a piece on social capital and management. It had been turned up by the outstanding library electronic facilities at the University of Melbourne, Buddy I think the system was called, which sought and obtained pieces in one go from its electronic databases. The piece, to which I will return in Section 7.3, was a draft by Adler and Kwon, and located on the World Bank social capital website, something of an establishment seal of approval. As a third-wave discipline, social capital now appears to be blossoming exponentially in management studies, as strongly as in any other field, exhibiting all the faults of its predecessors and adding some extra ones of its own.

Before getting to grips with these, I need to say something about the more general nature of management studies as a discipline (Section 7.2). For someone whose own discipline of economics lies outside its immediate domain, this is to court the danger of being both presumptuous and offensive. That's a risk I need to take, and I am more than ready to be corrected.[2]

Section 7.3 offers a selective overview of the vast range of applications that have been made of social capital across (critical) management studies. Once again, it is shown how this has the effect of degrading social theory and undermining the more critical content that might otherwise flourish within the discipline, especially in relation to capital–labour relations, a theme also taken up in Section 7.4. The concluding remarks repeat the theme of needing to beat social capital rather than joining it; there, and throughout, McDonald's-type metaphors are to be found.

7.2 'TWIXT HETERODOXY AND PARASITISM?

The stylised view of management studies for those from without is that it is intellectually lowbrow and normatively compromised by the very nature of its subject matter and the motivation of its practitioners. I do not doubt that, in some respects, these are important factors and they may even lie at the core of the discipline – possibly disciplines, since much the same is said of business, market and consumer studies, with which management has close and overlapping relations. It is a close-run thing whether the presumed parasitism of these fields leaves it suffering an even lower status than (human) geography.

But I am happy to report that these are dismissive assessments that I do not share, for a number of reasons concerning what I take to be some of the virtues of management studies, although others take them as vices. First, it tends to be more than usually empirically grounded, for obvious reasons in light of its subject matter. This is some protection, if not a guarantee, against ascent/descent into abstraction and over-generalising to the point of oblivion. Second, it is multidisciplinary and, as a consequence, is not bound by the variables, theories and methods of a single discipline and its traditions and professional practices. Third, whilst I suspect that theoretical dependency, if not parasitism, on other disciplines is strong, this does not mean an absence of theoretical challenge, either to those within management studies or to those seeking to incorporate its contributions from outside.

I can illustrate this most personally in two ways. On the one hand, whenever I have engaged in empirical work, this has almost inevitably involved visits to the libraries of business schools to solicit the necessary information. On the other hand, more specifically, I look back over my work on consumption and, having developed my own analytical framework that departs from those to be found within particular disciplines, judge in retrospect that I could not have reached my approach without engaging critically with business, consumer and marketing studies (Fine and Leopold 1993; Fine 2002a). Often with a simple naivety, these studies offer lessons about what to incorporate, if not always how to incorporate it, that would leave more grown-up theory floundering in its abstractions.

The final reason for rejecting the stylised and dismissive view of management studies is because of the presence of critique within the field, both of concepts and practices. At least in principle, critical management studies is neither intellectually nor ethically compromised, although this does not mean it is entirely independent of the mainstream core of the discipline, which might be characterised in these terms. Again, if I might offer a presumptuous and superficial assessment, management schools have prospered recently in the United Kingdom, not least through rapid growth in student numbers. Together with the application of pseudo-market forces within universities, this has offered them a position of strength in command over resources. Subject to satisfying certain vocational requirements, this has meant that what is taught within the all-encompassing notion of management is otherwise extremely flexible. At the same time, the McDonaldisation of social science across other disciplines in the wake of marketisation and research assessment exercises (RAE) has discouraged heterodoxy within those disciplines, especially amongst those inspired by the radical expansion of social science in the 1960s – many of whom are now in positions of some seniority, with generations of succeeding students seeking homes as prospective academics.[3] Together with reorganisation into schools and faculties, with management and the like often taking the nominal and intellectual lead, this has created a situation in which critical management studies has not only been able to thrive but has also occasionally and rapidly attained a degree of (tolerance of) heterodoxy and controversy that puts other disciplines, and especially my own of economics, to shame.

Somewhat more speculative is the idea that European management, with its greater freedom in the academic field, has yet to become as hard-nosed as its US counterpart. But, we have been advised, McDonaldisation of management is on the way, as is implicit in the suggestion of Starkey and Tempest (2004, p.78) that the more effective European methods of management are being undermined by Americanisation. This is destructive of social capital within management itself, the result being, 'unrestrained pursuit of self-interest, market fundamentalism, minimal state, low taxation'. Could this presage McDonaldisation of management studies?

Yet, the situation in the United States is not homogeneous and allows for some degree of heterodoxy. Management studies is so diverse and longstanding and there are so many different ways of funding it that there is plenty of room for critical management studies, as indeed there is for a department or two of radical political economy across the university system as a whole. On the situation in management studies elsewhere in the world I am not prepared to comment, for lack of knowledge and investigation. But the position, role and influence of critical management studies should not be dismissed out of hand.

7.3   IT AIN'T CRITICAL ...

Let me now return to the classic article of Adler and Kwon (2002), which in the United States is perceived to be part of critical management studies, and which first struck my attention in 1999. It stands alongside Nahapiet and Ghoshal (1998) as the leading article in management studies on social capital. Forsman (2005, pp.10–11) mentions that in 2003 it was the sixth-most-cited item amongst all those on social capital published between 1979 and 1999.[4] Adler and Kwon (2002) comes in as seventh-most-cited item of those published after 2000, one place below my own book; but the total number of citations for these two plus all others above them in rank are more than matched by those for Putnam (2000), which stands in first place.

In my book of 2001, I was critical of Adler and Kwon's article simply for being a contribution to social capital, but recognised that it had taken a position that was at the forefront of the literature, especially in terms of BBI. In this vein, they offer their own definition: '*Social capital is the goodwill available to individuals or groups. Its source lies in the structure and content of the actor's social relations. Its effects flow from the information, influence, and solidarity it makes available to the actor*' (p.23). On the basis of this definition, I conclude: 'In short, although there is a notable absence of power and conflict, the result is to throw everything into a gently bubbling analytical cauldron and expect social capital to result as accommodating synthesis' (p.111). In a later, unpublished and less kindly comment on the article after it was published in 2002, I suggest to myself that it represents, something commonly found in the literature, a case of 'the vanity of putting social capital straight'.

What is significant in the treatment of social capital within management studies is that the concept first appears (in Adler and Kwon's and Nahapiet and Ghoshal's articles) in what would generally be recognised as the critical branch of the discipline. This is not surprising for a number of reasons. First, the critically inclined within management studies are liable to be open to new ideas and so to be in the vanguard of incorporating them, even if they are subsequently turned to more mainstream purposes. Second, and a related but different point, the critical scholars are liable to be open to a more wide-ranging set of variables with a more progressive and relational content, for which social capital fits the bill in many respects. And, last, these early uses were themselves mindful of the critical potential in the use of social capital, not least in being sensitive to the approach offered by Bourdieu. Social capital offered the potential for critical leverage.

Indeed, it may be that the relatively early appearance of social capital with a radical content, through the auspices of critical management studies, may have impeded, if not discouraged, an earlier and fuller adoption by the orthodoxy in the discipline. But this could not last, and the goal of defining social capital meaningfully and progressively proved an impossible task. The attempt to tie social capital to social relations that can be used as resources has allowed others to use the approach of Adler and Kwon not only surreptitiously to bring back in *power*, but also to exercise it on behalf of the *powerful*.

Let me cite a study emanating from the Canadian Institute of Chartered Accountants, entitled *Stakeholder Relationships, Social Capital and Business Value Creation: Research Report* (Svendsen et al. 2003). It begins approvingly with Adler and Kwon's definition of social capital. But where does it end? It delivers two case studies essentially revealing how corporate stakeholders can prevail in their goal of value creation either through the incorporation of supportive social capital or through the exclusion of oppositional social capital. This is in the context of large-scale resource extraction corporations desperate to overcome local resistance, especially on environmental grounds. Let me quote the naive honesty involved in this. Under the heading 'Links from Relationships to Social Capital to Business Value', we find:

> MainstayCorp [a pseudonym] increased its social capital with community stakeholders by forging strong relationships. These relationships were characterized by active communication ties, mutual trust and mutual understanding. The corporation then used its social capital, in the form of (i) influence over stakeholders (ii) information to and from stakeholders and (iii) norm adherence by stakeholders *to avoid delays*.

The government stakeholders were particularly influenced by the state of relationships that MainstayCorp had with community stakeholders. The governments were disinclined to speedily approve an unpopular project. Mainstay removed this potential source of delay by interacting with community stakeholders to maintain their continuous support. (p.51, emphasis added)

And of the second case study, we are told:

GrowthCorp is a natural resource extraction corporation that has been rapidly expanding its operations in a northern rural area of Canada. Its stakeholders include environmental non-governmental organizations (ENGOs), First Nations and government regulators. The latest expansion received regulatory approval faster than anticipated. The corporation wanted to learn whether and how stakeholder relations contributed to, or detracted from, the speed of approval. (p.52)

Of course, these examples of social capital being used as a means to (specifically corporate) stakeholder value may be exceptional. Nonetheless, the parallels with the use of social capital by government as a policy tool to facilitate decisions against popular resistance are striking. For the deployment of social capital as a management technique is transparent: in this case to obtain approval of potentially unpopular and environmentally questionable projects – and ahead of rivals, as is made clear elsewhere in the report. More generally, social capital is pervasive as an element in management, across all of its functions, although its use is usually in the context of the functional attainment of some general goal of positive-sum outcome for all concerned, with only limited reference to the explicit pursuit of self-interest in the form of stakeholder value. It is not surprising to find in Hüppi and Seemann (2001) that social capital is offered as a management tool: the contribution is co-written by the CEO of Zurich Financial Services, one of the world's leading social capital consultants.

As such, the use of social capital seems to have little or no purchase in promoting critical management studies, either in and of itself as critical, or against orthodoxy, or in its wider application across the social sciences. Universality and neutrality of definition do allow for a critical content, but orthodoxy and conservativism, if not degradation of scholarship, almost inevitably prevail. For the critical to prevail, it is arguable that it must occupy the high intellectual ground by virtue of both its critical and its strategic content. These requirements are noticeably more important in the inevitable slippage between theory, analysis, policy and outcomes in the struggle against the deadweight of economic, political and ideological power.

Interestingly, though, business management has been more or less unique in addressing the relationship between globalisation and social capital, not least the need to negotiate – may I suggest bridge? – the relationship between the global multinational corporation and its local affiliate. Thus, for Frost and Zhou (2005), innovation depends upon social capital as the social relations within organisations. The more there is co-practice, absorptive capacity and social capital in the affiliates of MNCs, the more innovation there will be. In a case study of Fiji, which has affinities with the longstanding debate over enclaves and export production zones, Taylor (2002) discusses the issue of whether or not MNC affiliates build local social capital and, hence, local productive capacity. On a lighter note, Au and Fukuda (2002) assess the role of expatriates as a form of social capital, finding that they are both happier and more successful the more they bridge boundaries in the local community.

The negative side of social capital tends to be overlooked at the global level, just as it is at the domestic level. For, when big business restructures, this involves affiliate closures, loss of jobs and community health, and decline of the very civil society that social capitalists suggest should be used to compensate for such losses. Portes (1998), Heying (1997 and 2001) and Levi (1996) have all pointed to such 'delocalisation', the process by which affiliate restructuring undermines the viability of the communities that lose employment and, with it, their social capital. Goetz and Rupasingha (2006) offer a neat study of Wal-Mart in this respect, finding both that the retailer tends to be located where social capital is low and that social capital lessens in its presence. This is the reverse syndrome of delocalisation, as the provision of hypermarkets and the like destroy local trading communities. But, as Walker (2002) finds, there is always the social capital of business executives in providing the means for compensating for corporate restructuring through philanthropy!

As a second illustration of the application of social capital to management studies, I wish to dwell on formal network theory, which might be summed up neatly and idiosyncratically by the idea of the social capital of structural holes associated with Ronald Burt (2002). For Borgatti and Foster,

[p]robably the biggest growth area in organizational network research is social capital, a concept that has symbiotically returned the favour and helped to fuel interest in social networks ... [But] to a large extent, social capital is 'just' a powerful renaming and collecting together of a large swath of network research. (2003, p.993)

I would add that the favour has been returned, but without interest, rather with deduction. For I see this as hackademia pure and simple. First, the whole enterprise existed happily prior to anyone ever having heard of social capital. Second, it has been opportunistically attached to social capital. Third, the network theory deployed is purely formalistic in orientation, as indicated by its inelegant diagrammatic spider webs, and at most seeks to compensate for lack of substantive content and theory by BBI social variables on a piecemeal and arbitrary basis and degrading such variables and theory in the process. There is even a step back from the weak and strong ties of Granovetter, for example, let alone from the more considered network theory that incorporates social relations, structures and meaning of what is communicated.[5]

Ultimately, as an example of the purely formal use of networks, Burt (2005, p.4) defines social capital by reference to 'a person's location in a structure of relationships ... the contextual complement to human capital in explaining advantage'. But context merely seems to mean how and how many people are connected to one another. His approach is overtly functional, following Coleman and Putnam, in terms of 'advantage' to be gained, with individualism extended to people and groups, one of his own wrinkles being structural holes (thin but invaluable potential for communication). The problem is how to move beyond this metaphor without recognising the constraints that it imposes. The answer provided by Burt is to attempt to BBI what has been left out by a facile technicism, and thus to incorporate network brokerage, improved vision, and network mechanisms and returns around closure (decreased variation in connections). Thereby, social capital can bridge structural holes with vision, creativity, learning, embedding, trust, reputation, contagion, leadership, control, whether passive or active, and so on.[6] Similarly, Burt (2002) seeks the solution to the social capital syndrome in the structure and longevity of personal interactions, but in a purely formal manner. Despite studying the investment banking division of a large financial corporation over four years, he provides no discussion of what it is that is done there! Rather his concern is purely with bridging relations and how they are built or decay.

Contrast this with Willman et al. (2006), who suggest that there is excessive financial trading or noisy trading by traders themselves (as opposed to their taking advantage of the irrational noisy trading of others) in order to be able to make contacts for information, if not for insider dealing. In other words, both institutions and their agents (traders) generate as well as smooth risk, raising questions of how this is to be managed both by internal and external mechanisms and incentives; this is particularly apposite given the current financial crisis (see also Godechot 2008).

Further, indulging my own training as a mathematician, I cannot resist making the point that, with just a hundred or so individuals, the number of potential networks exceeds the number of molecules in the universe. As we ought to explain why networks do or do *not* exist, something generally overlooked in the empirical literature, which tends to examine only those that do, it becomes essential to take common *social* properties as the basis for networks in order to reduce dramatically the number that need to be explained.

Burt has his followers, of whom Lin is probably the most active and prominent. They have edited a book on social capital, together with Karen Cook (a rational choice theorist who was a contributor to the social exchange debate). In his own book, Lin (2001, p.10) asserts that, 'human capital can be seen as consistent with the theoretical scope of Marxian analysis', but that 'it challenges the classical (Marxian) theory in the definition of capital, it challenges the classical theory regarding who can or cannot acquire capital', 'with extensive cross-grade mobility possible, rather than a rigid two-class system'. Indeed, 'laborers can become capitalists, as they enjoy the surplus value of their labor … The confrontation and struggle between classes becomes a cooperative enterprise – "What's good for the company is good for the worker and vice versa."' (p.13). This is a truly astonishing misrepresentation and degradation of the intellectual tradition associated with Marxist political economy.[7]

For my third illustration, consider innovation, technical change and productivity increase. This has been a very popular topic for management studies and social capital, tending to focus upon the internal mechanisms by which such things as innovation are internalised, generated, and adopted or obstructed, although the literature has also addressed external relations – university connections, for example – as a source of social capital for innovation. Shane and Stuart (2002) find that pre-existing contacts are important for the success of university start-up businesses. Morgan (2002, p.66) suggests that 'universities can play a key role in the building of social capital ... as catalysts for civic engagement and collective action and networking'. But this is failing in Wales due to the presence of an elite model of university research that promotes it at the expense of application through outreach and diffusion. On the other hand, the leading cliche concerning social capital and technical change, Silicon Valley, is also open to alternative interpretation, as suggested by Feldman (2001), who recognises that cooperation there and elsewhere (his own case study is of the US Capital Region, Washington, DC) has much to do with government support and contracts and hence, unwittingly against the grain, suggests that 'one proxy for social capital may be governmental activity' (p.867). Similarly, Honig et al. (2006) understand firm social capital in Israel in terms of business connections to the military.

Casting the net wide in interpreting what falls under productivity increase, specialised journals such as the *Journal of Venture Capital* and the *Journal of Intellectual Capital* have been hackademic beneficiaries of the rise of social capital, with the latter adding to the plethora of (social) capitals with the addition of social intellectual capital (SIC). Particularly prominent in the management literature has been the rare consideration of ethics and its relationship to social capital (see, for example, Saxton and Benson 2005 for the non-profit sector; but, most obviously and more generally, social capital has found a home in the *Journal of Business Ethics*). The treatment of ethics primarily has a counterpart in other social capital literature in that concerned with religion, where the contributions have been scathing about the functional and limited interpretation of human motivation that is attached to social capital (religion being an association like any other that has fluidity to other activities and outcomes but is not assessed in its own right). This reflects an impoverished understanding of the individual within the social capital literature, a deficiency that tends to be overlooked by virtue of the vernacular of the social within social capital itself as well as its appeal to (social) trust, reciprocity, and so on (see also Chapter 8). Otherwise there is a profusion of management journals that have been beneficiaries of social capital, and whose titles give a fair indication of likely application. These include *Venture Capital, Journal of Small Business Management, Family Business Review, Small Business Economics, Entrepreneurship Theory and Practice, Corporate Reputation Review, International*

Journal of Entrepreneurial Behaviour and Research, Journal of Knowledge Management, Journal of Small Business and Enterprise Development, Career Development International, The Learning Organization, Journal of Management Development, European Management Review, Industrial Marketing Management, Journal of Strategic Information Systems, Journal of High Technology Management Research, Technological Forecasting and Social Change, and so on.

However, because of its close consideration of empirical issues, usually by case study of firms, and some acknowledgement that innovation requires attention to the nature of knowledge, this literature has from time to time offered some insight into BBI as far as social capital is concerned. This is to emphasise the importance of context in determining outcomes. Thus, Edelman et al. (2004) point out that each of bonding and bridging may be positive or negative in the context of the management of innovation. They advise the use of social capital with caution in light of 'the potential for unanticipated negative consequences ... [as] it can also grossly hinder the value-creation process by limiting trust, excluding new ideas and providing sub-optimal solutions to problems' (p. S68). In other words, it can be its own opposite. Bresnen et al. (2005) reckon that social capital inertia might attach itself to project-based learning in construction firms. Reagans and Zuckerman (2001) investigate whether the heterogeneity or homogeneity in the composition of 224 corporate R&D teams is a source of the success (or failure) of the teams. Ahuja (2000), in a study of innovation in the chemical industry, concludes that different types of network (dense/direct, indirect, structural holes) perform differently and with different effects in different circumstances. And Phillipson et al. (2006) offer the notion that as soon as the state seeks to intervene to sustain and formalise business networks, it may undermine their motivational basis, as the networks are attached to ideologies and symbolic actions around local identity and independence.

Further, by reference to Schumpeter's notion of creative destruction, for example, it is recognised that economic and social interaction that is conducive to change for one technology may be a barrier in the case of another, thereby implicitly questioning when and whether the same social capital is positive in what might be rapidly shifting circumstances. Westlund and Bolton (2003) show that local social capital can impede Schumpeterian creative destruction. Fuller (2005) argues that the research process can create social capital, but that it is destroyed by its being spread by teaching. And, in a purely model-building exercise for industrial spillovers, Soubeyran and Weber (2002) recognise that your social capital is also somebody else's, so that you have to weight your own gain against theirs, what they call 'co-opetition'. Thus, 'firms take into account the reciprocal nature of local spillovers: while reducing their own costs, the firms also reduce the costs of their rivals' (p.65).[8]

But, more generally, this literature, more by way of neglect than of degradation, lags a step behind what has been achieved in the study of technical change, especially from a critical perspective. For a start, there is little or no reference to the national system of innovations literature that is significant for its attention both to the wider socio-economic and institutional context and the evolutionary rhythm of accumulation. Thus, for Rycroft, we have the implicit displacement of the national, even global, system of innovation approach by social capital:

> Viewing globalization through the lens of the emergence and evolution of social capital points out that even in the most powerful technological innovation process, success depends as much on social factors (e.g. the key roles of trust, shared values, and community) as on economic, scientific, or engineering variables. (2003, p.299)

As I have argued elsewhere (Fine 1993), this approach is weak on questions of evolving class structure, power and conflict, and the specificity of the particular systems of accumulation attached to particular economies or sectors of the economy.[9] Not surprisingly, such omissions are reproduced in the social capital approach, as is the absence of more recent literature concerned with the nature and meaning of productivity change that can be derived from science and technology studies (STS), sociology of scientific knowledge (SSK), and even actor-network theory (ANT), though I have considerable reservations about the last (Fine 2003d and 2004c).

My fourth example is social capital in terms of the gains of cooperative relations between, usually small, firms or individual entrepreneurs. This has attracted attention outside management studies, not least with repeated reference, from Coleman onwards, to New York Jewish diamond traders – albeit without noting, as I am tired of pointing out, the wider context of the (internationally cartelised) diamond industry that makes their mutual trust over precious gems possible in the first place, nor the gender, ethnic and racial exclusion involved, nor the gains from tax evasion and avoidance. Another avenue for hackademia in this area has been the revival through rereading as social capital of flexible specialisation ('flec-spec'), industrial districts, externality spillovers, and so on. What each of these approaches shares in common is the positive-sum view of cooperation, and a tendency to idealise it across small-scale enterprises that often only survive on the margins through excessive forms of exploitation. This has become much more transparent in the literature on small-scale traders and finance, with Grameen banking being reinterpreted as social capital, and the condition of female success in these activities being shown to depend upon acceptance of the norms of gender oppression attached to the advantages from community interaction (see Chapter 4).

I have saved what is possibly my most salient example to the last. It concerns labour markets and work organisation. There is a significant literature on this outside management studies, concerned with access to, and advancement through, promotion. Not surprisingly, this has been taken up within management studies. This has to be put in context. It is over 35 years since I was a Ph.D. student at the London School of Economics, so I read the university's alumni magazine with increasing attention to the obituaries. In a recent issue, there was one, in a sense, for its Department of Industrial Relations, now renamed Employment Relations and Organisational Behaviour and located within the Department of Management. This is startlingly symbolic of the transformation of industrial into human relations management, and of a shifting emphasis from class, power and conflict into employment, organisation and cooperation. Social capital, from bonding within each of capital and labour to bridging between them, is an ideal conduit for this transformation, as is transparent from the literature that deploys it, in both its analytical approach and its managerial motivation. For Novicevic and Harvey (2001), social capital is now an important element of human resource development in a global world offering cooperation as opposed to a hierarchy of command.[10]

I suspect it is not necessary for me to highlight the significance of this illustration for those familiar with the origins and continuing dynamic and content of critical management studies. For the United Kingdom at least, one of the discipline's major inspirations came from the Marxist labour process literature of the 1970s. Grenier and Wright (2006, p.38) correctly highlight the absence of that tradition in the rise of social capital, and point out that '[t]he workplace has tended to be excluded from theories of social capital almost by definition'.[11] Unfortunately they continue by immediately

offering Coleman's New York diamond merchants as a notable
exception. In the rest of their contribution, there is no reference to
work (and none to trade unions) other than in the context of the
stress that arises out of (the threat of) unemployment, a potential
cause of weakened social capital, as feelings of trust are eroded
(with rising inequality in Britain also being a contributing factor,
possibly partially compensated for by burgeoning Internet use).
But it is in that tradition of studying the labour process, extended
and developed across all aspects of managerial control and conflict
within the firm and across capitalism, that the future of critical
management studies needs at least in part to rest. Social capital
cannot serve as an instrument in this respect.

7.4   … AND IT AIN'T MARXIST

And nor can it do so through Marxist political economy. Mercifully,
there are few who try to incorporate social capital into a critical
rejection of capitalism itself as an alternative to its critical
management. There are, of course, good reasons for this, as have
been laid out earlier in this book. Nonetheless, the use of social
capital as an instrument against capitalism, rather than within
it, is to be found across the literature. Not surprisingly, this use
of social capital can be traced across a sequence of the ways in
which capitalism destroys the beneficial social capital of the past
and impedes and distorts its formation in the present. The critical
rejection of capitalism can be effective in advancing working-class
interests in pursuit of future reform and revolution.

As detailed in Chapters 3 and 5, social capital has been located in
the past in historical studies of pre-capitalist societies and those in
transition. Generally, these studies are dictated by an understanding
of social capital that departs from its current use, focusing on the
aggregate or systemic economic properties that are heralded by
capitalism. This also has its counterpart in the understanding of
contemporary capitalism, with Bina and Davis (2000) and Bina
and Yaghmaian (1991), for example, deploying the notion of social
capital as the spread of capitalist relations, especially through the
internationalisation of circuits of capital.[12]

On the other hand, not least in terms of the corresponding reorganisation of the relationship between the economic and the social
that is brought by capitalism, there is the presumption that social
capital comes under assault from capital in general and commercialisation and monetisation in particular, hardly a novel insight

given Polanyi's 'double movement'. There can be the loss of social capital as the traditional knowledge of health remedies, under assault from pharmaceutical companies (Norchi 2000), and Trask (2000) similarly argues that the Hawaiian people's knowledge of their own colonised history is at risk from the need to present a welcoming face to tourists.

But the most wide-ranging contribution in this vein is offered by Ciscel and Heath, for whom social capital is destroyed by a combination of capitalism and patriarchy, not least through the process of commodification in shifting the boundaries against self-provision through the household. The relations attached to social capital, and the means and motives to achieve them, are taken away by the market. Thus,

> [a]lthough corporate capitalism has provided a measure of opportunities to families and women, the concomitant usurpation of the family's social role has been to the detriment of the family, society, and the market itself. The market has usurped those discrete aspects of social capital that are most profitable to itself, and left the remainder of social capital – the creation of the web of relationships – to the family, primarily women, to provide. Thus, the ersatz freedom flowing from the unfettered expansion of the markets in reality represents another form of oppression, confining women and their families to lives of market supporting activities. (2001, pp.407–8)

The market not only provides what was previously provided by the family, but also reduces motives around such provision to self-interest (pp.410–11). So capitalism not only depends upon the family's social capital for social reproduction but also undermines its creation and potential: 'the paradox within a paradox is now complete. The market not only free rides on the family's provision of social capital, the capitalist drive for profit makes that social capital increasingly impossible for the family to provide' (p.412).

What is at dispute here is not the significance of the rise of capitalism for family relations and social reproduction more generally (Fine 1992a). Rather, the incorporation of social capital as the way to address this has the effect of unduly homogenising what are a diverse set of differentially determined outcomes. Thus, Bateman (2003) usefully argues that as commercialised forms of microfinance appropriate profitable opportunities, there is both a loss of social capital in the way such services have been provided previously and the spread of Grameen banking initiatives to support such finance in places where the commercial sector will not go[13] (see earlier chapters for some discussion of the continuing inequities associated with this). But such an outcome is not replicated across other areas of provision in economic and social reproduction, especially given the role of the (welfare) state (see Chapter 9).

Significantly, then, Das (2006, pp.72–3) explicitly rejects my advice that the concept of social capital be jettisoned altogether and, instead, seeks to endow it with a 'class-based, political economy' content.[14] Now, given the BBI syndrome, it is hardly surprising that Das is able to incorporate class, power, the state, conflict and political economy in his own reworking of social capital. And he accepts that this is unusual and runs against social capital's predominant attachment to enlightened neo-liberalism or reformism and its neglect of the class and political economy aspects of capital as social. For him, in contrast, '[w]orking-class social capital is about mutual relations of trust and cooperation within working-class communities … It is *also* about relations of trust and cooperation between workers and reformist officials' (p.82). This is simply the bonding (within groups), bridging (between groups) and linking (across hierarchy or with the state) social capital to be found within the orthodoxy. But for Das, this is tied to the observations that social capital is limited in what it can achieve (because of class and the political economy of capitalism – something that is also accepted by much of the orthodoxy on its own terms); and that it can be used to promote workers' immediate (within mode of production) as opposed to fundamental (across mode of production) interests.

In addition, social capital 'will also be place-specific, because the balance between class constraints and class opportunities – and indeed, the balance of power between classes – will vary geographically' (p.83). So what we need to do is to analyse the balance of power within and between classes, constraints and opportunities, the relationship between reform and revolution, the role of the state, and so on, according to specific place. I suspect that we knew this already, and the appendage of social capital is at best superfluous and at worst unduly homogenising across specificity in lieu of appropriate attention to detail (although Das does offer detailed case studies).

But, as already argued on a number of occasions, the dispute is not simply about whether social capital is capable of offering an acceptable analysis on the basis of an individual contribution. Rather, whilst a Marxist (or other) version of social capital might deliver appropriate insights, these would certainly be lost amongst the orthodox juggernaut of contributions that dominate the literature. The proliferation of social capitalists in part reflects the process of bringing back in omitted considerations, not least in light of the concept's potentially variegated content (anything social) and universal application. Das might be interpreted as having fallen into this trap, with class, political economy, conflict, power, the state, and so on being appended, although these, however unsatisfactorily, were already there in Bourdieu's first use of the term, before they were systematically jettisoned. Whatever the intentions of individual authors in this regard, the overall effect across the literature is to legitimise the notion of social capital as truly universal and well founded. Look, it can deal with things like class, and even Marxists are able to accept it!

7.5 CONCLUDING REMARKS

How, then, are we to maintain a healthy analytical diet in response to the McDonaldisation of management studies, with critical management studies a potential victim as well? Two syndromes need to be avoided. One is the 'naughty but nice' syndrome, the jingle used to promote cream cakes to an increasingly health-conscious market. There are individual indulgences to be gained from deploying social capital, even from within critical management studies, such are the rewards for hackademia in a field that is inevitably heterodox, in face of a vocationally organised and conservative orthodoxy. But at the end of the day, naughty is naughty, and such indulgence cannot promote the cause of critical management studies more generally.

The other syndrome derives from the heavy/'lite' duality. As long as I have a Diet Coke, it's OK to have a hamburger. This is the position adopted by those who argue that they accept all the criticisms of social capital as it is, heavy, but believe they can lighten it up by their own particular use, especially BBI. There is, of course, at the individual level, the risk of the self-delusion of slipping back into being naughty but nice under the rationale of being heavy if tempered by being lite as well. The evidence from my own work on the nation's diet is that the impact of the availability of ranges of healthy-eating products in hypermarkets has been to increase the consumption of both heavy *and* lite foods, and, especially, to worsen the diets of those already having the worst diets, as lite consumption is virtue rewarded by heavy indulgence (Fine et al. 1996; Fine 1998b). Even if this can be avoided in an individual case or two, amongst those with the greatest self-control and determination, the impact is still to sustain the forward momentum of heavy consumption. As I have already suggested, social capital is intellectual repressive tolerance par excellence.

The thing about repressive tolerance is that it can be accepted or it can be fought but it cannot be avoided. The extreme and overt limitations of social capital have, however, tended to elicit two responses. One is to jump on the bandwagon, to become part of the social capital of social capital as it were, to be included alongside those who positively embrace it – to do so, but pretend to do otherwise; and to do so, but genuinely (and misguidedly in my view) seek to reform it from within. The other option is to seek to avoid it altogether in the hope that it will go away. Unfortunately, the latter is only too common, as evidenced by the silent majority who read my poem (Chapter 2), but who do not engage in opposition. As will have been apparent, I have sought to adopt a third way of my own, one of obdurate, even obsessive, criticism. As far as the prospects of critical management studies are concerned, I hope to have persuaded you that social capital should neither be adopted nor avoided, but critically engaged and rejected, from the unique intellectual and institutional position that the field occupies. If this does not happen, critical management studies will tend to become part of management studies, to the extent that its critique is acceptable; otherwise it will be marginalised.

8
Degradation without Limit

The range of applications of social capital is so diverse, extensive and voluminous that it defies systematic organisation. This is reflected in this chapter more than any other, possibly apart from the next. Three apparently disconnected themes are explored. Section 8.2 introduces Putnamenology, highlighting the extent to which the leading proponent of social capital has, in a sense, become an object of study in his own right and, as a result, has built his startling reputation and prominence despite, or even upon, having been open to devastating, extensive, almost universal criticism. To some extent, such critical treatment of social capital can be found amongst orthodox economists, if on economics' preferred terrain of technical and statistical modes of enquiry. Even on the narrow and flawed foundations of that discipline, as shown in Section 8.3, it is enabled to embrace social capital only, paradoxically, by both highlighting and disregarding its legion deficiencies. One of these is the way in which it conceives the individual. Whilst the social capitalist is nowhere near as reduced as the homo economicus of the dismal science, it is striking how shallow and incoherent is homo socio-capitalus, as is revealed by interrogating the meaning of trust within the literature in Section 8.4. Our concluding remarks ask once more whether social capital can be reformed or whether it would be better for it to be abandoned

8.2 PUTNAMENOLOGY

As reported previously, in trying to get a handle on the explosion of the social capital literature across a multiplicity of topics, I sought to allocate different contributions within and across a number of themes. I soon began to realise that much of the literature offered explicit critical reference to Robert Putnam. In addition, there was also much qualified acceptance of his work that might reasonably be categorised as at least implicitly critical. Such criticism has taken a number of forms, especially in empirical work. First, for example, are differences in methods of measurement and in the trends of social capital, either for the United States or for other countries. Second is the failure to replicate his results in other countries, or even in the United States (and Italy). Not only might social capital not have declined in the United States, but also any decline may not have had the consequences that he suggests. Third, as is often explicitly recognised, there is the problem of omitted variables that condition both the presence and effects of social capital. Putting these sorts of contribution together, the 'critical of Putnam' category becomes one of the largest. Quite apart from being the most cited of authors across the social sciences, he is also one of the most criticised. For McLean (2007/8, p.683), '[c]riticism of Robert Putnam's theory of social capital has become something of a cottage industry in political science'.

As observed in my earlier book (Fine 2001a, Chapter 6), these two characteristics of prominence and criticism often go together and induced me, for obscure reasons laid out there, to dub Putnam a 'benchkin': an academic who attracts attention in spite of the poverty of analysis and lack of validity of empirical work – attention whose result, far from the academic's rejection, is the promotion of a programme of work that qualifies and advances what has been shown to be a false starting point. As should be apparent, the weight, position and impact of such 'critical' work is a consequence of the nature of social capital itself, in terms of its burgeoning definitional chaos and its capacity to absorb more or less anything through 'bringing back in' (Chapter 4). Thus, the success of social capital is a striking illustration of the benchkin phenomenon, with Putnam at its core.

Such scurrilous mocking is hard to avoid and is even thrust upon us by what might be termed the Putnam phenomenon, or Putnamenon to which it might now be shortened, given the failure of the benchkin terminology to catch on.[1] For Putnam has himself bordered on the ridiculous in his claims, grand historical or otherwise. Whilst social capital was laid down in twelfth-century Italy, with the comparative disadvantage of the south continuing into the twentieth century, it could be restored in the United States in the immediate wake of 9/11 (Putnam 2002).[2] As cited in the *Financial Times* of 14 April 2001, Putnam claims: 'There is less social capital than there used to be. From that you can predict higher crime, lower levels of health, lower educational performance.' His website has claimed, without evidence, that the impact of going out and joining an association is as good for your health as giving up smoking. Upon appointment to the University of Manchester to lead a team, jointly with Harvard University, to study civil society, he was asked in a radio interview, after breakfast with the prime minister, Tony Blair, what he would do about the veil problem in British schools. The stunning response was that more bridging, rather than bonding, social capital needs to be built. In the renewal of his work on social capital and ethnic diversity (2007), Putnam sees one as being at the expense of the other, outflanks potential future criticism (as well as criticism from the past) by constructing and answering his own criticism, and somehow manages to avoid any discussion of racism, other than to claim that it has been eliminated from the US armed forces. Hero (2007) offers a detailed rebuttal of Putnam's earlier work, counterposing a racial diversity hypothesis to a social capital one for the United States. In contrast with Putnam's historical account of decline in social capital and its impact upon outcomes, Hero finds that racial diversity is a far more powerful explanatory factor than social capital. In popular parlance, social capital is a 'white man's story'; in more academic terms, he points to 'the tendency of civic republican accounts of American politics generally to understate the legacy of the racial or ascriptive hierarchy tradition' (p.9).

In part, in more popular discourse, Putnam's appeal to the bowling club, in practice and as metaphor, is doubly unfortunate given both Timothy McVeigh's use of a bowling club to organise the Oklahoma bombing conspiracy and the rather different image of bowling presented in the film *The Great Lebowski*, in which neither the idea of capital nor of the social readily spring to mind in contemplating the dude, played by Jeff Bridges, or any of the other dysfunctionals involved. Putnam continues to offer opportunistic hackademicisms in ways that are liable to make even his fellow social capitalists cringe. I recall one interview in which he was told that more men were going to the pub in Britain, so he welcomed this as evidence of growing social capital in the United Kingdom; but when told this was to watch football on the TV, he immediately retracted. But the 'surprising' headline 'fact' to be found on the Bowling Alone website (www.bowlingalone.com), itself inspired by Putnam's now already classic contributions (1995 and 2000), is that '[j]oining one group cuts in half your odds of dying next year'. This is a benefit that I too offer to those who gain social capital by absorbing my criticisms (and why not visit www.iippe.org/wiki/Social_Capital_Working_Group?). Incidentally, the study with which the World Bank launched its commitment to social capital suggested that joining a burial society in Tanzania was six times more effective than female education in reducing poverty, both for those that joined and for the villages as a whole in which burial societies prospered. Putting these two results together, it seems that joining a burial society means there is less need to do so!

But death is a serious business, especially when it comes to violent crime. Consider the contribution on social capital and firearm ownership in the United States by Hemenway et al. (2001), of which Putnam is a co-author.[3] This regresses individuals' firearm ownership against the number of times in the previous year they went bowling, played cards, entertained at home, sent greeting cards, and attended dinner parties. It accepts that issues such as race, urbanisation and poverty were omitted from the study and that correlation and causation have not been distinguished.[4] The National Riflemen's Association does not warrant a mention (although going to church is found, if insignificantly, to raise possession, suggesting that firearm ownership and religion may have some values in common).[5] These conclusions also have to be set against the civilian possession of 270 million firearms in the United States, compared to 7 million in Italy, and a death total by firearms 40 times higher relative to population than that in the United Kingdom – for all of which, explanation in terms of dinner parties and the like might seem to be slightly misplaced.

For these and other reasons, given the McDonaldisation of social theory by social capital, it is irresistibly attractive to place Putnam in the role of the Ronald McDonald of social theory, a metaphor that warrants considerable deconstruction, given the complexity of both the Ronald image and the use to which it is put. Inevitably, though, there are more serious, and academic, takes on Putnam's deficiencies. First and foremost, he is perceived as being reactionary or conservative in his approach, not least through reference to generally unacknowledged antecedents.[6] Whilst there is both reliance upon, and distancing from, Coleman's rational choice (and corresponding neo-liberalism), Putnam is appropriately seen by Grix as deploying outmoded notions for societies that have moved on:

> Traditional social capital indicators, developed in the early 1990s, fail to take account of the technological revolution, the major shift in working patterns and modes of production, the effects this has had on citizens' mobility and families and the channels through which citizens articulate their interests and engage in civic affairs. (2001, pp.200–1)

Similarly, Urry (2002, p.264) questions whether Putnam's social capital has acknowledged the physical mobility and interaction characteristic of the current age of the Internet and international travel – not least in citing Putnam's appeal for neighbourliness:

> Let us act to ensure that by 2010 Americans will spend less time traveling and more time connecting with our neighbors than we do today, that we will live in more integrated and pedestrian-friendly areas, and that the design of our communities and the availability of public space will encourage more casual socializing with friends and neighbors. (2000, pp.407–8)

Urry observes the irony that 'Putnam also ignores what his own practice as an academic shows, the widespread *growth* of longer-range mobility especially by air, as conferences, holidays, family connections, diasporic relations and work are increasingly internationalized'. And, whilst ethnic diversity has always figured within Putnam's horizon once he had shifted social capital to the United States, its presence is not deeply analytically rooted. MacKian appropriately sees the Putnam model as

> increasingly divorced from the realities of postmodern society, comprised as it is by a variety of cultural identities, affiliations and behaviours, populated by a wider constituency than the white, middle-class, churchgoing nuclear families so often found in the popular social capital literature. (2002, p.205)

This all corresponds to the predisposition on Putnam's part to inhabit and restore the supposedly lost world of associational civil society. This reflects a structured analytical starting point in which civil society is separated from the economy and the state, before, possibly, they are allowed to interact once more. As Skocpol (2008, p.117) cautiously puts it: 'At first glance, and in some of the original scholarly incarnations, social capital research seemed to be a reversion to social–cultural determinism, pushing state actions and political organization back into the province of dependent or intervening variables.' Ironically, though, this passage is taken from Skocpol's 2007 Johan Skytte Prize Lecture; Putnam (2007) had won the prize in 2006. The two complement each other, one bringing back in civil society, the other bringing back in the state, and neither the economy!

Couto points to the extent to which such structural separation leads to a stripped down version of the separated elements, comparing this position with that of the conservative sociologist Edward Nisbet. For, imposing a social capital interpretation on him, Couto writes that 'Nisbet relates the failure of intermediate associations to provide the psychological and symbolic functions of social capital – that is, its moral element – directly to their diminished capacity to perform the material and economic functions of social capital' (1999, p.53).[7] By contrast,

> Robert Putnam's work supported the conservative revision of the political role of mediating structures. It ignored and diminished the economic function of mediating structures and the material side of social capital. Social capital, in Putnam's work, consists almost exclusively of moral resources. Defining social capital as moral resources expresses a limited criticism of market economics.

This is part and parcel of a dual absence in Putnam's work, that of the agency and mechanisms by which social capital accrues benefits even within civil society itself, and of the constraints and interactions that these involve with state and economy. As Anheier and Kendall put it:

> [H]ow do we explain the intermediary step of actual trust generation? This mechanism appears as the crucial link in the implied causal chain ... what is it about voluntary associations that facilitates trust? ... the 'intervening factor' in trust generation is, however, largely left unspecified by current sociological thinking. Putnam and others ... tend to remain silent on how and under what conditions voluntary associations generate and preserve trust for their members and more widely for society as a whole. (2002, p.345)

That social capital is a resource that is mobilised merely by virtue of its existence is a consequence of a terminology in which we all become capitalists merely by belonging to (civil) society. This necessarily glosses over the different circumstances in which we engage in political activity and the moralities which we attach to it. Consequently, for Smith and Kulynych, the social capital terminology celebrates the individualism, competition and pursuit of wealth that is characteristic of capitalism, but only by seeking, inconsistently, to promote the universal civic virtues that are its antithesis. For,

> [a]s suggested by Putnam's use of the term *social capitalists* as well as by his claim that working-class solidarity is a form of social capital, the term *social capital* imposes a universalizing logic on political activity that minimizes the historical context that gives much of this activity its meaning and impedes normative theorizing. (2002a, p.151)

Not surprisingly, they also take offence at Putnam's (2000, p.351) citing the *fraternité* of the French Revolution as a form of social capital!

Similarly, DeFilippis recognises that Putnam too readily writes out power, relation to economic capital, and conflict within civil society, in order to be able to focus on win–win opportunities. Thus:

> In Putnam's understanding of the term, social capital becomes divorced from capital (in the literal, economic sense), stripped of power relations, and imbued with the assumption that social networks are win–win relationships and that individual gains, interests and profits are synonymous with group gains, interests, and profits. (2001, p.800)

Further, there are questions of the distribution and use of social capital, for why would an elite give up their advantages in these respects any more than they would their economic capital?

> Why would those who benefit from the current structures that produce and distribute social capital willingly turn over their privileged access to it? We would not expect rich people to willingly turn over their mutual portfolio funds or, less hypothetically, embrace poor and nonwhite students in their schools without a confrontation. Why should we expect that this form of capital would somehow be different from others? People who realize capital through their networks of social capital do so precisely because others are excluded. (p.801)

As a result,

> [i]nner-city neighbourhoods have social networks and trust between members of those networks, and they possess many

nongovernment, community-based organizations. What they lack is power and the capital that partially constitutes that power [over the flows of economic capital]. They are not likely to realize either without confrontation or within a Putnam-inspired framework of community development. (p.801)

And there is a welcome reference to the lack of attention to the (declining) social capital of the wealthy, in contrast to the focus on those who might be deemed to be able to help themselves through more community spirit:

Why are the American elites, who have gone through 35 years of civic disengagement, doing so well financially? Affluent and professional Americans have enjoyed a virtually unprecedented period of prolonged prosperity, and the current gap in wealth between rich and poor is greater than it has been since before the Great Depression. Putnam's theory just does not make sense in, let alone explain, this reality. (p.801)

In short, even where there is social capital in US inner cities,

these networks and support are unable to generate capital ... the ability of most of these community-based organizations to generate long-term economic growth for their communities has been rather limited ... it is also clear from this experience that simply creating community-based organizations in inner-city neighbourhoods does not, by itself, generate economic prosperity or even economic security for the residents. (p.797)

Thus, as Navarro suggests, Putnam displays a 'remarkable absence of *power* and *politics*' (2002, p.427), with social capital being deployed to replace the language of race, class and gender. Siisiäinen (2000) highlights how Putnam also neglects conflicts of interest of various types, deploying a romantic and universal notion of trust that can be 'posited as disinterested ... a euphemism concealing the hidden, but underlying specific interests of the powerful'. Significantly, then, in examining political democratisation in Taiwan, Marsh (2005, p.613) finds that increasing civic participation is associated with illiberal values and hierarchical organisations, indicating the extent to which 'the theory [of social capital] takes the politics out of political behaviour and attitudes', as well, it should be added, as offering a positive morality to be attached to associationalism (despite its potential for exclusion and the dark side).

As has been fully revealed in Chapter 3, the social capital literature in general, and Putnam in particular, have studiously ignored earlier and explicit uses of social capital (as a macro-social economic aggregate) that do not conform to its current imperatives. In addition, as seen above, some concerted criticism has been directed at Putnam for the influences, whether these are conscious or not, that he does not acknowledge. And there are also those that question his use of both putative and explicit influences. Across each of these elements in the formation of the thought of Putnam, a common theme is the reduction and degradation, to suit his purpose, of what has gone before. This is revealed, for example, by Hospers and van Lochem (2002), who are critical of Putnam for departing from a rounded interpretation of the contributions of Jane Jacobs, a heralded pioneer of social capital, and for failing to see her as emphasising diversity, creativity, entrepreneurship and innovation within cities. But decisive in this respect is the treatment of the classic contribution of de Tocqueville, which in many ways Putnam takes as his starting point for the decline of social capital.

For Fried, then, Putnam totally misreads de Tocqueville, through insufficient attention to inequality and by neglecting the wider structural context and dynamics around economic, social and political life as an influence on political participation; and Putnam's survey methods neglect individuals as interviewees, failing to tease out how they perceive and interact with institutions, as opposed to simply deriving bland quantitative measures of participation in civil society. In any case, associational life occupies only 6 of the 700 pages of the de Tocqueville volume *Democracy in America*. Thus,

> [d]espite Tocqueville's status as (according to Putnam) a patron saint of social capitalists, Tocqueville's ideas and approach have a more partial than robust presence in *Bowling Alone* ... a more fully recovered Tocqueville casts attention to the issue of equality as a main element influencing American democracy, encourages scholarship that is contextual, institutional, and historical in nature, and invites methodological approaches oriented towards structural analysis and interpretative exegesis. (Fried 2002, p.40)

Similarly, Ehrenberg accepts social capital as an analytical concept, but considers that it is hard to create in practice, suggesting that 'Bowling Alone would be considerably stronger if it took Tocqueville seriously. The fact that it doesn't shouldn't be surprising. Unfortunately, a moralized, depoliticized, and self-righteous communitarianism is a perfect ideological reflection of contemporary disengagement, materialism, individualism, cynicism, and inequality' (2002, p.71).[8] Or, as Crenson and Ginsberg observe, it is not the decline of civil society that is involved, contra Putnam, as Americans do not bowl alone. Rather, '[t]hey continue to bowl together, but they take part in politics alone and with far less frequency and enthusiasm than their forbears' (2006, p.210). On the other hand, for Schultz, Putnam's 'appropriation' of de Tocqueville proceeds by emphasising 'group membership as a means of enhancing individual social capital, psychological attributes, and participation', as opposed to de Tocqueville's own pluralist focus on 'critical structural forces essential to maintaining a stable democratic system' (2002, p.73); and, once again, attention is drawn to the significance of equity for de Tocqueville. Putnam ignores structural forces and, in seeking to 'build social consciousness from the individual up reveals an incomplete vision of democracy and human nature, as well as an incomplete understanding of human intersubjectivity' (p.76; see also p.83). Further, Putnam is seen as combining the inner-directed individual governed by inner values and motives with the other-directed individual who seeks guidance from others (p.92–3, following Riesman et al.1953). For Riesman and his co-authors, the period under scrutiny by de Tocqueville was, indeed, dominated by an inner drive with values derived from the family. But from the 1950s, outer direction came to the fore in a pernicious form, with individuals subject to malign influence, not least from McCarthyism. In contrast, Putnam harks back to the 1950s as a civic golden age, despite its McCarthyism, consumerism and racial segregation (see below).

Not surprisingly, even without reference to de Tocqueville, the absence of equity and equality in Putnam's work is a common criticism. Savage et al. (2005) emphasise the need to disaggregate social capital in terms of who gets what and how because, for example, '[p]eople in disadvantaged positions are more likely to obtain situational social capital from informal neighbourhood relations, whilst those in advantaged positions are more likely to have social capital from social networks and civic engagement' (p.120). They draw the conclusion that there is a need to situate social capital in the context of both stratification and inequality (p.121).

Much the same position is taken by Kisby (2007), who rehearses criticisms of social capital in terms of what it excludes. He argues both that citizenship education was introduced in the United Kingdom by New Labour to promote social capital and also that it will fail because of its 'reluctance to challenge the entrenched inequalities that undermine the promotion of social inclusion and thus prevent the development of social capital' (p.84). Across these two contributions, there is a mix of presumption that inequality might be more important than social capital, that it certainly conditions it, and that social capital will not contribute unless this is all recognised.

In a slightly stronger vein, and with the added motive of suggesting the use of social capital to put inequality on the back burner, O'Connell emphasises that equality plays a more important role than social capital in explaining effective participation in political institutions across the European Union, but that the latter has become more popular, because 'the difficult task of challenging powerful vested interests to redistribute wealth can be avoided in building cohesive societies' (2003, p.247). And, he continues, and closes, as follows:

> Rather, an active interest in their local football club will suffice to turn 'ghetto mums' into 'soccer mums'. Vibrant birdwatching associations, busy rotary clubs, and regular philatelic conventions will start the wheels of progress rolling. This is not a caricature of the position [of Putnam]; in *Bowling Alone*, these are precisely the sorts of measures set forth for 'renewing the stock of social capital'.

These are, of course, if we add a firearm or two, astonishingly apposite premonitions of Sarah Palin.

A rather different critical perspective on Putnam derives from Durlauf (2002a), who has long sought both secure micro-foundations for social theory and more rigorous use of statistical methods in deriving empirical results.[9] For him, Putnam 'is in many ways very deeply disappointing, particularly when judged from the perspective of rigor or analytical depth', a problem being 'lack of clarity as to what constitutes social capital' (p.260). Indeed, Putnam 'suffers from a problem that pervades social science, the overstatement of the implications of particular empirical studies', and 'one finds a statistically significant coefficient of a particular sign far too often treated as justifying a claim that the associated variable is a causal determinant of the process under study' (p.266). The fallacies involved are precisely those that have been pointed out more informally in Chapter 2, with omitted variables, model specification, identification problems, and so on. In short, Putnam 'has not come close to the appropriate standard for drawing firm inferences …[and he has shown] little ability to discriminate between a social capital explanation versus some other' (p.269); he has failed to offer 'an explicit description of the joint determination of social capital and socioeconomic processes' (p.270).[10]

It is hardly surprising, and is already apparent, that Putnam's work should have been subject to extensive criticism, if not always in these hard terms, in its portrayal of the (nature of the) decline of US civil society and the causes for it.[11] One major element in such reassessments, if not so explicitly put, is that Putnam looks forward from the past rather than the other way around. If we suppose that social movements come and go, in and of themselves, and reflect their times, this inevitably offers a bias towards the hypothesis of decline, since the measured social capital of the past will have given way to the unmeasured social capital of the present, unless attention is paid to new forms. In other words, supposing we undertook the exercise the other way round, the result would be to find that there has been an explosive growth in social capital, as low levels of activity in the currently new are found to have been minimal in the past. This is so whatever new form of social capital we take, whether it be the rise of consumerism (as activism), the 'grey panther' movement (organisation of the elderly in the United States),[12] environmental campaigning, or something else.[13]

In addition, of course, it is not just the projection of the loss of the past onto the inevitably different future that is at stake, but also that this is done from a necessarily conservative and limited perspective. An outstanding critique in these respects is offered by Arneil (2006). She emphasises how Putnam's generally positive view of the women's temperance movement as responsible and reciprocal overlooks its powerful role in racist oppression of non-Protestants in its drive for homogeneous assimilation and hegemony. Putnam's associations were often exclusionary, in many instances on the basis of race and ethnicity, so that Arneil questions whether their decline should be deplored, especially given the changing situation of women (p.48). Where it does exist, the generational decline in social capital from the 1970s is better seen in terms of 'economic turmoil and inequality … crises in political leadership … [around the] Vietnam War and Watergate … and dashed hopes of cultural and racial politics' (p.145).[14] In this light, Steger (2002) admires, I take it sarcastically, Putnam's (2000) panache in setting up the death of civic America as a whodunit, with answers in terms of the pressures of two-career families on time and money (10 per cent), commuting and urban sprawl (10 per cent), the privatising effects of electronic equipment (25 per cent), and the almost-as-important generational change between 1910 and 1940. Yet, Putnam's 26-page index has no entry for globalisation, and the 541-page book devotes just two pages to the global economy. Equally, there is no mention of deregulation, privatisation, marketisation, neo-liberalism, and so on.

The thrust of these and many other writings is the need to bring back in the substance of politics explicitly, and on a wider and different frame than allowed for by Putnam.[15] As Trigilia argues in the case of Italy:

> Contrary to the hypothesis put forward by Putnam, social capital is less absent in the south than one could expect by defining it in terms of a civic culture inherited from a distant past ... it is not the lack of these networks which seem to have hindered development in the south, but the lack of a modernized politics. While in the centre and north a modernized politics favoured a productive use in the market of social networks, based on kinship and community ties, in the south it fostered political capitalism: the use of social networks for a collusive appropriation of public resources. (2001, p.437)

And, on a grander and more general scale, Navarro (2002) offers a critique of Putnam's understanding of the US progressive era as deriving from social capital rather than from social movements, and of the way in which he rejects solidarity within the labour movement as a purpose in itself, within and against capitalism. The recent decline of social capital within the US trade union movement is a reflection of repression and the shift in balance of class forces rather than a loss of cultural values amongst the young (as a result of watching television, for example). For Muntaner (2001), US exceptionalism (in the nature and decline of social capital) derives from the lack of a strong working-class movement, one capable of creating a welfare state. On a slightly different tack, McLean (2002b) simply suggests that the rise of mistrust in government (as a loss of social capital) may be stronger amongst those who are more active in civil society, especially in newer movements and newer forms that are liable to be overlooked in counting decline in moving forward in time.

In short, as in the social capital literature more generally, there is a paradox, or at least a tension, in the extensive criticisms offered of Putnam, not least as these range over conceptualisation, theory, measurement and the empirical, both in cause and effect and in what happened. The paradox arises because the critics both accept social capital as an organising principle and, at the same time, reveal how the concept is too weak and chaotic to be sensitive enough to the complexity of the factors involved. And the same applies in the contextual content over the questions of whether social capital has gone up or down and whether this has been good or bad.

8.3 THE DISMAL (SOCIAL) SCIENCE

As previously revealed, it is a significant but easily overlooked fact that the first major economist to use the term 'social capital' was Gary Becker (1996) – not surprisingly, given his association with James Coleman at the University of Chicago (Fine 2001a). As a pioneer of economics imperialism of the old type (treat everything as far as possible as if reducible to individuals optimising given utility over given goods in an as-if-perfectly-working market), his use of social capital has been more or less totally discarded, for it is an embarrassment to the new type of economics imperialism, which is still founded on such ideas as that of optimising individuals, but in the context of imperfectly working markets and the non-market as the response to those imperfections. The reductionism may be less than for Becker, but the scope of application becomes much wider and more appealing whatever the subject matter (Fine and Milonakis 2009).

A neat application of Becker's approach is provided by Borcherding and Filson (2002). The idea is to explain reciprocity (a form of social capital) on the basis of pursuit of self-interest, and they take the custom of buying a round of drinks as an example. They find, through a model explicitly based on Becker, that

> [i]nformal reciprocity agreements are more likely to be used when transaction costs are high, the unit cost of the good is small, each consumer's demand is not too responsive to price changes, the group is likely to continue to interact, the consumers are patient, the time between transactions is short, and the group is small and homogeneous. (p.239)

That is, down the pub. For Borcherding and Filson, though, social capital through 'socialization shapes the utility function to encourage consumers in the group to internalize price externalities' (p.257). This reflects another aspect of Becker, the idea that apparently changing preferences are nothing of the sort, simply fixed ones modified in application in light of experience. But Borcherding and Filson see economists as reluctant to embrace social capital for, as a latent variable, it is difficult to measure. Yet, 'there is every reason to believe that since social constraints and spontaneous informal coordinating are ubiquitous, economists will find the will and the wit to make sense of it'.

They have, however, also found the will and the wit to move beyond Becker. Nonetheless, one feature of his approach to social capital does, unsurprisingly, tend to survive amongst economists into more rounded approaches. This is the attempt, not always in pure form, to incorporate wider economic and, especially, social factors, but by retaining the uncritical use of prevailing concepts and techniques. Thus, Ray et al. (2001) are not alone in deploying social capital (A) as an input in a production function, generating increasing returns to scale within a new growth theory model:[16]

> A is the stock of 'social capital' the economy has developed in the context of history and geography. It includes institutions like compulsory primary education, civil societies, free press, independent judiciary, effective law enforcement authority, and public policies relevant to: basic research; investments on transport and telecommunication networks, which generate network economies; health care; protection of environmental resources; promotion of competition as well as coordination among economic agents; and macroeconomic management of the economy. It also includes culture, such as thrift, work ethic, valuing knowledge or education beyond its market value, morality and ethical standards, and geographic factors such as climate and natural resources. It can be deliberately produced from a coordinated action of groups of individuals in a society for some collective good or is autonomously generated in the form of knowledge network economy. (pp.497–8)

Note the breadth and diversity of factors covered by a simple symbol A, to which I return below.

Piazza-Georgi also offers a striking illustration of social capital as business as usual as far as economics is concerned, first of all when he defines any capital as '*a productive resource that is the result of investment*' (2002, p.462).[17] Otherwise, the more or less automatic procedure is simply to seek to reduce social capital to a form of physical capital, including everything from informal associations to (Douglass North's) institutions. Thus, the search is on for assets

> producing income without being consumed by the production process (but being subject to depreciation, thus needing maintenance and eventual replacement) ... created and maintained by people at a theoretically measurable cost, thus fulfilling the condition that distinguishes capital from natural resources ... [and] they 'reside within' human beings – in this case in the relationships between them rather than in the individual minds. In addition, institutions and social capital have important public good characteristics, which are shared by the 'stock-of-knowledge' form of human capital. (p.476)

Robison et al. adopt a different tack, acknowledging that the definition of 'social' has suffered from expansion of scope and, as such, 'is at risk of becoming the ether that fills the universe' (2002, p.1). They see the attempt at abolishing the use of social capital as being futile (getting the social capital cow back in the barn, as they put it), but they do at least seek to confine it to the pasture of 'sympathy', since this is the only way of making it capital-like. Sympathy itself is defined as a relationship that affects one only by affecting others, so that social capital produces benefits to others beyond those provided by exchange (p.6). By this means, social capital is capital-like, since it shares all of the properties of physical capital – transformation capacity, durability, flexibility, substitutability, decay, reliability, ability to create one form of capital from another, opportunities for (dis)investment, and alienability (p.9). Indeed, Robison et al. find that social capital has a market value, since farmers sell land to their neighbours at lower prices than to strangers (see also Robison and Flora 2003), although this is a value to the buyer rather than the seller and might be explained by other factors.[18]

But appealing to sympathy as being equivalent to social capital, whilst this is an extraordinarily narrow definition, is indicative of how social capital functions for economists in its fullest form. First, traditional economic analysis fills out as much as is possible. Second, this is then extended to the non-economic. Third, anything else left out after this can be incorporated as complementing what has already been provided. As seen in Chapter 5, institutions play a similar role, especially for those economists who are prepared to accept that there is a bit more out there than the optimising individual. Social capital becomes a relatively broad application of 'freakonomics', or the economic theory of everything (Fine and Milonakis 2009). As Temple (2001, p.82) puts it, 'for some economists (not all) the intuition that "society matters" is strong enough to outweigh the current absence of much in the way of a theoretical understanding'.

But lack of theoretical understanding does not get in the way of theory (abstract mathematical models), and this can even be of a critical bent. For Farmer and Kali (2007), for example, the Putnamesque decline in social capital is a reflection of development in the positive sense of the greater efficiency of market provision in place of the non-market at higher levels of income – social capital declines as it is functionally displaced by the more efficient, and honest, market. The decline of social capital is modernisation. On the other hand, Mogues and Carter (2005) provide micro-foundations which model 'social capital as a real capital asset with direct use and collateral values'. These, however, tend to stick to wealth, and '[f]ar from being a distributionally neutral panacea for missing markets, social capital in this model may itself generate exclusion and deepen existing economic cleavages' (p.193). And an exemplary illustration of the use of social capital in the hands of economists is provided by Bartolini et al. They jump on the economics of happiness bandwagon (see Johns and Ormerod 2008 for a critique) and seek to explain the decline of happiness by adding social capital as an explanatory variable. For them:

By SC we mean the stock of both 'non-market relations' and 'beliefs concerning institutions' that affect either utility or production functions. More precisely, in what follows we will distinguish between *relational social capital* (RSC), i.e. the non-market relations component of SC, and *non-relational social capital* (non-RSC), i.e. the 'beliefs concerning institutions' component of SC. We further distinguish two parts of the RSC component: intrinsically and extrinsically motivated RSC. The concept of extrinsic motivations refers to the incentives coming from outside an individual. By contrast, intrinsic motives issue from within an individual. (Bartolini et al. 2008, pp.4–5)

This is relatively sophisticated in allowing for the individual to be intrinsically motivated; but it is merely a prelude for a statistical exercise on large-scale data sets. They find that, 'at the individual level, the intrinsically motivated part of relational social capital is positively correlated with reported happiness …[but] the extrinsically motivated part of relational social capital is negatively correlated' (p.23), i.e. you are happier the less you are economically rational! But they do advise:

> In principle, the problem of endogeneity could affect most of our regressors, including for instance absolute and relative income and, of course, social capital variables. However, in order to carry out a meaningful IV [instrumental variables] estimation we would require a large number of instruments that, in turn, would require a long list of additional assumptions about their relationships with both regressors and happiness. We are skeptical about the feasibility of such an IV estimation with our dataset. Thus, our analysis is limited to correlations and imputations and cannot support any claim about causality. (p.25)

Such honesty is as welcome as it is rare.

In my earlier book (Fine 2001a) I devoted the best part of Chapter 10 to the implications that could be derived technically from mainstream economic theory for the theory and measurement of social capital. This is because economics has long agonised over how to define aggregate capital across its different components in a way that is independent of its effects. The orthodoxy demonstrates that the associated problems are irresolvable – hardly surprising given that multidimensional categories cannot be reduced to a single concept or measure without anomaly or even inconsistency. In particular, I made use of the theory of social choice and the Cambridge critique of capital theory to demonstrate the hurdles that would have to be overcome[19] before using a concept like social capital (ranging over social as well as physical assets, the latter alone proving troublesome enough).

This all involves devastating criticisms of the use of social capital by its current practitioners, who simply draw upon standard results from within orthodox (economics) reasoning. Conveniently though, within economics itself, these difficulties have been set aside as if they do not exist – a reflection of the rigour of economics taking second place to its substantive content whenever there is conflict between the two (Fine 2007g; Fine and Milonakis 2009). It is hardly surprising that these criticisms of social capital within economics should suffer the same fate as across social science more generally. I know of not one reference to this aspect of my critique of social capital. In this light, can we place intellectual trust in social capital?

8.4   IN SOCIAL CAPITAL WE TRUST?

One of the advantages, at least in some respects, of mainstream economics is that it does at least have few pretensions of *conceptual* sophistication and complexity. And, precisely because of its deductive, axiomatic and statistical methods, what it has to say is reinforced in its clarity. As is apparent, for example, the reliance upon methodological individualism of a special type (utility maximisation) is a fundamental starting point, within and then beyond the market, ultimately being supplemented by a range of other more or less arbitrary motivations to suit particular applications. But what of the individual in the wider social capital literature, outside of economics?

Shorn of its origins in Coleman's rational choice, the individual within the social capital literature tends to become a little, if not too much, more rounded. The pursuit of self-interest remains paramount. But, as with economics, this can be supplemented by other motivations *and* by social determinants at different levels, ranging from the family and neighbourhood through community to national culture of one sort or another. None of this tends to be closely examined. Instead, there is a presumption of relatively fixed mechanisms for relating the individual to the social, as well as for their co-evolution. And, not surprisingly, this is all underpinned by a positive spin. It is not just nostalgia for the lost world of social capital that has been romanticised, but also the role that individuals can currently play if they (or circumstances) would only bring out their sociability. As Tomer (2002) observes, social capital corresponds to the higher aspects of human life and functioning and, for Thomson (2005), it is a device for handling the alienation and anomie of the isolated individual, which can be traced back to Durkheim. For 'social improvement through increased social capital does not require any fundamental economic or political transforma-tions'. In short, this is all because 'American social theories both assume individualism and fear its excesses' (p.443).

The result, as already hinted, leaves individual motivation and its social origins underexplored. As Lebow (2005, p.287) notes, social capital shares this propensity with liberal institutionalism, at best describing secondary processes as a manifestation of an underlying and unexplained propensity to cooperate (although institutions are required to preserve property against violent pursuit of self-interest). In short, 'in their desire to offer parsimonious and "scientific" explanations for cooperation, both approaches denude the more complex framework from which they derive their deeper explanatory power'. There is a need to add reason and emotion and not just to rely upon the microeconomics of egoistic individuals primarily responding to external stimuli.

On reflection, these considerations raise serious questions about the nature of individual identity, how it is determined, how it is translated into action, and what subsequent consequences flow from this. As Servon (2003, p.15) observes, social capital, especially bridging social capital, is (or should be) inevitably bound up with identity and, '[i]n the anthropological literature, communities like this are said to be characterized by a plethora of cross-cutting ties – everyone is connected to everyone else in myriad ways'. There is also the issue of the origin of the needs served by social capital, for (citing Fraser 1989, p.163) these are formed with meaning, and are themselves interpreted by others, and filtered through socially legitimised discourse and practices. More generally, Body-Gendrot and Gittell (2003) argue that the much broader and richer notion of the individual encompassed by social citizenship – national identity, social status, participation and republicanism – is being substituted for by social capital. This is not unrelated to the hollowing out of social citizenship in practice by the rise of identity politics in the context of loss of welfare provision.

The vast majority of the social capital literature is cavalier on these issues. As Brickner (2000, p.105) puts it, 'the capital in Putnam's social capital is an underdetermined term with its moral stimulus cloaked in socioeconometrics ... The problem with social capital is that it seductively presents itself as socioeconometrics while omitting its moral predilections'.[20] Both an escape route from, and an illustration of, this veil of omission, is popularly provided through social capital's use of game theory in general as a way of resolving these conundrums, with the prisoners' dilemma to the fore (social capital is a solution, not least for Fukuyama (2001)).[21] Klabbers (2001, p.476) even suggests that our growing knowledge of game theory is itself a form of social capital for, 'the participants become the co-owners of that knowledge. What a simulation and/ or game produce is to a large extent their social capital'. In other words, we learn about others and ourselves through game theory, not least since, for Carpenter, experimental games can pin down behavioural patterns in response to incentives:

> We have identified four experiments that are (relatively) easily adapted for use in the field, the trust game which measures trust and trustworthiness, the ultimatum game which measures the strength of norms and fairness and reciprocity, the dictator game which measures altruism and generosity and the voluntary contribution game which measures the propensity to cooperate. (2000, p.15)

Of course, 'in the field' signifies an enormous and unbridgeable gap between game theory and context (other than as defined by the game itself). There is no reason why behaviour should not vary as you move from game to game or, indeed, from game to real life, so fluid is behaviour by context.

But, as Murphy (2002, p.615) recognises, 'it is imperative that we more closely examine and better elucidate the cognitive processes that enable individuals to trust outside narrow groups'. In other words, individuals reflect upon their circumstances and create understandings of them, and with which there are very complex relations to action and positive or negative outcomes. Thus, Roberts and Devine (2004) suggest that civic volunteering poses issues of formal participation and activism that may or may not be embraced by individuals who simply want to help out as opposed to being more widely and/or politically involved. Is activism motivated by commitment or antipathy to formal politics? – the answer surely depends both upon the substance of the politics itself and how this is internalised by the individual. And there are differences across socio-economic strata: Williams (2003, p.75) discusses differences in how social capital might be mobilised 'as sociability vehicles for higher income populations. Lower income households, perceiving these groups to be for people other than them, instead relying on one-to-one reciprocal exchange ... to access material support'. And, at a much grander level, Roberts (2004) refers to the isolated reciprocity of capital and labour under capitalism (suggesting resonances with possessive individualism). This imposes limitations on the extent to which there can be trust and reciprocity, given differences in the ethos of universal welfare systems: redistribution of wealth and democratic control of public services for labour as opposed to profits, flexible labour and private control of public services for capital – although each, of course, attempts to persuade the other, with varying degrees of success, of its own ethos.[22]

These various observations about how the individual is poorly and weakly situated by the social capital literature come together in the treatment of trust. At one level, trust is simply seen as social capital. Individuals like to trust one another; they tend to do so within the family, but less so in the remoter layers of civil society. Trust is mutually reinforcing, and the more we experience and gain from it, the more of it we accrue and deploy. No wonder that Stolle (2003) no longer sees it as necessary to define social capital. It derives from everywhere – voluntary associations, the family, the state and political institutions – and, like the rain, it falls indiscriminately.

But, before unpicking this rosy picture of trust, it is worth questioning why it should have become more prominent in the social capital literature than other similar variables, most notably reciprocity and, especially within anthropology, the gift relationship.[23] There is no reason in principle for this. Durston, for example, explicitly citing Mauss's essay on the gift, asserts that

> the concept of reciprocity is a central element of the social capital paradigm ... For this reason, although reciprocity might at first sight seem to be a minor social phenomenon among many others, it is in fact the basis of social capital institutions in contexts like that of a peasant community. (1999, p.104)

However, as already argued in Chapter 5, by virtue of their origins in anthropology, gift and reciprocity sit uncomfortably within the social capital paradigm, once it has discarded Bourdieu and, with him, concerted attention to a coupling with both context and meaning.[24] Trust, on the other hand, seems to have been much more amenable to the designs of social capital.

And, once again, we see within the literature how social capital degrades the concept of trust, but is not rejected as a consequence of this. First, Delhey and Newton (2003) unpick the notion of trust into two broad categories, as a property of individuals or of society. Individuals trust out of socialisation or out of pursuit of well-being. Society garners trust within individuals through voluntary organisations, networks, communities or social factors such as extent of conflict, extent of democracy, and so on. Different types of trust are associated with different outcomes in different countries, and '[t]he study of trust is bedevilled by the problem of cause and effect' (p.102). This necessarily casts doubt on the idea of a single measure of trust and a single relationship between trust (as social capital) and outcomes. Indeed, Delhey and Newton conclude that 'individual social–psychological and demographic character-istics are less likely to explain trust than objective and subjective measures of macro-social conditions and the strength of informal social networks' (p.114). This complements the conclusions of an earlier study: 'the theory claiming that there is a close connection between social and political trust, and a close connection between both of these and voluntary organizations on the one hand, and democracy, on the other, seems highly questionable' (Newton 2001–2, p.207).[25]

The thrust in these contributions is not to reject social capital so much as to qualify its influence. The same is true not only of different types of trust but also in how it is generated and deployed. But to ask for the mechanisms is to unravel the nature of trust and identify its different types: the deferential as opposed to the reflexive, the thick or dense versus the thin (Anheier and Kendall 2002, p.348). Trust also differs by place, time and context (p.350), and in whether it is character-based (from background identity), process-based (from experiences of one another), or institutionally based (pp.350–1). To recognise the complexity of trust is essentially to set about reconstructing the breadth and complexity of social capital through its medium.

Such an exercise is bound to fail because, however far and wide, and deep, social capital is cast, it will prove unable to grasp the missing link that is essential to trust, as is brought out by Möllering (2006). He carefully lays out the nature of trust in terms of three standard approaches: one involving rationality or calculation of strategy in light of what is expected of others; a second focusing upon routine derived from attachment to institutions; and a third also inducing routine, but arising out of response to experience. Individually, or taken together, none of these is adequate to get to grips with trust. Indeed, each might be seen as a ground-clearing exercise in determining what is not trust. For Möllering, trust is something where calculation is *not* enough, where institutions need to gain or sustain credibility, not where they already have it, and where experienced routines retain elements of vulnerability and uncertainty (without which trust would not be necessary). Trust is not independent of rationality, calculation and routine, but requires something over and beyond each and all of them.

This issue is, however, cleverly addressed, if not entirely resolved, in a remarkable earlier paper (Möllering 2001). Here he observes that most treatments of trust approach it from a functional perspective and, of these, relatively few examine its origins. Thus, across the literature, '[t]rust can be defined, first of all, as a state of favourable expectation regarding other people's actions and intentions' (p.404). It is derived from the experience of others. By contrast, drawing on a reading of Simmel on trust, it is perceived to include 'a mysterious further element, a kind of faith, that is required to explain trust and to grasp its unique nature'. It is related to confidence, which can be given by money, but in its own dealings lies somewhere between complete ignorance and complete knowledge, the presence of either of which would eliminate the need for, or the possibility of, trust. Hence trust is highly nuanced and heterogeneous; it depends on a mixture of knowledge and ignorance and also, crucially, is not entirely inductive. Through Simmel, Möllering posits three elements that constitute trust – expectation, interpretation and 'suspension'. The latter is associated with a leap of faith. By contrast, 'current trust research is concerned predominantly with the land of interpretation assuming (wrongly) that "good reasons" will inevitably produce trust (without a leap)' (p.412).

Whilst suspension, then, departs from rational choice, nor is it blind hope. It involves 'a duality of individual self-interest and social/moral embeddedness', but one wedded to the interpreting individual: 'The process of trust as such, however, ends with a state of expectations and begins with *interpretation*' (p.415). This is to be distinguished from

> probabilistic perspectives (from game theory to rational choice and so on) and positivist methods (quantitative methods and most types of survey or experiment) [which] are limited, because they predict a singular model of human interpretation. They cannot capture the arbitrariness of 'good reasons' which Simmel's notion of trust entails ... The challenge is to grasp what from the point of view of the trustor constitutes ignorance, or the 'unknowable' ... [Thus] [t]rust is in danger of becoming an insignificant sociological concept, one that is easily subsumed under decision making and exchange theories, unless it is recognised that the problem of the 'leap' represents more than a quirky defect of an otherwise 'reasonable' concept' (pp.416–7).

A number of points can be made about this reading of trust, and of Simmel. First, there is a wonderful and continuing parallel with trust as money. Simmel is (in)famous for having construed money as the great homogeniser (although, more accurately, he argued that the idea of money gives rise to the *idea* not the actuality that everything can be reduced to it). Like money, trust can be spent where you will. Second, the idea that trust depends upon a leap of faith, and resides within the individual (rather than deriving from external events), has parallels with Mauss's treatment of the gift,[26] and reciprocity, a term that is heavily used as innocently and crudely as trust within the social capital literature. Third, whilst posing a deeper understanding of trust by virtue of an added subjective element, one that breaks out of the circle of the past to embrace new experience, the idea of suspension points to the problem rather than resolving it. What is this leap of faith, why does it arise in some people and not in others, and in some but not other circumstances, and why is it transferred, or not, between practices? No answer can be found within the individual alone, even if the question is located at this level and with suspension of (dis)belief to generate trust. For, fourth, already implicit in Möllering's account is the dependence of suspension upon the individual's ideology, how the world is interpreted. Fifth, Möllering's account reveals what a simple view of humans has been constructed within the social capital approach, not least because of its predominantly functional foundations. They respond to the external world but they do not interpret it, and they recreate it in thought in highly contradictory ways. In reality, the meaning and exercise of trust, for example, is heavily bound up with the formation of identity, the understanding of self and its extrapolation, or not, onto others. At best, the social capital literature recognises associational activity and values that are sources of trust as involving identification with self (bonding), others (bridging) and those at other levels, possibly opponents (linking or vertical). But even joining a single association (from marriage to a trade union), or holding to a single value (from vegetarianism to freedom of speech), is highly complex, contradictory and shifting in meaning. Trust is not at all like money, with its homogeneity in transferability between objects in exchange.

Last, that trust depends upon ideology and how the system is understood by its participants means that analysis can only legitimately proceed from the sources of that ideology in the social system itself. This cannot be reduced to judiciously chosen measures of associational activity, questions about values, trust, or neighbourliness (usually for purposes of regression). Rather, any proper treatment of trust must locate individuals in their economic, political and social context – their class, gender and race, and so on.

8.5   CONCLUDING REMARKS

In closing their contribution, Foley et al. (2001, p.273) ask 'Is It Time to Divest Ourselves of Stock in the Social Capital Concept?' and offer 'a qualified "no"', as long as 'the context-dependent and social structural/relational approaches of Bourdieu and Coleman' are adopted (p.274). Although not intended as such, this is a destructive amendment, certainly in practice and possibly in principle also. It depends upon a chalk-and-cheese combination of Bourdieu and Coleman, with the weaknesses of each, let alone the chaos in taking them together.

As this chapter has demonstrated, as soon as we look at Putnam, economics, the individual or trust, we find problems raised by social capital that, rather than being resolved, grow worse the more we pursue them. Unlike the stranger asking directions for a destination, who is told that it would be better to start the journey from somewhere else, we do have that option in theory. It is preferable, then, to divest ourselves of our stock in social capital.

9
W(h)ither Social Capital?

This chapter has four purposes. First, Section 9.2 samples some of the new, and not so new, applications of social capital, to give a sense of the widening spread it has experienced, and continues to experience, as well as the critical tasks that face social theorists in undoing the damage it has caused. Topics covered include consumption, leisure, migration, the family, welfare, disaster, disability, gentrification and religion. At most a taster is offered of each, in the hope, as suggested in the final section, that others with expertise in these areas will carefully deconstruct the way in which social capital has generally degraded both the subject matter and the literature that has previously been associated with it and will point to alternative ways of proceeding.

Second, Section 9.3 offers a discussion of some of the problems that have attended the measurement of social capital. These are recognised to be legion, but the nature of these problems is shown to derive from those of social capital itself rather than the more general problem of operationalising abstract concepts within social theory, which is often used to excuse the definitional and measurement issues surrounding social capital. Third, the failure, or inability, to measure social capital in any coherent way has also meant, as discussed in Section 9.4, that its deliberative presence within policy has been extremely limited, as opposed to its being used as a discursive rationale for policies that are, in a wide-ranging and substantial literature, found to be located somewhere between Third Wayism and neo-liberalism, at least to the extent that these are not identified with one another.

Last, the final section of the book reiterates the necessity of rejecting social capital, as it stands as an impediment in the way of understanding contemporary capitalism, including its preferred terrain of civil society. The most glaring symbol of social capital's failings is that the global financial crisis has crept up upon it without so much as an inkling of acknowledgement. At least the same cannot be said of globalisation. The most pressing problem facing civil society is whether it will allow itself to continue to be the slave of bankers and to pay for its own slavery, whilst individuals, no doubt, continue to reside in families, (mis-)trust politicians and one another, and engage in associational activity of one sort or another, with the partial promise of betterment within limits through cooperation. It was once said of socialism, and is now said of capitalism in joking, that it is all very well in theory but it just doesn't work in practice. Sad to say, social capital is one step worse, and does not even work in theory.

9.2 FLAVOURING BUT NOT FAVOURING SOCIAL CAPITAL

As previously discussed in Chapter 5 in the context of (social) history, there are a number of topics in which social capital has made little headway, especially where more rounded social theory is liable to be present and/or required. This includes consumption.[1] This is despite the sociability that is involved, especially for food and eating (Hess 2007), from the family meal through dinner party to formalised banquet (and despite the highly publicised dictum that the family that eats together sticks together).[2] Nonetheless, Bian (2001) puts forward the notion of *guanxi* capital, garnered from Chinese banqueting or social eating, and Pietrykowski (2004) poses the slow food movement as a form of social capital. This neglect, though, is unsurprising once recognising the postmodernist influence on the consumption literature albeit moving more recently to approaches based on material culture that continue to emphasise the social construction of the meaning of consumption (Fine 2002a and 2005a). On a small scale, consumption has entered into the social capital literature through a set of contributions on its connection to leisure, especially gyms, but this has tended to focus on the role of leisure as source of network. There is though a small but lively, and generally reasonably circumspect, literature on leisure and social capital, in part inspired by the rise of leisure studies and in part by the rise of the gym as a site of sociability (see Blackshaw and Long 2005). The literature, mainly US, on social capital and sport in schools tends to be less critical (but see Arai and Pedlar 2003; Langbein and Bess 2002).

These are exceptional entries of social capital into the world of consumption and, presumably if implicitly, there would be more sympathy in the field for the judgement of Warde and Tampubolon (2002, p.155) that 'social capital is a flawed concept and that greater appreciation of the complexity and diversity of network ties is required to understand how personal connections influence consumption'. Otherwise, with the neglect of ethnography, the gift, Polanyi, and context as meaning, history, anthropology and consumption are marginalised by social capital, confined to casual reference and more likely attuned to Bourdieu, aptly dubbed the ghostly Banquo at the social capital banquet (Baron 2004; and see below).

Migration might be thought to be a fertile location for social capital, given its emphasis upon networks in both sending and receiving migrants. But it too benefits from considerable ethnographic and cultural input, which would discourage application of social capital as it has become; an early intervention stressing the limitations of the concept in studying migration was made by one of the leading scholars in the field, Portes (1998). Nonetheless, and unsurprisingly, there are excellent accounts of migration that jump the social capital bandwagon whilst offering sophisticated analyses of material and cultural factors that run against its common grain (see Babou 2002 for an outstanding example; also Griffiths et al. 2005 for a critical use of social capital, BBBI in the context of refugees).

But the spread and depth of social capital is not only uneven by topic, the same is true of its geographical application. For some reason, possibly due to individual proselytisers, it has been especially prominent in Scandinavia and Australia.[3] The appropriation and homogenisation by social capital of the cultural forms of sociability is unsurprising. It ranges from *ujamaa* in the context of coastal management in Tanzania (Torell 2002) to *blat* in eastern Europe (Korosteleva 2006); Boström (2002) likens the social capital underpinning lifelong learning in Sweden to Japanese *kokuru*. Whilst Zhao (2002) examines the role of social capital in finding re-employment in China, measured in part by the number of new year greetings cards sent and received, Knight and Yueh (2008) use own or parental membership of the Communist Party.

The nature of social capital as equivalent to an oxymoron induced me to suggest 'It Ain't Social and It Ain't Capital' (Fine 2001b); but subsequently I extended this to 'It Ain't Social, It Ain't Capital, and It Ain't Africa' (Fine 2002c), examining the chaos that surrounds the application of the concept to the dark continent – a peg for research that could be used for other parts of the world. For social capital can only be applied in context by exposing its limitations. There is a significant literature on social capital and India, but for Morris (1998, p.8), it is '[l]ike heat in the chemistry experiment, social capital speeds up the rate of reaction, making the system run faster and more smoothly'. And for Islam (2005), social capital provides the framework for BBI everything from Marx to Putnam to Indian rural organisation and social theory.[4]

Yet most of the literature finds it necessary to depart from traditional concepts of social capital, if not from social capital itself, in order to make it work for India.[5] For Bhattacharyya (2002), it is a matter of making *local* democracy work, deploying 'a redefined notion of social capital most suited to the specific situation ... as democratic consciousness about citizens' right as well as the state performance regarding the same' (p.34). Putnam's form of civil society is seen as unnecessary and, equally, as less likely to arise in non-western societies in light of their capacity to draw on 'historical movements (national liberation, labour, peasants, socialism, ecology, students and so on)'. These may become formalised through the state and political parties and organisations as a condition of democratic electoral success. The result is that '[f]or the post-colonial societies, "democracy without associations" may be the rule rather than the exception' (p.36). Indeed, 'Without denying the importance of associations in making democracy work, this study has shown and argued that this act of associationalism may be performed by agencies not typically civil societies.'

Similarly, Dash (2004) takes his model from Kerala, with its need 'for mobilization and cooperation of government, political parties and civil society organizations' (p.190): Kerala was declared the first totally literate state in India in April 1991 – before, it should be emphasised, social capital had ever been heard of. It is unfortunate that Heller's outstanding study of Kerala (1995, 1996, 1999a and 1999b) should have used social capital as a point of reference. His analysis, and his emphasis upon the role of class forces and state relations, runs entirely against social capital's thrust, as is apparent from his reference to Kerala as a developmental state and to 'Social Capital as a Product of Class Mobilization and State Intervention', the title of the earliest of these three pieces.[6] Das (2004 and 2005) also wishes to endow social capital with a class content in the context of rural India (see Chapter 7). Less explicitly in relation to class, Krishna (2001, 2002a, 2002b and 2007) has been concerned with the nature of the politics and the unique agencies that give rise to outcomes in India.

More generally, as it has evolved or, more exactly, expanded in scope of definition and application, social capital has become chaotic in content, and subject to the problems associated with distinguishing cause and effect, and the conflation of determining, determined and conditioning variables. This has increasingly brought the salience of context to the fore, although this too has been deployed in weaker and stronger forms, raising the issue of whether one instance of social capital has any resonance with, let alone implications for, another. Indeed, one significant avenue along which the social capital literature has strolled, if not galloped, with at least implicit criticism of Putnam as a by-product, is the way in which the presence or taking account of some extra variable has the effect of nullifying or even reversing the supposed impact of social capital. I have dubbed this the plus/minus syndrome. It is recognised in principle in the social capital literature itself most explicitly through the idea of negative social capital, the distinction between bonding (within groups) and bridging (between groups), and the corresponding acknowledgement that social capital includes only by excluding, by whatever social characteristics, and that it is only romanticised as a positive-sum resource by setting aside power and conflict, across both those it includes and those it excludes. Considerations of class, race, gender, poverty, inequality, politics, morality, ethnicity and much more besides, inevitably allow all of this to be transparent. BBI these variables both adds to the social capital juggernaut in practice, on an individual case-by-case basis, and undermines it in principle if case studies are encompassed as a whole.

One area in which the tensions accommodated by social capital have been prominent is religion. On the one hand, there are those who wish to see social capital as a major source of beneficial outcomes, seeking to elevate the partnership of religion and social capital to a more prominent place (whether in emphasising and regretting mutual decline or in suggesting that the decline of social capital is not so dramatic if religion is properly taken into account). On the other hand, and increasingly so, emphasis has been placed on the complexities and diversities of religion itself and the ways in which it functions within society. (The religion and social capital literature has, however, had a decidedly Anglo-Saxon Christian bent.) The idea that religion is reducible to one element in the social capital lexicon becomes patently absurd. Thus, for Wuthnow (2002), religious involvement is not only civility, but also a source of status and presumed access to hierarchy, with social capital too amorphous 'in reducing the complexity of the social world to a single concept' (p.682). Further, Dodd and Gotsis (2007), to quote the abstract to their paper, examine 'the interrelationships between religion and enterprise. The authors find that these are highly context-specific, and will vary markedly over time and social setting, mediated by other sociocultural variables such as political structures and ideologies, and religious symbolism in the workplace' (p.93).

Indeed, the good/bad (allowing for the dark side) and plus/minus syndromes are inevitable, with the corresponding nature and impact of social capital heavily contingent. I do not wish to demonise 'fundamentalism', itself socially constructed; Lam (2002), however, amongst others, shows that religion, even the fundamentalist, has a positive association with civic activity.[7] Schwadel (2005) points to the complexity of the role of the church, with the beliefs of conservatives often militating against wider social participation, other than on their own terms. 'Simply put, what is preached from the pulpit and talked about in the pews influences church members' activities, not just in the church but also outside the church' (p.169).[8] Unruh and Sider (2005), for example, appeal to the notion of religious social capital deriving from corporate social action, individual civic action, sharing of resources, and evangelism, as opposed to spiritual social capital based on beliefs, acknowledging that the drive for one may not be entirely compatible with the other. In other words, the reduction of religion to a resource is hopelessly simple-minded. On the other hand, religion has played a significant role in progressive liberation movements and the struggle against racism (and, obviously, in the fight against South African apartheid). All of these factors can only be taken into account by looking at the substance of belief and practice as well as at context – each of which tends to be obliterated by a homogenising social capital. Otherwise, how do we explain, as reported in C. Wood et al. (2007), that the trend to convert to Protestantism from Catholicism in Brazil reduces infant mortality by 10 per cent? How do we bridge, analytically let alone politically, even within the Christian tradition, let alone with other religions, across the divide created by the right to life? Social capital is too blunt and inappropriate an instrument for this and other matters.

And the same applies to discussion of social capital and welfare provision. Does social capital substitute for the latter's absence? – or vice versa? For Rothstein raises the question of whether the welfare state serves as a destroyer of social capital:

Have, as many have argued, the numerous and encompassing welfare programs made not only voluntary organizations but also other forms of informal social relations and networks between individuals unnecessary and thereby fostered social isolation and anomie? Is there something like a 'carving out' effect so that more social programs mean less civil society and thereby less social capital? (2001, p.208)

On the contrary, he argues that social capital and social welfare go together in Sweden, because the latter is more of an all-inclusive 'insurance', without class-segregated, Bismarckian-type stigma and, he concludes, 'people receiving support from the government cannot be portrayed as "the others" ... and compared to means-tested programs, universal ones are far less likely to create suspicion that people are cheating the system' (p.234).

This suggests that if we are to allow social capital, its relationship to welfare provision can only be unpicked by a sufficiently sophisticated study of the latter in its own right – something that is extraordinarily complex, and is contingent on both what is provided and how, to whom and where it is provided (see Fine 2002a for a critique on this score of the welfare regime approach and Fine 2005b specifically in the context of social capital). Thus, Käärläinen and Lehtonen (2006) find different relations between various types of social capital and various types of welfare regime, and similarly for van Oorschot et al. (2005), who refer to the substitution and reinforcement hypotheses in the context of formal and informal 'solidarity'.[9]

Similar issues of contagion, and hence complexity, contingency, and context, apply across other favoured areas of application for social capital. We need to unpick the family, for example, with Edwards (2004, p.16) making a start by opening up rather than, as has happened, '[closing] down on a range of issues concerning gender and generation'. She sees this, however, not as 'a call for the jettisoning of social capital as a concept ... [but as] a call for greater reflexivity in the use of social capital, intellectually and politically'.

The aim is welcome, but whether it would be realised in practice through social capital is a moot point. As Furstenberg suggests:

Before we can determine the relevance of social capital to the sociology of family and kinship, we must fill the gaps in our theoretical knowledge. For example, we still do not know how couples, parents, children, and groups generate, accumulate, manage, and deploy social capital. Neither do we know the consequences of social capital for the welfare of families and their individual members. To investigate these areas, we must replace the makeshift measures currently in use with measures that do not confuse social capital with the presumed consequences of access to same. With this attention to theoretical elaboration and careful measurement, we will discover whether the idea of social capital is fruitful or merely decorative. (2005, p.809)

There must be doubts about whether these worthy aims have been or can be achieved with social capital, with the literature (pushing to the extremes) more likely focusing on specific variables at finer levels of detail – social capital, for example, perceived as making for better fathering or step-fathering (Fagan et al. 2007 and Marsiglio and Hinojosa 2007, respectively). And familial social capital is itself a determinant of criminality. For Williams and Sickles (2002), deploying the presence of father and working mother as proxies for social capital, suggest that '[p]eer influences from youth have an enduring influence on criminality in adulthood ... family structure is an important factor in criminal choice, with men in common law marriages more likely to engage in crime' (p.505). Similarly, by perceiving crime as akin to a form of work, McCarthy and Hagan (2001) find that youth crime pays greater dividends in the presence of social capital (willingness to work cooperatively with others).[10]

Yet, crime is also a function of neighbourhood, itself a function of constructed space. Saegert et al., writing about New York, say that while their study demonstrates 'the important role that within-building social capital plays in preventing crime in low-income housing, there is still the broader question of preventing neighborhood crime' (2002, pp.119–20). They go on, reasonably, to ask:

Is it the case, for example, that in buildings having higher levels of social capital, within-building crime is simply displaced to contiguous buildings having less social organization? Or do many well-organized buildings in a particular neighborhood lower neighborhood as well as within-building crime? These are clearly important questions, and, at the moment, we do not have the answers. However, the questions themselves raise important conceptual and policy issues.

Glaeser and Sacerdote (2000) suggest that large apartment blocks have more social capital through close association with immediate neighbours, but this leads both to less civil participation because of internalised management and to crime being displaced to the street. And self-contained, high social capital apartment blocks may be associated with gentrification and opting out of neighbourhood schooling for private education elsewhere at the expense of the associational life that supports local state schooling (Butler and Robson 2001). In short, as Butler, concludes in a study of social capital in Barnsbury, 'Gentrification has not so much displaced the working class as simply blanked out those who are not like themselves: they do not socialise with them, eat with them or send their children to school with them' (2003, p.2484). Indeed, 'only about half of the middle-class children are attending primary schools in the areas in which they live and none is in the borough's secondary schools'. Not too much bridging social capital between the classes there then to promote educational achievement![11]

Similarly, Carter (2008), in a study of Southwark in London, offers a heady and fascinating mix of gentrification, ghettoisation, crime, slum clearance, the dilemmas attached to provision of insufficient levels of public housing, intra- and inter-class and ethnic divisions, migration, and the politics and economics of urban renewal. He suggests in his abstract that 'the narrow community that is capable of creating strong social capital will often be unwilling to share the benefits it creates' (p.155). This might appear to offer an ideal example of bonding at the expense of bridging social capital. But the term 'social capital' does not appear again throughout his piece, and this is hardly surprising, for the explanatory factors listed preclude simple nostrums like appealing for more bridging social capital to overcome intense rivalries over access to resources, which are themselves played out against broader and national processes of economic, social and political change. Indeed, Carter appropriately concludes that, with housing programmes, for example, designed to support the worst-off, a negative outcome 'was by no means inevitable; rather, it was an unintended, and cruelly ironic, consequence of 50 years of social intervention designed to build social solidarity' (p.155).

Cyberspace offers equally insurmountable challenges to the social capital sledgehammer and has attracted a strong and rapidly growing set of contributions over the most recent period. There is an earlier presumption that Putnam had rounded up the Internet with television (because each uses an individualised screen perhaps), but his later work has become a little more sophisticated. As Williams puts it, scholars investigating the relationship between the Internet and social capital have been stymied by a series of obstacles, some due to theoretical frameworks handed down unchanged from television research ... For example, the social interactions that occur through television are prima facie different from those that occur online. (2006, p.593)

Yet, Field reports,

Putnam devoted an entire chapter of *Bowling Alone* to this subject. Although he [now] accepts that the internet removes barriers to communication and thus facilitates new networks, he remains sceptical about its influence. In particular, he notes the emerging digital divide between those who are connected and those who lack the skills and equipment to enter cyberspace. Second, because online communication is casual and lacks the instant feedback of face-to-face encounters, it discourages reciprocity and facilitates cheating. (2003, p.101)

But the thrust of much of the literature is that these qualifications do not begin to get to grips with the complexities involved.

In the case of the digital divide, for example (or should that be digital divides?), Korupp and Szydlik (2005) find that, in Germany at least, this is related to reunification, ethnicity, gender, income, household composition, and class; and Borgida et al. (2002) suggest that the nature of and response to the digital divide depend upon whether the Internet is perceived as a private or a public good and, as such, is political in content. Numerous studies show that the Internet expands or reduces social capital with results that can be positive or negative, and are always contingent: for example, Sullivan et al. 2002 for (community) electronic networks; Aalto-Matturi 2005 for trade unions and NGOs; Barzilai-Nahon and Barzilai 2005 for the complex relation to religious fundamental-ism; and de Vreese 2007, p.207, for whom, '[c]ontrary to common wisdom ... the young online consumer is also politically active'. Indeed, somewhat uncontroversially, '[i]t is not the time spent online ... that matters but rather the activities that are undertaken' (p.214). As Quan-Haase and Wellman (2004, p.126) put it, '[t]he fact that people are not interacting in visible public spaces does not mean that they are isolated'. And, for Huysman and Wulf (2006), it is a fallacy to separate the Internet from its environment, the individual from the group. The result is to acknowledge the salience of Bourdieu's approach to social capital and to bring in power and conflict, trust, cognition and embeddedness, and so on, with the Internet subject to the BBI syndrome (see also Fischer et al. 2004, Oxendine et al. 2007 for the importance of politics and context in how the Internet is introduced and used; Bærenholdt and Aarsæther 2002 for the idea that locational proximity is not necessary for forming social capital; and Miyata and Kobayashi 2008 for the greater sociability associated with emailing by mobile phone as opposed to the Internet!)[12]

Not surprisingly, on the other, dark side of the digital divides, given its overtones of self-help and improvement through both costless cooperation and disregard for deeper determinants of disadvantage, social capital finds itself open to application for those in the more, or most recently, straitened circumstances. This began with the World Bank using social capital as the means to poverty alleviation, estimating that joining a burial society in a Tanzanian village might be six times more effective than female child education. Social capital has now become attached to disaster research, as observed by Carson (2004), including relief following the Asian Tsunami of 2004. Those with more social capital do better (no doubt illustrated by the fate of the black population in New Orleans following the 2005 flooding) – an observation which pays little attention to where disadvantage derives from in the first instance and whether it might not be better to address such underlying determinants. So social capital has been seen as an element in 'coping' strategies (Carter and Maluccio 2003; Jóhannesson et al. 2003, for example), and the same applies to those with disabilities (Pavey 2006; Bates and Davis 2004, for example). And environmental management is benefited by social capital. Pretty and Ward (2001, p.209) observe that in recent years over 400,000 groups with around 10 million members have emerged in 'watershed, irrigation, microfinance, forest, and integrated pest management, and for farmers' research'. These naturally make up social capital.[13]

9.3 MEASURE FOR MEASURE[14]

An extraordinary proliferation of empirical case studies has accompanied the social capital phenomenon, ranging from the highly specific and local to the general and national (although rarely the international). Consequently, it has been necessary to provide some empirical evidence for social capital in order to identify its presence or not (and, thereby, to gauge its consequences, and less frequently, its causes). Not surprisingly, then, there has been a mini-industry setting about measuring social capital – individual researchers for their own case studies as well as concerted large-scale national surveys. Such proliferation of measurement has attracted remarkably little critical attention. Researchers have just got on with it in individual case studies or even for (inter)national (government) agencies. In a rare exception, van Deth observes that the measurement of social capital in practice has been far less diverse than its conceptualisation, which, as has been seen, varies across almost every aspect of individual and social life. Van Deth himself points to the conceptual ranging over a number of divides, such as structural–cultural, individual self-perception as opposed to observer observation, individual–collective – and these too could be broken down into separate components. He concludes:

> Surprisingly, the conceptual heterogeneity is much less reflected in operational and empirical heterogeneity than expected. The field is characterized by several orthodoxies, mainly related to the dominant position of polling methods and the use of straight-forward survey questions. Available alternative approaches are limited to the use of official statistics as inverse indicators and to some experiments. (2003, p.79)

He appeals 'for multi-method and multi-level strategies in order to strengthen the role of empirical evidence in the debates on social capital, civil society, and citizenship'. But, as has been emphasised throughout this volume, rescuing social capital by such devices is to acknowledge that it is not the homogenising, or unifying, concept that it purports to be from its initial starting point.

In addition, as Devine and Roberts (2003) observe, van Deth's account is almost exclusively concerned with quantitative, as opposed to qualitative, measures of social capital. They reasonably point to the possibility that someone belonging to an association may participate but be alienated (although some degree of participation, if not its exact nature, can presumably be counted on in addition to membership itself). Once the qualitative is restored, measurement of social capital is, or has the potential of being, more or less as diverse as its conceptualisation, further compounding the problem of identifying what it is, does and how it is created. Yet, even on the quantitative side alone, van Deth accepts that 'for many authors the actual meaning of the concept cannot be fixed *a priori*, since it arises in definite situations only' (p.81). This seems to provide a rationale for measuring social capital before, or as a means to, defining it.

As a result, van Deth is able to point to 'a number of nasty questions that go far beyond the conventional quality assessments of measures in terms of validity and reliability' (p.86), listing these as one pitfall after another: using proxies from existing data sets, and relying upon surveys designed for other purposes; substituting (self-)perception for observation (validity of self-reporting); using aggregated measures for collective concepts; using putative consequences of social capital to measure it; using the same index in different contexts; and using single instead of composite indices.[15] On this basis, it would be appealing as a critic of social capital to put forward a model of research (not followed by the literature) in which concepts are first defined, and then placed within theory that offers hypotheses to be tested against the evidence garnered from well-designed empirical work.

Whilst I do not want to go down this route, because neither individual nor collective research is or can conform to this model (not least because there are necessary tensions between concepts, theory and measurement, and corresponding relations between them that are interactive and continually reconstructed), it is significant how far social capital research diverges from established empirical procedures, and cannot converge upon them, so diverse and chaotic is social capital in definition. In short, it is not satisfactory simply to claim that the measurement and empirical problems that beset social capital are common across all social theory, since they are particularly severe for social capital. This is not just because of such problems in general, either in principle or in practice, but reflects the inadequacies of social capital itself as a concept and the way in which it has evolved. A promising area of research is to deconstruct how social capital has been conceptualised, measured and tested in light of the mutual interaction between these analytical procedures in a particular intellectual, ideological and policy context (see below).

One response, which I tend to favour in empirical work, is to use factor analysis to address the variables involved or, as van Deth puts it, to handle multi-dimensionality 'by using sophisticated data reduction techniques' (p.82). He is right to recognise that this is very rare in social capital research. What it would do is to take the various elements that purportedly make up social capital and test whether they do or do not mutually co-exist amongst themselves and across other factors that might not be construed as social capital. But this is only to discover empirical regularities in particular circumstances and with particular causes, consequences, mechanisms and meanings that have to be examined, with little or no presumption of generalisation to other circumstances.

In other words, to put it in technical terms, it is possible to define the principal components in a factor analysis of a mix of variables as social capital. But that would mean that social capital would be different in each and every application, and the causes and consequences of such correlations would still require explanation. In more mundane terms, we are left with conclusions of the sort that: obesity is more prevalent amongst men with lower trust, but this is not the case for women; and smoking is more prevalent for both men and women with lower trust, but this is less significant if other factors are taken into account. These conclusions derive from ranges of survey questions (on levels of social capital) of the sort concerning safety in going out at night, loud parties in the neighbourhoods, drunks or tramps on the road, and so on.[16] Such are the conclusions of a major household survey of social capital and health in the United Kingdom (Boreham et al. 2002). It's a long way from 'it's not what you know but who you know that counts'. The journey would appear to have been wasted, possibly in and of itself in terms of teasing out the socio-economic and socio-cultural determinants of health, but certainly in taking social capital as guide and companion.[17]

9.4 SOCIAL CAPITAL AS POLICY?

Despite its prominence across the social sciences, and its role as a panacea in curing all social and individual ills, there is remarkably little literature on social capital and policy. I mean this in the following very special and possibly narrow sense, because there is much literature saying that things, including policy, turned out well because social capital was present, and badly because it was not. But, where is the literature that says policy set out to create and/or to deploy social capital and demonstrably succeeded with the positive impact that was expected and intended? It is practically non-existent, and none springs to my mind as particularly prominent and convincing.

To some extent, this is to be expected, because social capital is at the outset supposedly located apart from the state and hence from policy. But getting things done through social capital is a little indirect and possibly ineffective. As Raymond puts it in the context of the urgency of protection of an endangered species:

> institutional mechanisms and political leadership can play an important role in encouraging collective action without relying on trust among cooperators. Besides their theoretical implications, the results suggest policymakers might spend more energy on creating incentives and assurance mechanisms to encourage collaboration, rather than the potentially fruitless task of building of social capital among rival stakeholders. (2006, p.37)

In addition, the presumption that social capital derives from civil society as opposed, or in opposition, to the state is wrong, with Brewer (2003), for example, finding, not surprisingly, that public servants have more civic attitudes than citizens in general. And, interestingly, Tittensor (2007) raises the issue of how social capital is created in light of its correlates such as health, employment and education. It might be better to provide these directly rather than through social capital. No one seems to be inclined to make such calculations.

Accordingly, it is not surprising that social capital should not have been authoritatively shown to be a positive instrument (and goal) of policy. It has, though, been extraordinarily prominent in policy discourse, from the highest down to the humblest levels, not least in offering both analytical and policy panaceas. As if to parade both its neo-liberal credentials and its aversion to them, social capital has been successively adopted by Bill Clinton and George W. Bush, not least through the social capital entrepreneurship of Robert Putnam, who is often reported to have enjoyed breakfast audiences with the (Anglo-Saxon) world leaders. As Arneil (2006) reports in detail, in the wake of 9/11, something that Putnam (2002) saw to have the potential to restore US social capital, the notion was explicitly and slavishly adopted by the Bush administration, which demanded, and heavily funded, voluntary public service for civic action (closely identified with national security), as well as making the sinister exhortation that one should keep an eye on one's neighbours.

More generally, the policy literature on social capital has been explicitly and most heavily associated with discursive support for neo-liberalism in action. For Mohan and Mohan (2002), it is a flag of convenience used by centre-right governments as a means of setting aside material circumstances in addressing social problems. Cheshire and Lawrence (2005) see social capital, community, and democratic participation as the complicit responses to the individualism of neo-liberalism, deploying the example of regional policy in Australia, where social capital has been unusually prominent. But, appropriately in light of the timing and content of its rise to prominence, it is more usual for social capital to be critically seen either as a marriage with, or as formed by, Third Wayism. Craig and Porter (2005) and Robison (2003 and 2004) have explicitly interpreted it as a way of promoting some form of compromise between neo-liberalism and Third Wayism. For Amin, in its use of social capital 'the Third Way has thrown its weight behind the prosperous, redefining its duty of care to the less prosperous as a duty of moral improvement and community empowerment' (2005, pp.629–30). He generously suggests that, in a sense,

> the *unwitting* result has been to squeeze the social into a narrow channel depositing social capital and the like as a tonic for those in need of regeneration, accompanied by an impoverished and utilitarian but largely ineffective understanding of the political and the democratic. (p.630, emphasis added)

Edwards (2004) notes that Third Way social capital approaches to the family have replicated stereotypes rather than challenging them.[18] Merrett (2001), in a case study of non-metropolitan areas of Illinois, disputes the idea that the decline of welfare provision under neo-liberalism can be compensated for by the spontaneous rise of social capital to fill the gap, as neither organisation nor finance exists to support it. And for Lister (2003), social capital underpins the Third Way shift to social investment in the child as citizen–worker of the future as opposed to being a policy perspective guided by the more progressive and welfarist notion of the citizen–child.

Similarly, for White (2002) for example. He notes that social capital serves as a metaphor for social relations, but with an incompatibility between the approaches of Bourdieu and Putnam, and perceives the latter as furnishing the basis for Third Wayism. He advises heeding Foucault's insight, 'Power relations are rooted in the system of social networks' (p.268). The intellectual pendulum has, however, swung so far against Foucault in the retreat from postmodernism that, despite the social engineering associated with social capital, his presence is almost totally absent in the literature, including the critical.[19] It is to be suspected in addition that, from a Foucauldian perspective, social capital is too easy a target to warrant the trouble of taking critical aim at it.

Nonetheless, the role played by social capital in defining away power and conflict, and both highlighting and marginalising the disadvantaged whilst rendering the privileged invisible, is a persistent theme. As Purdue (2001) acknowledges of social capital in the context of leadership in neighbourhood regeneration partnerships, there are problems of trust and collaboration, from planning to implementation, from one leader to another and across different parts of the community, and both inside and outside.[20] Hence, 'social capital was used in competition and conflict as well as in collaboration and community development' (p.2222). More critically, for Baron, who sees social capital as a Macbeth of sorts,[21]

> [t]he Banquo at this new policy feast was, of course, Bourdieu. There is little sense in [Gordon] Brown's vision of the social and cultural mechanisms by which dominant classes maintain their dominance and how these power processes articulate with economic power. (2004, p.8)

This gives rise to a pathology of 'good' and 'bad' social capitalists and the dispossessed and problematic 'social proletarian', with both social science survey design for social capital and policy suffering an elision 'from being defined in terms of the literature's triad of networks, trust and norms into an ever expanding metaphor for "social problems"' (p.11). Saegert (2006) emphasises how building cooperative community initiatives is liable to be at the expense of marginalised groups, who need to organise to challenge existing power structures rather than to cooperate with, or defer to, them.

There is, then, a sense in which social capital borders on the utopian in its vision of individuals, communities and politics. For Avis (2002, p.315), 'social capital ... has a number of weasel-like qualities'. He suggests that, in the face of the knowledge economy, Third Wayism is an amalgam of post-Fordism, collective intelligence and learning (all also weasels), and has a radical content and appeal in its democratic objectives. But it is limited, because it 'seeks to create a moral community organised around a settlement based upon a collective intelligence, a settlement that would apparently reconcile the conflicting interests of a range of constituents – labour, capital, ecological movements and so on – enabling economic competitiveness' (p.321), with social capital (and Third Wayism) conveniently forgetting to suit the systemic dependence of capitalism upon extraction of profitability.

Walters (2002) pinpoints all of this and more in terms of social capital as 're-imagining politics'. Social capital is located both at individual and collective (cultural) levels but, 'social capital assesses politics in terms of social norms of performance rather than ideological legitimacy' (p.386), not least because 'a key presupposition of social capital theory is of the actor as a self-interested maximizing individual'. In the context of a state–society duality, social capital also holds out the promise of self-governance, as opposed to 'an image of politics as a system defined by the poles of elites and the governed. With social capital this stark polarization gives way to an image of the polity as a much more *horizontal* space of multiple communities' (p.388). He describes this in terms of a shift from a bio-politics – governing health, education and welfare in all its aspects – to an etho-politics, involving the population's trust, civility, volunteering, communalism, and so on, which become manageable aspects of the system. 'Social capital brings the ambition of positivity and calculability to ethopolitical discourses … it offers a quantitative rendering of the ethical field, all the better to enhance its governability. It purports to make trust and civility measurable' (p.390). It conforms comfortably with divisions between normal and pathological, sane and insane, social and antisocial, employed and unemployable, excluded and included, and civic and uncivic (p.392). And, unlike previous political theory, 'with social capital, this stagist, developmental trajectory is not evident. Across space and time, all societies are analysable in terms of social capital' (p.395). And, as far as the World Bank and other international agencies are concerned, 'it could be that social capital will offer them another way to express concern for social injustices, but in such a way that they are not required to address the thorny matter of economic exploitation' (p.394; see Chapter 6).

With social capital a cure-all confined within civil society, it has captured discourses about communities, decentralisation, participation, and so on, in this rose-coloured and analytically blinkered etho-politics, albeit posing, in Blair's words, as tough but fair. The critical literature, attached to close case studies, has demonstrated how the processes and outcomes do not match the rhetoric. Mooney and Fyfe's study of development around a swimming pool in Glasgow is representative of a growing but heavily outnumbered literature on the dark side of the force around social capital. In it they argue that,

[a]gainst a background of globalization, neo-liberalization and the demise of the Keynesian/Beveridgean welfare state, neighbour-hoods are largely viewed ... as arenas where developers, realtors, lending institutions, and a host of other private ventures extract profit and instigate a particular vision of the city ... Arguments advanced from within the community about use-value of the pool in terms of its contribution to local social welfare were simply deemed illegitimate. (2006, p.148)

For Flint and Kearns (2006), in a study of housing policy in Scotland, especially the creation of registered social landlords, the emphasis on social capital has to be set against the arguably more important impact of material deprivation, and the corresponding role that might be played in mobilising consent and cooperation if this were addressed. Even so, heightened tensions can arise out of conflict between marginalised groups for access to improved facilities, suggesting that both bonding and bridging capital are insufficient and ambiguous in their effects unless account is taken of the broader internal and external conditions. Flint and Kearns observe the tension 'between the emphasis on social cohesion and community empowerment at neighbourhood level and a neo-liberal economic focus on competitiveness and entrepreneurialism at city and national levels' (p.52).

In a more favourable vein, Bridgen (2006) suggests that attention to social capital means that addressing health inequalities and primary health care may be put on the agenda, but acknowledges that this is placed in jeopardy by high workloads, auditing and performance targets, and the search for quick fixes at the expense of local public participation. In contrast, Gewirtz et al., in the context of English 'education action zones', conclude that

progressive sentiments are not enough ... policy and practice needs not only to be responsive to the material constraints faced by those defined as socially excluded but also must be based on, and informed by, respect for the values and choices of these people. (2005, p.670)

Similarly, in the context of leisure services and the prospect of communitarianism that underpins social capital as policy, Blackshaw and Long perceive 'an inconsistency in the protestations of promoting trust at the local level while successive governments have centralised power' (2005, p.254). In contrast to responding to how people live their lives, a mythical world of civic communitarians is created. For

> the once emancipatory welfare services can too easily become a second-rate and repressive regime, subject to the 'gaze' of those employed by the state: the social services officer, the community sports development worker, the doctor, the social worker, the probation officer, and so forth that collectively 'police' the 'flawed consumers'. (p.254)

Further, Shortall (2004), in a study of Northern Ireland, concludes that 'the social capital debate gives renewed impetus to a romantic naive view of rural communities, where civic harmony and inclusion triumphs and there is little room for power struggles, exclusionary tactics by privileged groups, or ideological conflicts' (p.110), with these being 'transferred by the state to sub-national levels' (p.120), and having limited power for addressing problems at the local as opposed to the central level of government. Shortall questions whether partnerships are empowering simply 'because they are local and moving power away from centralised bodies' (p.120). Jones and Gray (2001) see social capital as potentially underpinning the positive side of decentralised employment initiatives; but, in practice, this turned out to be little more than Third Way rhetoric wedded to local 'workfarism', with benefits conditional on employment activity. Lowndes and Wilson (2001) note that Putnam is light on the mechanisms through which social capital does its work and, in particular, neglects the role played by state institutions and politics because of his society-centredness. In the context of local government, they point out that participation in practice is not the same as benevolent social capital in principle, but can be managerial (what do 'customers' want?), instrumental (meeting statutory requirements), tokenistic (window-dressing) or cynical (to legitimise the unpopular). Even the local museum can no longer be taken for granted in the age of social capital; for 'current government policy aimed at "building social capital" in both Britain and Australia expects museums to prove that they "make a difference" in terms of long-term social impact', rather than being valued for their intrinsic worth as public goods (Scott 2006).

The Third Way and the Third Sector also come naturally together with social capital, Fyfe (2005) possibly unwittingly suggesting a two-Thirds society. The consequences are at their sharpest in transition economies. For Korosteleva (2006), in much of the new

Europe social capital plays the role of impeding the formation of genuine democratic rights, and it undermines protest for human rights and against abuse and oppression by offering 'a method of keeping discontent under control by diverting the grievances and dissatisfaction to informal infrastructures that can deal with specific concerns more efficiently' (p.186). And for Kovách and Kučerová (2006), a 'project class' has emerged to benefit from, and take advantage of, attempts to build social capital in Hungary and the Czech Republic.[22] Of course, NGOs as well as favoured donor recipients benefit from the social capital they garner and promote. For Sundar (2001, p.2009), in the context of Indian forestry and the World Bank's search for local-level bridging social capital, 'in practice neither the Bank nor state governments have made attempts at wider consultations with forest dependent people', preferring contact only with experts and bureaucrats. Much the same story is true for linking social capital, with selective exclusion of NGOs and people's organisations except where these are small and uncritical. Further, current policies of devolution are now being opposed by those who have long campaigned for lower-level democratic participation, as this is being manipulated to legitimise the displacement of local inhabitants from forest land and the reallocation of this land to the forestry department (see Chapters 5 and 6 for more on development and transition).

And last, but by no means least, as Harrison (2006) puts it in an article about the 'new regionalism', social capital takes time to cement and cannot be put in place by fiat and, whilst it can be used to gloss over complexity in policymaking, 'an economic and democratic dividend can be achieved through the occupation of the institutional voids by weaker economic groupings and civic based third sector organisations' (p.35). Indeed,

> although concepts such as social capital are not always deployed accurately, its place is relatively secure as a useful mechanism for both academics and policy-makers ... many of the relations and concepts that new regionalists promote do indeed have inherent flaws, but bearing these in mind and not shelving their existence can still enable pertinent theoretical insights to avail from the pens of scholars prepared to engage in such debates. (p.43)

Given both the depth and breadth of the flaws appropriated by social capital and its role in legitimising rather than making policy, this is more wishful thinking than anything else.

9.5 THE LAST WORD – AGAIN

Throughout this book, the recurring theme has been how social capital has degraded social theory. In part, this is because it has failed to acknowledge, let alone to debate with, its critics. But, on occasion, the problems with social capital are recognised by its proponents and the concept is defended, although this is much rarer in print than in person. I want to focus on two responses that are particularly prominent. The first is that social capital is no different from other concepts used widely across the social sciences. Rothstein and Stolle put it as follows:

> Whilst much of this criticism has been valid and necessary to improve the research, it is also obvious that social capital does not differ from many other central concepts in the social sciences when it comes to problems of definition, let alone measurement. (2003, p.2)

The 'other concepts' include 'power', 'oppression' and 'violence'.

The implication is, of course, taken to be obvious, that just as we would balk at removing power, oppression and violence from the social science lexicon, so we should refrain from discarding social capital. But this is not a valid argument. Our commitment to these concepts is not because they are difficult to define and measure but because they capture a universal reality that we wish to incorporate. Nor would these concepts be deployed as an analytical starting point; but they would always be endowed with context and substance. The problem with social capital is not that it is hard to define and measure, but that why and how this is so is a reflection of the legion analytical deficiencies that it displays in practice, not least that it tends to preclude the presence of power, oppression and violence other than as an afterthought. The validity of concepts must surely be disputed on the basis of their substantive content, not the unfortunate, possibly inevitable, properties that they do or do not share in common.

Secondly, social capital has been defended on the grounds that it gets to grips with an aspect of social theory and reality that would otherwise be, or has been, overlooked. It addresses the role of civil society as opposed to the state and the market. I consider this to be sheer mythology in two separate senses. On the one hand, the literature on civil society is extremely extensive and has anticipated everything that social capital has had to say and much more besides. On the other hand, social capital has parasitically replicated such contributions through reducing their content. In any case, if civil society is our object of study, social capital is not the way to go about it.

That is unless the social is to be understood, incorrectly, as founded upon the three separate elements of state, market and civil society. Then we can make a start with social capital and BBI economy and the state. One problem, as seen within the social capital literature itself, is that the boundaries between these three elements become blurred, with social capital reaching out to incorporate its determinants and consequences as part of itself. By the same token, social capital is fractured by the standard divisions of social theory across class, race, gender, and so on. As is only too apparent, without a proper specification of the social and of capital, and their mutual interaction within capitalism, social capital promises what it cannot deliver – cooperative gains without reference to properly specified power, oppression and violence.

These remarks are brought home forcibly by the severity of the financial crisis that continues to unfold at the time of writing. Is it too much of, and too unfair, a pastiche to suggest that the way out of the crisis is for there to be more bridging and linking capital between finance and the rest of us, and between governments and finance? And, otherwise, for the rest of us to help one another out as best we can? I am reminded of my favourite quote from Sir Josiah Stamp, formerly a director of the Bank of England, and reputedly the second-richest man in England in the 1930s:[23]

> Banking was conceived in iniquity and was born in sin. The bankers own the earth. Take it away from them, but leave them the power to create money, and with the flick of the pen they will create enough deposits to buy it back again. However, take it away from them, and all the great fortunes like mine will disappear and they ought to disappear, for this would be a happier and better world to live in. But, if you wish to remain the slaves of bankers and pay the cost of your own slavery, let them continue to create money.

Is it accidental that the social capital literature should have engaged scarcely at all with either globalisation or finance, let alone the elites they serve?

What Stamp is pointing to are the illusions created by the failure to see the bigger picture, not least the powers that reside in the establishment, even if in his case this was confined to banking. But like money, globalisation and McDonald's in the age of financialisation, social capital is getting everywhere.[24] Some, often producing outstanding analyses, have argued that social capital can be rescued from its deficiencies by BBI whatever has been left out. Others have been more opportunistic, accepting that social capital has a presence, and so they might as well join it rather than fight it. I beg to differ, and insist not only that social capital should be critically addressed, but that it should be discarded as a result. This is not simply a matter of occupying the intellectual high ground; if social theory is to flourish, it is a necessity.

Notes

1. I also used 'male' and 'female' in place of 'gender'. The search engine used in this case, provided by BIDS (Bath Information and Data Services), recognised an asterisk (*) in search strings to specify truncated versions of similar words – 'segments' and 'segmentation', and 'consumer' and 'consumption', for example – and an ampersand (&) to specify that both terms are to be present.
2. For similar exercises, see Fine (1990) on the British coal industry, and Sato (2005) on the South Korean steel industry.
3. As Akçomak interestingly reports, '20 years ago there were about 0.1 social capital articles per human capital article but now there are 1.2 social capital articles per human capital article' (2009, p.2).
4. See also Laird (2006) on social capital as 'pull', with a historical reductionist narrative reduced to this notion, ranging over magnates, the success, but also the exclusion, of women and Afro-Americans, stereotyping and how to use it, affirmative action as 'synthetic social capital', and self-help. In short, as Laird writes in closing, 'Revealing the existence of social capital and how it works embeds individuals' stories into their social and cultural context. These newly enriched narratives highlight the consequences of differential access to social capital and the benefits of synthesizing it on behalf of the meritocracy of our ideals ... It may be that reaching the perfect balance of individual and social factors for success in business – making America truly the land of equal opportunity – is a dream. But it remains the American Dream' (p.338). See McNamee and Miller (2004) for a different take on the meritocracy myth.
5. Not surprisingly, the longest 'chapter' by far in this book is the last, the references!
6. Further mini-surveys were undertaken as the book was being completed around the end of 2008.
7. See Islam (2003), Durlauf et al. (2005) and Rodriguez (2006), for example. There is a stunning parallel with the literature on total factor productivity, in which its change over time tends to be explained by the incidence of, for example, market imperfections, contradicting the basis on which what is to be explained has been constructed. See above on South African coal.
8. Actor-network theory (ANT), for example, has tended unscrupulously to abuse others for deploying an artificial division between the social and the natural, reading the literature through the very division that it itself rejects (Fine 2004c).
9. Unfortunately, copyright obstacles prevented the use for the cover of this book of the image of Morgan Spurlock spewing out McDonald's chips (French fries), modified by labelling each chip 'social capital'; for the original image, see, for example, www.celebritywonder.com/wp/Morgan_Spurlock_in_Super_Size_Me_Wallpaper_3_1024.jpg.

10. On Becker and Bourdieu, see Fine (1999b). For fuller account of economics imperialism, see Fine and Milonakis (2009) and visit www.soas.ac.uk/economics/research/econimp/ for more references.
11. See also my earliest published piece on social capital (Fine 1999a).
12. See especially Fine et al. (2001) and Jomo and Fine (2006), but also Fine (2008c).
13. Here is another typical example from Schuller (2007, p.15), citing Halpern (2005), the leading adviser to Blair and New Labour on social capital: 'Halpern uses the vitamin metaphor to argue that a healthy and effective community ... needs a blend of different types of social capital, just as a body physically needs a mix of different kinds of vitamins. Excessive ingestion of any single vitamin will not only not produce good health; it can also have the opposite effect. Similarly, a single form of social capital ... is not enough on its own, for meaningful measurement or for the development of effective policy.' So, as long as McDonald's is part of a healthy diet ...
14. There are, of course, defenders of McDonald's, including those who would wish to discredit Morgan Spurlock (see www.spurlockwatch.typepad.com/). But see also Tschoegl (2007), whose abstract boasts, 'McDonald's brings training in management, encourages entrepreneurship directly through franchises and indirectly through demonstration effects, creates backward linkages that develop local suppliers, fosters exports by their suppliers, and has positive external effects on productivity and standards of service, cleanliness, and quality in the host economies', all of this in the context of development. It seems that social capital plus McDonald's is the missing link to all success.
15. In googling on 'social capital' and 'turtle' to obtain this address, I turned up numbers of academic articles on social capital and turtles (frequently in metaphoric conjunction with hares). See Lei (2008), for example, on how to be successful in business in China.
16. But, by the same token, Pagett (2006) sees social capital as an inducement to neglect the language of home or origin and, presumably, the same can apply to accents.
17. Possibly to be pipped at the post by the study of the social norms on the *Titanic* which allowed for 'women and children first' (Frey et al. 2008). (This was discovered through the excellent social capital website run by Fabio Sabatini at www.socialcapitalgateway.org/; see the list of the new papers organised under the umbrella of social capital at http://lists.repec.org/mailman/listinfo/nep-soc for evidence of the concept's widening scope of application and influence.)
18. The idea of middle-range theory derives at least from Merton (1957), but is hardly explicitly prominent these days. For its application in the case of segmented labour market theory, and the corresponding dangers of becoming middle-brow, or even low-brow, see Fine (1998a).
19. See Schuller (2007, p.14) for an implicit account of social capital as middle-range:
    1. One of the key merits of social capital is that it shifts the focus of analysis from the behaviour of individual agents to the pattern of relations between agents, social units and institutions.
    2. It offers a link between micro-, meso- and macro-levels of analysis.
    3. It encourages multi-disciplinarity and multi-professionalism, through its broad appeal and potential application.
    4. It reinserts value issues into the heart of social science discourse.
    5. It has significant heuristic capacity.

20. Despite their emphasis on the chaos, they explicitly reject my recommendation to discard social capital, preferring to modify it by bringing back in sounder foundations (but see Chapter 4).

21. By contrast, see Hauser (2007, p.84) for whom '[s]ocial capital is not an appropriate term for empirical analyses because it consists of multiple independent dimensions. Scientific hypotheses should be formulated with respect to specific dimensions rather than to the too general notion of social capital'.

22. See below for a plethora of capitals, with relational capital and systemic capital as likely candidates. See also Lorenzen (2007, p.801) who, in the context of the relatively narrow goal of analysing localised learning, offers a 'relatively *narrow* definition' as '"social relations" ... connections among two or more agents ... persons (individuals), but these often represent the organisations (firms) in which they are employed'.

23. For Onyx (2005, p.3): 'The point is not that some of these definitions or components are correct and others incorrect. Social capital, we are coming to understand, is a complex and multi-layered concept. Within the broad scope of social capital there are probably some elements that are core and others that are effects of the core. We are not yet in a position to clearly delineate the boundaries of the concept (any more than we can do so for concepts such as "beauty" or "governance" or "intelligence".' Together with Dale (2005a and b), Onyx sees a need for social capital to address or incorporate inequality, power, exploitation, political economy, wider structural, economic, political and national factors, and vested interests, expertise, alienation, distrust, disconnection, anomie, separation, empowerment, relationship, connection, reciprocity, communication, deliberative dialogues, reconciliation, engagement, trust, cooperation, collective norms, knowledge diffusion, shared futures, voice, commitment, stakeholders, diversity and leadership – all in pursuit of a dynamic balance between social capital and sustainable community.

24. See 'The Foresight project on Mental Capital and Well-Being' at http://carycooperblog.com/2008/10/23/the-foresight-project-on-mental-capital-and-well-being-delivers/. But note how Wieloch (2002) appeals to the idea of 'oppositional capital' in the context of pro-drug groups and their use of popular culture. And Sabatini (2005, p.13) notes that the *Dictionary of Political Economy* at the beginning of the twentieth century includes 'the Law, the Church, Literature, Art, Education, an Author's Mind'. So, presumably, each of these is a potential source of (social) capital.

25. Note that Freitag (2003) finds that, as a result of its cantons, Switzerland has high levels of social capital in the form of trust even though it is extremely impoverished in associational life. See also Akkerman et al. (2004) for the Netherlands. In the business world, hierarchical ties to social capital are networked very differently (Jack et al. 2004, for example, and in EU governance for water provision, Kaika 2003). See discussion of linking social capital in later chapters as a way of bringing back in the state, vertical relations and hierarchy, especially Chapter 9 on social capital and policy.

26. See Moore (2001) for a more general critique of the incorporation of such notions as empowerment and participation into social theory in anaesthetised forms.

27. Note that Ritzer (2003) himself has now moved on to the idea of 'globalisation of nothing' indicating both that the local remains salient and that the global is degrading.

CHAPTER 3

1. Bourdieu's understanding and critique of mainstream economics seems to have remained anchored in its simplistic representation as pro-market, with no recognition of the market-imperfection varieties of economics and their increasing significance over the past 20 years.
2. Interestingly, Merton (1957) proposes middle-range theory as a compromise between these two extremes, on both of which he is tart in commentary.
3. Although this is fully documented in Fine (2001a, ch.5). For a partial exception, see Lazega and Pattison (2001) and Seppola (2004, p.31); the latter suggests that social exchange theory 'has been used extensively by marketing scholars to explain business-to-business relational exchange'.
4. Quoted in Amadae (2003, p.151).
5. For fuller discussion, see Fine and Milonakis (2009).
6. Discovered through citation in Amadae (2003, pp.151–2), emphasis added.
7. James Buchanan, 'Moral Community, Moral Order, or Moral Anarchy', Abbot Memorial Lecture, no.17, Colorado College, Colorado Springs, 1981. The title gives away all you need to know, that social morality (of which social capital is a part), not the market, is the foundation of society, and that the United States is losing it. Note that this lecture was delivered a few months after President Reagan took office.
8. As evidence of his extraordinary conservatism, Coleman (1993, p.1) begins this contribution on the rational reconstruction of society with a vision of the past, as he accompanies his son in 'a canoe trip down the Wisconsin River and a portion of the Mississippi ... in a setting much like that experienced by Indians', invoking family bonds in a world without commerce, urban life and, it should be added, native Americans.
9. For the opposite view, in which social capital compensates for the market, see Marysse (1999, p.24) for, 'in an era of triumphant and unrivalled capitalism' in which 'unfettered pursuit of self-interest is overlooking a whole domain where people's well-being in markets, liberalisation and globalisation do not have a solution ... Social capital brought cultural, social and historical factors back in the picture saving us from a disease that could be called the reduction of society to monoeconomics'.
10. See Fine and Milonakis (2009) and references therein.
11. The 'newest' economics imperialism takes the form of adding supplementary factors to the newer, whether based on the individual or not, giving rise to dirty models (Fine and Milonakis 2009).
12. See Stevens et al. (2006) for the lack of association between wealth of social capital and more localised coverage by the media in Minnesota, 'one of the nation's "social capital capitals"' (p.61). More generally, explorations of television as an explanatory factor in the (decline of) social capital pay little attention to its commercial imperatives and corporate origins.
13. For the (contextualised) significance of class for any study of social capital, see Anderson and Miller (2003) and Pichler and Wallace (2009).

14. Their answer is that social capital is, 'the god-thing in a secular power-religion, the one true measure into which we can empty all that is complex and puzzling, the embodiment of all our bravest ambitions and secret desires for a society that reflects our very own values' (p.206).

15. Significantly, Putnam and Goss (2002, p.5) claim, totally erroneously, that 'Hanifan's account of social capital anticipated virtually all of the crucial elements of later interpretations of this concept, but his conceptual invention apparently attracted no notice from other social commentators'.

16. On Austin (and social capital), see also Gabrielson (2006), who notes, however, that '[l]ike many progressives, Austin's theory weaves together arguments for democratic inclusion and justifications of racial and class discrimination' (p.661).

17. Interestingly, Pinnock (2007) cites Dubé et al. and suggests that the weakness in current usage of social capital reflects its failure to have introduced the physical practices and facilities that underpin it.

18. See Idahosa and Shenton (2006, p.71), who cite Marx's use of social for aggregate capital, observing that 'Coleman's crediting of Loury as the originator of the concept of social capital was, of course, wildly erroneous for the simple reason that it has long been a staple of classical political economy'.

19. A fascinating example is provided unwittingly by Malinvaud (2003) in his discussion of Wicksell's contribution to neoclassical capital theory. He finds that Wicksell was unable to reconcile the marginal product of (social) capital as a whole with the multiplicity of marginal products of individual capitals (in the absence of the real rate of interest as its price in inter-temporal general equilibrium).

20. See also Smith and Kulynych (2002b).

21. Until Godechot (2008), who offers a fascinating account of the social capital of a financial team able to threaten departure from a major bank in order to be able to leverage higher compensation. Heads of dealing rooms are seen as internal subcontractors for their teams, following Marglin (What Do Bosses Do?), Schumpeter (creative destruction), and Marx (revolutionising the instruments of production, although, in this case, exchange), allowing for an account of the conflicts between individualism as a goal and the collectivism required to achieve it, given the individual and team knowledge attached to financial trading. Social capital meets insider trading! See also McNamee and Miller (2004, pp.84–7) who, in the context of the 'meritocracy myth', point to the glass ceiling and insider knowledge in the stock market as well as the negative effects of social (and cultural) capital in relation to nepotism, fitting in social climbing and snobbery, which, together with oil networks, led to the presidency of George Walker Bush!

22. Cited in Oishi (2001, p.23).

CHAPTER 4

1. See also Rothstein (2000).

2. See Stein (2001) for the idea of social capital as a black box that needs to be filled by being placed in the context of institutions.

3. See Chapter 8 for more on social capital and game theory.

4. Similarly, for Anderson and Jack (2002), who interviewed three entrepreneurs about the operation of their businesses, social capital is both 'glue and lubricant', a process of forming structures with their own etiquette.

5. See Taylor and Leonard (2002) for a series of case studies in different countries examining social capital in the context of the embeddedness of local enterprise. They conclude that the power to exclude is important in defining success and failure.

6. See also Allen (2006, p.98) who, in the context of community-based disaster preparedness, concludes that, 'social capital cannot be created or shaped independently of structured inequalities and the political agendas of local and external actors'.

7. By way of contrast, for an outstanding study of the changing nature, meaning and gendered personnel of a market (for illegal foreign exchange in Kinshasa), see De Herdt (2002).

8. I hesitate to engage with these socially constructed regressions, but the absence of significant gender effects may be due to simple self-selection bias in a market context – necessarily disadvantaged women who do survive as traders may enjoy some compensating but unobserved 'advantage' – the most obvious (and most observed in the critical literature) being to gain it through conformity to oppressive gender roles. Thus Friedemann-Sánchez (2006) finds that Colombian female flower producers do better the more social capital they have, but this is seen as a way of avoiding male domination (Friedemann-Sánchez is oblivious to the irony that the latter may itself be a form of social capital).

9. See also Lyons and Snoxell (2005), who observe that informal traders use different social capital by gender, and so warrant different policies, but without questioning whether this may consolidate undesirable gendered relations.

10. Jackson (2000, p.17) raises the question of whether men are engaging in 'leisured decadence' or 'diversifying into non-agricultural work' in so far as social capital promotes women's taking over their roles in agricultural labour.

11. Note that for Fonchingong (2006, p.137), the success of social capital as communitarian networks in advancing women's position in Cameroon grasslands 'hinges on efforts at erasing cultural stereotypes that project women as domestic workers, improving literacy, increased access to productive resources especially land, direct support to women's agricultural activity and improved rural infrastructure (roads, water supply, and electricity) that is compromising women's participation and empowerment drive'. With these preconditions for the success of social capital, it is arguable whether it would then be needed!

12. See also Ghazali (2003) for social capital and micro-credit (*kut*) in Penang, including the downside, especially for women; Takhar (2006) for gender blindness of social capital, in the context of its tension with, and diverse effects in the presence of, 'multiculturalism'; and Hope Cheong (2006) for the limitations of social capital's impact upon impoverished ethnic minority families.

13. It has long been noted that social capital is seen by corporate capital as a preferred solution to its own downsizing and the impact this has on local economic and social decline.

14. See Chapter 7 for women in business.

15. See also Park (2007), who finds for South Korean academic biochemists that formal rules for advancement, far from leveling the playing field, need to be more fully satisfied by women.

16. Note that Idahos and Shenton (2006) give an excellent account of how the position adopted by Loury (1977 and 1987) on US black disadvantage derives from an inherited history of slavery and racism rather than from any deficiencies in black culture. This has been ignored by the social capital literature. Coleman credits Loury for introducing him to the idea of social capital.

17. See Mullis et al. (2003), Crowder and South (2003) and Caughy and O'Campo (2006) for the limited impact of social capital as opposed to race in explaining educational performance.

18. See also Foley and Hoge (2007), who emphasise the shifting meaning of ethnicity itself and its relationship to Americanisation. Complexity covers the geography and culture of ethnicity as well as its economic and non-economic aspects, the enormous variation among worship communities, organisational culture, external relations, and the different circumstances and reception of immigrants. Significantly, their chapter on the sources of social capital manages to mention the term only six times!

19. Her earlier piece (McClenaghan 2000) argued that '[s]ocial capital is used in such a way as to place the main emphasis on social cohesion; an emphasis which gives the analysis a profoundly functionalist and socially conservative bent in that it discounts community organisation and mobilisation in defence of citizenship rights and the political articulation of rights-based demands which inevitably generate conflict, in favour of activities designed to enhance social cohesiveness and, by implication, social control. Such an approach only serves to conceal and obscure the expanding social divisions incorporated within social capital's sister concept, "community"' (p.580). See also Mowbray (2005, p.257) on social capital as a spray-on solution to Brigadoon communities that has 'facilitated a move to depoliticize social problems'.

20. See Smith (2004) on reducing faith communities and religion to social capital.

21. See also Alex-Assensoh (2002) for emphasis on context in understanding civil community engagement.

22. They might equally have referred to a 'deficit *theory* syndrome'. Mitlin (2001), in recognising that the rise of social capital has reflected a shift of expectation from NGOs to civil society more generally in order to make up for 'deficits', suggests that critical issues have been abandoned, such as representativeness, motives, and leader dominance in community organisation. See also Everingham (2003), who views social capital as both capturing a mood of reaction against economic rationalism and also as blaming the poor for being so through social capital deficit. There is a corresponding need to go beyond social capital to understand how community is constituted and contested, without exclusively relying upon concepts and measurements drawn from the supposedly universal values of western democracies.

23. Commenting on Putnam, Sundar (2001, p.2009) asks 'why a country whose citizens are as trusting as they are claimed to be, would need to build up the largest nuclear arsenal in the world'.

24. See Chapter 9 for brief further discussions of social capital and each of religion, the Internet and the welfare state.

25. Brooks and Lewis (2001) find that low trust in government can encourage volunteering.

26. See Maloney and Rossteutscher (2007) for a close study of social capital as associationalism across six European cities. The diversity of sources and forms

has the paradoxical effect of leading to the almost complete absence of social capital even where it is supposed to be explicitly addressed. It is not mentioned in Maloney and Rossteutscher's conclusion, for example, and there is no entry for it in the index.

27. For a more sophisticated and less politically and ideologically compromised version of BBI (or not), centred on the United States, see Saegert et al. (2001). In the introduction (by Warren, Thompson and Saegert: Warren et al. 2001), they BBI context, racism, power, conflict, bonding and bridging, synergy with financial and public institutions, culture and gender. The foreword by Putnam concludes: 'comfortable Americans must summon up a more capacious sense of "we", an interpretation of "our" communities and "our" children that extends beyond the neat front lawns of suburbia' (p.xvi).

28. Interestingly, his own historical study of health and social capital in Britain appends the latter as an afterthought whose absence explains all deficiencies and for which New Labour Third Wayism needs to take more note.

29. See also Bridgen (2006), who appeals to Bourdieu's approach to social capital and health as a way of incorporating social stratification into the study of social networks. And for Flint and Rowlands (2003), housing tenure incorporates different forms of social, cultural, symbolic and cultural capitals, with these deployed to label multiple deprivation and, hence, notions of antisocial behaviour.

CHAPTER 5

1. This chapter draws in part upon Fine (2008b).

2. The study of Dennison and Ogilvie (2007), on serfdom in Bohemia and Russia, deploys the notions of horizontal (communal) and vertical social capital in a way that is replete with reference to a coercive apparatus for internal and external social control and brutal extraction of surplus. They regard 'claims such as those so widely advanced by the World Bank that lavishing resources on the social capital of horizontal community institutions will automatically bring beneficial economic outcomes with considerable scepticism. Such resources may simply be appropriated by a local oligarchy with centuries of expertise in profiting from collaboration with exploitive vertical hierarchies' (pp.542–3). Ironically, and presumably to her horror, Ogilvie (2003) is cited by Meadowcraft and Pennington (2007) as a rationale for neo-liberalism's rescuing of social capital from social democracy. This is because nasty, state-supported guilds in Germany are a contrast to the 'more liberal economies of the Netherlands and England' (p.3).

3. There is also the issue of globalisation. Does it make sense to talk of the impact of social capital within Russia when '[r]eportedly, the Russian Mafia is operating in Poland, Italy, and Spain'? (Varese 2004, p.148).

4. If only. Fukuyama (2004, p.37) is lured into the definitional honey pot, 'One of the weaknesses of the concept of social capital ... is that there is still no agreement as to what it is. I will use my own definition ...' Further, he does recognise the role of social capital for the World Bank: 'the failure of the Washington consensus was one of omission; the problem did not lie with the policies themselves ... The problem with the Washington consensus was not that it was misdirected, but rather that it was incomplete. One of the ways in which it was incomplete was its failure to take social capital into account' (p.34).

5. There is no guarantee against the McDonaldisation of history by historians. See the astonishing approach to the industrial revolution offered by Sunderland (2007, p.208), for whom '[t]rust changes over time and it seems likely there exists a trust equilibrium, a level of social capital that facilitates growth and social stability ... As the economy accelerates, trust will continue to rise, but will eventually overshoot the equilibrium level and give rise to structural impediments that damage growth.' And, smoothing over context: 'Turning to present-day trust levels. These appear to be low and falling, and the social capital problems of the Victorian age are therefore arguably as relevant today as then' (p.209).

6. See Fine (1998a and 1995b) for example. Note that flexible specialisation ('flec-spec') is a natural application for the idea that the small-scale can survive, compete and prosper by non-market cooperation. Alongside its treatment of small-scale traders and finance, often involving women (see Chapter 4), the literature has blossomed by discovering non-market sources of market success. However, the blood diamonds of the New York dealers provide the classic starting point (again, see Chapter 4). But the flec-spec literature has been sluggish in embracing social capital, despite the latter's obvious uses in explaining cooperation between small producers. This is probably because flec-spec itself emerged prior to social capital, and it has been extraordinarily weak in addressing such cooperation in terms other than those of commercial operations (as an antidote to a stylised Fordism). For a relatively early exception, not apparently pursued, see Bazan and Schmitz (1997), where trust is preferred as the missing link. And, for other examples of social capital in this context, see Nel et al. (2001) and Milone and Ventura (2000) for the agricultural, Bellandi (2001) and Molina-Morales and Martínez-Fernández (2006) for industrial districts (the latter for 'relational capital' in Valencia), Wølneberg (2002) for Argentina's tanning industry supply chain, Bertolini and Giovannetti (2006) for agri-food industries in Modena, Molina-Morales (2005) for Spanish tiles, OECD (2006b) for clusters in transitional eastern Europe, and Annen (2001) for Pakistani manufacture of surgical instruments! See also Larance (2001) for the Grameen Bank. Interestingly, the flec-spec approach has now given way to global value chains (with global commodity chains en route). It offers another example of BBI as it uncomfortably attempts to handle ill-fitting case studies to its ideal types. Social capital has only just begun to appear (see Vasileiou and Morris 2006; McPhee and Wheeler 2006).

7. Nonetheless, in explicitly asking if social capital is capital, he offers only a weak response (pp.243–4).

CHAPTER 6

1. This chapter draws upon Fine (2003c, 2007d and 2008a).

2. Note that the shift from the Washington to the Post-Washington Consensus, with social capital as conduit, is at best limited and at worst obfuscating for Bergeron (2003) on women, for Wong (2003) on empowerment, and for Robison (2004) on combating neo-liberalism.

3. Given Woolcock's excellent article (1998), it seems that mole's condition three is operative on occasion for others, with Woolcock soon to become a leading social capitalist employed at the Bank.

4. I cannot resist pointing to the answer that might have been given by a World Bank 'lead economist', Bonnel (2000, p.849), who in discussing social capital, argues that '[r]eversing the spread of the HIV/AIDS epidemics and mitigating its impact' requires three sets of measures: (1) sound macroeconomic policies; (2) structural policy reforms; and (3) modifying further the systems of incentives faced by individuals. But what about HIV/AIDS?

5. See foreword to Fine (2004b).

6. See also the Deaton assessment of Collier and Gunning, 'Explaining African Economic Performance' (1999); and, for more detail, Fine (2008e). In response to the question, 'Are the conclusions consistent with the research findings?', it offers the answer, 'No. The paper jumps to conclusions about social capital, while there is nothing in previous research or even in this paper that suggests that social capital is a major factor.' For a corrective on social capital as the key (to entrepreneurship) see Meagher (2006, p.579): 'The weakness of African small-firm networks does not arise from excessive state intervention or from perverse cultural blueprints but from state neglect and the instability of the wider institutional context in which these networks are embedded ... where the state fails to contribute appropriate institutional support, strains on informal enterprise networks provoke a fragmentation of informal organization which impedes growth and exacerbates differentiation, uncertainty, and opportunism. This negative production environment undermines the development of collective efficiencies in small-firm organization and limits the formation of subcontracting links with the formal sector ... [and] weak formal institutions and the lack of incorporation into the formal economic framework encourage informal firms and occupational associations to turn to cliental forms of economic and political incorporation.'

7. These issues are taken up again in the specific context of the individual and trust in Chapter 8.

8. The ambiguities are neatly expressed by D'Hernoncourt and Méon (2008) in terms of their subtitle, 'Does trust increase the size of the shadow economy?' The informal as well as the corrupt economies (often the same!) depend upon social capital as much as the formal.

9. Note that these two authors appeal for openness and participation amongst those engaged in studying social capital, but essentially make no reference to the critical literature themselves.

10. Like many others, Grootaert and van Bastelaer see human capital as a model for social capital to follow, with its initial difficulties being overcome through neglect rather than resolution (but with no sense of the overwhelming deficiencies of each) (p.345). For an outstanding critique of the creation of the myth of the Robinson Crusoe economy, see White (1982).

11. This might be explained to some extent by the lag in getting into publication. It is notable that Bebbington's continuing contributions on social capital are much more hedged and lacking in confidence than formerly. Bebbington (2007) might be thought to be a little bit late for BBBI and BBI gender as correctives. See below for his views on social capital and the developmental state. As late as 2002, Woolcock insists on 'the ever-accumulating weight of evidence documenting the significance of social capital ... it allow us to rule *in* several decades' worth of careful research by sociologists and economists on communities, networks and associations that, while not deploying the social capital terminology as such, nonetheless most certainly can and should be read as foundational work

in this field' (2002, p.23). In addition, Woolcock in 2004 is leading a charge to have social capital installed in the vanguard of study of the social determinants of health (see Fine 2008e for a full account and critique).

12. Note this is also complemented by Bebbington et al. (2006) which, despite being later, engages much less with critics. There is every reason to believe this is because of forced scholarly standards on the earlier refereed journal article.

13. Bebbington himself seems to be able to do well enough without social capital (2000)! His paper 'Social Capital/Social Development/SDV' (2002b) reveals its appeal for him at its height, before the subsequent decline.

14. See also Hewison (2002) and Jayasuriya and Rosser (2001).

15. Thus, Isham and Kähkönen (2002) advocate a policy of 'no water without (the right amount, and pro-privatisation type of) social capital', to reiterate, (p.184): 'The allocation of investment resources for water services may need to be adjusted to take account of the fact that water projects are less likely to be effective in villages in which the level of social capital is low. Donors may want to avoid investing in community-based piped water systems in villages with low levels of social capital.' This establishes the link between social capital and social engineering, something that reaches absurd proportions with the suggestion that mental health clinics should be located in regions of low social capital (Lofors and Sundquist 2007).

16. Is it a coincidence that social capital came to the fore just as the World Bank proposed the reallocation of billions of dollars for infrastructural funding from International Development Assistance (IDA), which makes concessional loans to governments, to the International Financial Corporation (IFC), which lends exclusively to the private sector? See Bayliss and Hall (2001).

17. Also omitted by BGOW is globalisation, itself generally absent from social capital analysis, and significant for the extent to which, unlike social capital, it has been won away from orthodoxy and with an economic content (Fine 2004a).

18. Methodological individualism over political economy.

19. The problem is not quantitative versus qualitative analysis, but how to combine the two satisfactorily – this in general being precluded by Bank economists on the basis of their own often appalling quantitative analysis (see Deaton et al. 2006 for a friendly slaughter of Bank 'advocacy' on this score).

20. 'I am an economist, I can analyse anything.' See Ferguson (2000, p.995) for a humorous take on economics and language, an important but flawed input to the economic (Collier's) analysis of civil war, for example.

21. One of the remarkable myths propagated by social capitalists is that they are innovative in understanding civil society and in bringing it back into consideration – whereas in reality they are selectively parasitical on, and distort, what has long been there. The mirror image of this myth is that economists resist consideration of the social – whereas in reality they are currently embracing it on their own terms, for which social capital has proved an ideal conduit, handed to them on a plate by the missionary social capitalists from other disciplines.

22. See Dannreuther and Dolfsma (2003) on the relationship between social capital, globalisation and the shift from the Washington to the post-Washington Consensus, all at the expense of the developmental state.

23. One element in this is external journal publication, where this is paradigm-conforming. Am I right in thinking, from casual observation, that this is growing, possibly motivated by a wish for fluidity of position between Bank

and academic employment, especially amongst non-economists, for whom the outside academic world is somewhat more critical than within the Bank?

24. This section draws on Fine (2007d). See Smith and Kulynych (2002a) for an assessment of social capital as a keyword, with a history of its use as such.

25. The critique of social capital from *within* mainstream economics is possibly the least acknowledged part of my work (Fine 2001a, ch.10).

26. Significantly, Lincoln's quote is deployed by Thomas J. Sargent in an explanation of rational expectations, the neo-liberal economist's version of not fooling any of the people any of the time (www.econlib.org/library/enc/RationalExpectations.html, accessed 20 March 2009).

27. And the World Bank's social capital website is both a disgrace and a barrier to the pursuit of knowledge, given its chaotic inclusion of anything and anyone as illustrative of the (usually unwitting) use of social capital (Fine 2001a, p.125).

28. As Deacon (2007, p.170) puts it: 'The problem, however, for those within the Bank who have struggled long and hard to reform its social policies in a more progressive direction, is that they are working in an institution that does not have global legitimacy. Far better that their efforts and their money had been directed to the UN social agencies whose work they have undermined.'

CHAPTER 7

1. This draws upon the keynote address to the 2007 Critical Management Studies biennial conference in Manchester (Fine 2007a).

2. For discussion of the issues involved here, see the contributions in *Organization*, vol.9, no.3, 2002.

3. See Lee (2007) for an outstanding account of the destruction of heterodoxy within economics as a result of the RAE. But his comparable conclusions for management studies is unduly pessimistic, not least in referencing interpretations primarily from the orthodoxy itself.

4. In a footnote to my earlier book (Fine 2001a, p.221), I describe how Nahapiet and Ghoshal 'throw everything from their field into social capital, including a good dose of Bourdieu, to explain how social capital supports intellectual capital within organizations'.

5. For an account of the potential richness of network theory, see Tindall and Wellman (2001).

6. See Taylor and Leonard (2002) for critical takes on the use of embeddedness in industrial development; they point especially to the absence of power, place, time and context.

7. Further, in the context of labour markets and harmony, for Lin et al. (2001, p.ix), '[t]he principal argument is that social capital should benefit both employers and employees'. For more of the same gobbledygook, see Lin and Erickson (2008) in their appropriately ambitious 'International Research Program'.

8. They find any number of equilibria by outcome for firms and their locational dispersal.

9. See Dovey and White (2005) for exceptional recognition that learning, creativity and innovation depend upon negotiating social capital as power relations.

10. But see Moerbeek and Need (2003), who offer social capital as a means by which networked 'foes' at work can impede your progress.

11. See Meulemann (2008b) for a rare attempt to address whether social capital leads to empowerment at the workplace (as opposed to political participation), although differences in country legislation are of importance. Yet, for Rothstein (2001, p.222), '[o]f all Swedish organizations, the union movement is the one with the most members and that is, next only to the sports movement, activating most people'. For Sánchez (2007), political motives are more important than social capital in explaining participation in trade unions. See also Gomez et al. (2002), who find that youth preference for unionisation in Canada is more influenced by peer pressure and other family attachment (social capital) and concerns over workplace issues than for their parents.

12. This may also be the intent of Hean et al. (2003), who offers an otherwise bizarre understanding of social capital as the circuit of money capital, M–C–M'. Equally peculiar is the articulation of Burt and Wallerstein in Sacks et al. (2001).

13. See also Quinones and Seibel (2000).

14. See also Das (2004 and 2005).

CHAPTER 8

1. And, just to prove that I am not the crudest in criticism and humour involving Putnam, it has been suggested in light of his neglect of gender that '[a] feminist critic might ask, for example, whether Mrs Putnam is doing the washing up and minding the children while Mr Putnam bowls alone?' (Witz and Marshall 2004, p.15).

2. Kapucu too (2006) looks to social capital as a positive factor in responding to 9/11.

3. As is Ichiro Kawachi, one of the leading (mainstream) scholars of the social determinants of health, who has actively embraced social capital and who also moderated the World Bank's social capital newsletter for a time.

4. Would you play cards with, or invite to dinner, someone with a gun? Or as Messner et al. (2004, p.882) put it more scientifically, on the basis of their own study, in critique of Putnam on crime: 'Systematic empirical evaluations of the links between the multiple dimensions of social capital and violence are limited by the lack of adequate measures ... findings show that many forms of social capital highlighted in the literature as having beneficial consequences for communities are not related to homicide rates. Two dimensions of social capital, social trust and social activism, do exhibit significant associations with homicide rates, net of other influences. However, in the latter case, the relationship is positive, and in both cases, simultaneous equation models suggest that these dimensions of social capital are consequences as well as causes of homicide. The results underscore the importance of examining the different dimensions of social capital and assessing their reciprocal relationships with homicide and other social outcomes.'

5. Firearm ownership aside, Kunitz (2004, p.70) implicitly observes the impact of social capital through 'the destruction of President Clinton's plan for health care reform by a coalition of voluntary associations including the National Rifle Association, the Christian Coalition, the National Federation of Independent Businesses and the Health Insurance Association of America'. Muntaner (2004, p.675) appropriately suggests that if social capital had been dubbed social anarchy in view of its potentially negative effects (or social socialism because

it is beneficial), it would have received short shrift even though, it should be added, reference could be made to negative social anarchy (or socialism).

6. The affinity between his work and Banfield's on Italy has long been pointed out (Fine 2001a, pp.83–4).

7. On Putnam and Nisbet, see also Brickner (2000).

8. See the essays collected in Edwards et al. (2001) for critical perspectives on both Putnam and broader neo-Tocquevillean perspectives and applications. These essays also place considerable emphasis on how economic restructuring is a major influence on the vitality of community life. See also Lichterman (2006) and Mouritsen (2003, p.650); the latter claims of Putnam that 'in four ways, he misses the more "political" understanding of ... republican writers, including his hero, Tocqueville'.

9. See also Durlauf et al. (2005).

10. Interestingly, Durlauf perceives the popularity of social capital as a consequence of the limitations of conventional economic analysis, essentially its inability to derive the social from the individual. His own remedy, superior statistical methods aside, is a combination of game theory and a more rounded individualism, so that cooperation is not derived from self-interest alone: 'trustworthiness means something quite different' (p.262). But see Fine and Milonakis (2009) for the limitations of this attempt to improve upon economics.

11. I will not run over the extensive critique of his extraordinary claims for Italy; but note that Mutti (2000) acutely observes that Putnam on southern Italy is part of a long tradition of locating the region in terms of particularism, the exceptional that impedes development, especially familism and clientelism, without attention to the universals that might have been expected to promote its development.

12. Sander with Putnam (2006) might be considered too little too late.

13. See Boggs (2002) for Putnam's self-serving choice of associations and movements, etc., and how they have engaged in politics. He also points to the complete neglect of corporate change, and its increasing reach into every arena of life, and of international agencies such as the IMF and World Bank.

14. Snyder (2002) also points to a lack of substantive politics in Putnam – who fought for civil liberties and economic justice, and who labelled such efforts communist? Is McCarthyism a form of social capital? – in which case its decline might be welcomed!

15. Thus, for Montero and Torcal (2006, p.339) 'politics matter', not least because 'the relationship between social capital and political disaffection varies according to the political context and, moreover, interacts with political factors'. Not surprisingly, the collection edited by Torcal and Montero (2006) is focused on explaining the US disaffection with politics as being much more complex than the decline in social capital. See also the essays in Maloney and Rossteutscher (2007) for European studies, in which there are many different processes involved in associationalism, different organisational forms and practices, no systematic relationship between nature of association and levels of resources and efficacy in action or mobilisation (including the myth that small is beautiful), the significance of gender, ethnicity, religion, welfare, leisure, politics, and so on. And, possibly most important, associations are far from being apolitical (so the notion of going from associational to political life is misleading) (Lelieveldt and Gaiani 2007, p.175), for 'the most intense interactions seem to take place between socially connected, subsidized, well-funded associations and local

government' (p.190). Indeed, 'we should not consider the civic fauna to be an apolitical haven, but devote ... much attention to differences in [associations'] political clout'.

16. See also Paldam and Svendsen (2004), for example.

17. He also suggests, 'It was sometimes found useful to define capital – as Marx did – from another angle, namely as the inputs which share in the residual profit'. This, of course, is the complete antithesis of Marx, for whom capital embodied a social relationship of the exploitation of labour, from which a system of remuneration derives and in which profit is systemic not residual.

18. A rather different form of commodifying social capital is offered by Strathdee (2005) in the context of networks facilitating the passage of youth into employment in New Zealand, with network facilitators paid by results!

19. Ironically, Putnam and Goss (2002, p.8) refer to the Cambridge controversy, but only to highlight the diversity of social capitals, like that of its physical counterparts – as if this offered rather than undermined credibility! Note that the collection to which this is an introduction (Putnam 2002) provides, in its case studies of different countries, much by way of empirical refutation of Putnam.

20. Brooks (2005, p.1) finds that '[c]haritable giving appears to be a beneficial consequence of some types of social capital' (p.1). But what about correlation, causation and omitted variables?

21. Note that Herreros (2004, pp.1–2) sees social capital as poorly defined and examined, and seeks to resolve this through appeal to the prisoners' dilemma and assurance game (pp.48–9 and 119). But he finds it necessary to introduce the state as a crucial external agent to act as guarantor for the creation of social capital and the shifting from a vicious to a virtuous circle (p.72).

22. In this light, Roberts sees social capital as a legitimate concept, since he locates it at a different level of abstraction than capital as such.

23. For an exception that proves the rule, see Everett (2008), which sees the social capital relationship between authors and editors in accountancy as a gift relation.

24. See also Hadjimichalis (2006) for the relationship between reciprocity, properly understood, and power.

25. Note that Newton (2006, p.82) identifies a number of synonyms for trust – 'mutuality, empathy, reciprocity, civility, respect, solidarity, toleration, and fraternity'. Each of these points to trust's complexity and contextual content, and each has the potential to change rapidly on its own and in relation to the others over time and circumstance.

26. A difference is that Mauss perceives the spirit of the gift to reside in the object itself rather than in individuals who give and receive.

CHAPTER 9

1. For some exceptions across management studies, see Yli-Renko et al. (2001) on social capital as the knowledge to be gained through relations with customers, Harvey et al. (2003) on the need to be in touch with the global consumer, and also Menguc and Barker (2005), who claim that theirs 'is one of the few studies that explores the strategic role of salespeople in creating a competitive advantage and links the sales management literature to the literature on the

RBV [Resource-Based View] of the firm and social capital/human capital theory' (p.885).

2. See Klooss (2001) for food and eating as a means to a community of inclusion *and* exclusion.

3. For Scandinavia, see the special issue of *Scandinavian Political Studies*, vol.26, no.1, 2003. On a personal note or two, I was asked to chair the panel of international experts for the Finnish equivalent of the Economic and Social Research Council (ESRC) for its funding programme on social capital. They have to have an international panel since the country is so small that all the academics know one another and would have difficulty in giving objective assessment. I saw this as a damage limitation exercise, but, just to make some of you scrabbling for funding feel bad, let me report that we seemed to be advising on handing out hundreds of thousands of euros to particular projects on the basis of applications that were little more than an abstract and a bunch of CVs. By contrast, in the United Kingdom only 40 per cent of alpha-rated ESRC proposals, themselves equivalent to fully fledged articles in substance and effort, benefit from much less generous funding. I wrote my previous book on social capital in Australia. At a conference there, for even challenging social capital's validity in principle and use in practice, I was personally attacked for having 'read too much and thought too little'. I do like to think I have been excessive in both respects. This was in front of a plenary audience of 500 and delivered by Eva Cox, a renowned feminist and labour radical, ardent promoter of social capital.

4. Samal (2007) has a self-contained chapter on social capital, which does not appear elsewhere in the book. It acknowledges that local organisation is essential for natural resource management but points out that 'modernisation and free play of market forces have been damaging these components of social capital' (p.230).

5. See Fine (2001c).

6. Galab et al. (2006) appeal to 'maternal social capital' as a means of improving child nutrition in Andhra Pradesh, but conclude: 'Higher social capital may help to enhance households' access to food, uptake of health services or knowledge about appropriate caring practices of young children, but our initial findings suggest that social capital levels are unlikely to replace the need for these three core inputs' (p.29).

7. See Harrigan and El-Said (2008) for the idea that neo-liberal welfare policies have promoted alternative provision through the equally, if unwittingly, promoted medium of fundamentalist civic organisation. There is a case, of course, for a treatise on 'It Ain't Social, It Ain't Capital, and It Ain't the Middle East'. For a start, see Liverani (2007) on how the Algerian state has used social capital for its own internal and external purposes; and for Jamal (2007), in the context of Palestine and 'centralized clientelistic settings', associations attached to the governing regime incorporate high levels of trust but low levels of democracy and civic engagement (p.13), not least mirroring the presence of corruption (pp.42–3; see also pp.55–6 for further examples).

8. Williams and de Mola (2007, p.233) report: 'In Immokalee, churches provide access to new social networks that can facilitate the accumulation of social capital, but these networks tend to favor more established immigrants over migrant farmworkers and sometimes reinforce the segregation of groups along ethnic and regional lines. In other words, churches facilitate "bonding"

social capital but often neglect "bridging" social capital. In contrast, a secular organization, the Coalition of Immokalee Workers, is more effective in bridging ethnic and regional differences among immigrants and in generating "political capital" that seeks to affect political and social change.'

9. Note that Scheepers et al. (2002) test for the impact of welfare regimes on social capital (family and neighbourhood contact) across 13 European countries, finding the lowest level of impact in social democratic regimes. And Hyggen (2006) concludes that social capital is not significant in facilitating access to social assistance.

10. Crime too is contextual; Hagan and Coleman (2001, p.353) observe that as a consequence of the war on drugs 'half of all the parents in [US] state prisons are African American, and about 7 per cent percent of all African American children currently have a parent in prison'.

11. Tony Blair was infamous for being a gentrified resident of Islington (in which Barnsbury is situated) whilst eschewing the state schools in the borough for his own children.

12. No study of the Internet should overlook the thwarted ambitions of the free software movement and the presence of that overwhelming social capital otherwise known as Microsoft.

13. See also Selin and Pierskalla (2005). And for social capital as the way to manage fisheries, see OECD (2006b) and Bennett and Clerveaux (2005).

14. Heading taken from the title of Shakespeare's play, from which we learn, 'Some rise by sin, and some by virtue fall' (II, i).

15. See also Catts (2007), and Sabatini (2007, p.88) for a similar acknowledgement of 'six main weaknesses affecting almost all the empirical studies'. Note that Paldam (2000) suggests that there is a trade-off between how *close* measurement of social capital is to theory and how *easy* it is to measure.

16. See Coulthard et al. (2002, app. B) for the 50 or so questions that make up the investigative content for social capital.

17. For the impact of social capital on the understanding of the social determinants of health, see Fine (2008e).

18. See above and also Holland et al. (2007), for example, for children as makers as well as beneficiaries of social capital. For Crozier and Davies (2006), the *extended* family is a form of social capital in Bangladeshi and Pakistani families, although its potential role has to be set against the considerably more significant impact of institutionalised racism. Parcel and Dufur (2001) and Stolle and Hooghe (2004) examine social capital as one element in the socialisation of children. Gillies and Lucey (2006) see older brothers and sisters as social capital to their younger siblings, and Schoen and Tufis (2003) posit children as a source of social capital to their mothers, and hence a motivation for having them, in or out of marriage.

19. See Blackshaw and Long (2005) and Walters (2002) for rare exceptions, with Coole (2009) also suggesting how social capital came to Camden Council: 'sticking together', to use the expression offered by Khan and Muir (2006).

20. See also Gray et al. (2005) on the tensions between leadership and social capital once the notion of power is introduced.

21. Social capital has not divided Gordon Brown and Tony Blair. For the former associates social capital with the Third Way and cites Tony Blair: 'the third way "will build its prosperity on human and social capital"', quoted in Prabhakar (2002, p.55). Blackshaw and Long (2005, p.239) report that Putnam was

required reading in Downing Street during the Blair years, with a social capital unit and with David Halpern as a senior policy adviser to the prime minister (Halpern 2005). See Runnymede (2005) for a rare confrontation between Halpern as a social capitalist and myself.

22. See also Jeffrey (2007) on the issue of NGO accumulation of social and cultural capital to access donor funding and local state confidence in Bosnia and Herzegovina.

23. See http://en.wikipedia.org/wiki/Josiah_Stamp,_1st_Baron_Stamp

24. For 'social capital' in action in this respect, in the wake of the financial crisis, consider the following cartoon from the *New Yorker*, 9 March 2009, cited in Wade (2009, p.539):

> Two executives sit at a conference table studying documents, and one says to the other, 'These new regulations will fundamentally change the way we get around them'.

Bibliography

Aalto-Matturi, S. (2005) 'The Internet: The New Workers' Hall. The Internet and New Opportunities for the Finnish Trade Union Movement', *Working USA*, vol.8, no.4, pp.469–81.

Abom, B. (2004) 'Social Capital, NGOs, and Development: A Guatemalan Case Study', *Development in Practice*, vol.14, no.3, pp.342–53.

Adkins, L. (2005) 'Social Capital: Anatomy of a Troubled Concept', *Feminist Theory*, vol.6, no.2, pp.195–211.

Adler, P. and S. Kwon (2002) 'Social Capital: Prospects for a New Concept', *Academy of Management Review*, vol.27, no.1, pp.17–40.

Aghion, P. and S. Durlauf (eds) (2005) *Handbook of Economic Growth*, vol.1, Amsterdam: Elsevier.

Ahuja, G. (2000) 'Collaboration Networks, Structural Holes, and Innovation: A Longitudinal Study', *Administrative Science Quarterly*, vol.45, no.3, pp.425–55.

Akçomak, I. (2009) 'Bridges in Social Capital: A Review of the Definitions and the Social Capital of Social Capital Researchers', UNU-MERIT Working Paper Series, no.2009–002, available at www.merit.unu.edu/publications/wppdf/2009/wp2009-002.pdf, accessed 20 March 2009.

Akerlof, G. (1990) 'George A. Akerlof', in Swedberg (1990).

Akkerman, T. (2004) 'Deliberation and the Interactive State', *Political Studies*, vol.52, no.1, pp.82–95.

Alex-Assensoh, Y. (2002) 'Social Capital, Civic Engagement, and the Importance of Context', in McLean et al. (2002).

Allen, D. and C. Reed (2006) 'The Duel of Honor: Screening for Unobservable Social Capital', *American Law and Economics Review*, vol.8, no.1, pp.81–115.

Allen, K. (2006) 'Community-Based Disaster Preparedness and Climate Adaptation: Local Capacity-Building in the Philippines', *Disasters*, vol.30, no.1, pp.81–101.

Amadae, S. (2003) *Rationalizing Capitalist Democracy: The Cold War Origins of Rational Choice Liberalism*, Chicago: Chicago University Press.

Amin, A. (2005) 'Local Community on Trial', *Economy and Society*, vol.34, no.4, pp.612–33.

Anderson, A. and C. Miller (2003) '"Class Matters": Human and Social Capital in the Entrepreneurial Process', *Journal of Socioeconomics*, vol.32, no.1, pp.17–36.

—— and S. Jack (2002) 'The Articulation of Social Capital in Entrepreneurial Networks: A Glue or a Lubricant?', *Entrepreneurship and Regional Development*, vol.14, no.3, pp.193–210.

Anderson, C. and A. Paskeviciute (2006) 'How Ethnic and Linguistic Heterogeneity Influence the Prospects for Civil Society: A Comparative Study of Citizenship Behavior', *Journal of Politics*, vol.68, no.4, pp.783–802.

Anheier, H. and J. Kendall (2002) 'Interpersonal Trust and Voluntary Associations: Examining Three Approaches', *British Journal of Sociology*, vol.53, no.3, pp.343–62.

Annen, K. (2001) 'Inclusive and Exclusive Social Capital in the Small-Firm Sector in Developing Countries', *Journal of Institutional and Theoretical Economics*, vol.157, no.2, pp.319–30.

Arai, S. and A. Pedlar (2003) 'Moving beyond Individualism in Leisure Theory: A Critical Analysis of Concepts of Community and Social Engagement', *Leisure Studies*, vol.22, no.3, pp.185–202.

Arcodia, C. and M. Whitford (2007) 'Festival Attendance and the Development of Social Capital', *Journal of Convention and Event Tourism*, vol.8, no.2, pp.1–18.

Arestis, P. and M. Sawyer (eds) (2004) *The Rise of the Market*, Camberley: Edward Elgar.

Arneil, B. (2006) *Diverse Communities: The Problem with Social Capital*, Cambridge: Cambridge University Press,

Arriaza, G. (2003) 'Schools, Social Capital and Children of Color', *Race, Ethnicity and Education*, vol.6, no.1, pp.71–94.

Atria, R. and M. Siles (eds) (2004) *Social Capital and Poverty Reduction in Latin America and the Caribbean: Towards a New Paradigm*, Santiago: ECLAC, United Nations.

Au, K. and J. Fukuda (2002) 'Boundary Spanning Behaviors of Expatriates', *Journal of World Business*, vol.37, no.4, pp.285–96.

Avis, J. (2002) 'Social Capital, Collective Intelligence and Expansive Learning: Thinking Through the Connections. Education and the Economy', *British Journal of Educational Studies*, vol.50, no.3, pp.308–26.

Aye, M. et al. (2002) 'Economic Role of Solidarity and Social Capital in Accessing Modern Health Care Services in the Ivory Coast', *Social Science and Medicine*, vol.55, no.11, pp.1929–46.

Babou, C. (2002) 'Brotherhood Solidarity, Education and Migration: The Role of the *Dahiras* among the Murid Muslim Community of New York', *African Affairs*, vol.101, no.403, pp.151–70.

Badescu, G. and E. Uslaner (eds) (2003) *Social Capital and the Transition to Democracy*, London: Routledge.

Bærenholdt, J. and N. Aarsæther (2002) 'Coping Strategies, Social Capital and Space', *European Urban and Regional Studies*, vol.9, no.2, pp.151–66.

Baiman, R. et al. (eds) (2000) *Political Economy and Contemporary Capitalism*, Armonk, NY: M. E. Sharpe.

Baker, W. (2000) *Achieving Success through Social Capital:Tapping the Hidden Resources in Your Personal and Business Networks*, San Francisco: Jossey-Bass/Wiley.

Bakker, M. et al. (2006) 'Is Trust Really Social Capital? Knowledge Sharing in Product Development Projects', *The Learning Organization*, vol.13, no.6, pp.594–605.

Bankston, C. and M. Zhou (2002) 'Social Capital as Process: The Meanings and Problems of a Theoretical Metaphor', *Sociological Inquiry*, vol.72, no.2, pp.285–317.

Baron, J. and M. Hannan (1994) 'The Impact of Economics on Contemporary Sociology', *Journal of Economic Literature*, vol.32, no.3, pp.1111–46, reproduced in Swedberg (1996).

Baron, S. (2004) 'Social Capital in British Politics and Policy Making', in Franklin (2004).

Barsky, R. and J. Bradford DeLong (1990) 'Bull and Bear Markets in the Twentieth Century', *Journal of Economic History*, vol.50, no.2, pp.265–81.

Bartolini, S. et al. (2008) 'Did the Decline in Social Capital Depress Americans' Happiness?', available at www.econ-pol.unisi.it/quaderni/540.pdf, accessed 20 March 2009.

Barzilai-Nahon, K. and G. Barzilai (2005) 'Cultured Technology: The Internet and Religious Fundamentalism', *The Information Society*, vol.2, no.1, pp.25–40.

Bateman, M. (2000) 'Introduction: The Policy Framework for Reconstruction and Development', *MOCT–MOST*, vol.10, no.2, pp.137–52.

—— (2003) 'New Wave Micro-Finance Institutions in South-East Europe: Towards a More Realistic Assessment of Impact', *Small Enterprise Development*, vol.16, no.3, pp.176–91.

Bates, P. and F. Davis (2004) 'Social Capital, Social Inclusion and Services for People with Learning Disabilities', *Disability and Society*, vol.19, no.3, pp.195–207.

Bates, R. and E. Yackovlev (2002) 'Ethnicity, Capital Formation, and Conflict: Evidence from Africa', in Grootaert and van Bastelaer (eds) (2002).

Bayliss, K. and B. Fine (eds) (2007) *Whither the Privatisation Experiment?: Electricity and Water Sector Reform in Sub-Saharan Africa*, Basingstoke: Palgrave MacMillan.

—— and D. Hall (2001) 'A PSIRU Response to the World Bank's "Private Sector Development Strategy: Issues and Options"', University of Greenwich, available at http://www.psiru.org/reports/2001-10-U-wb-psd.doc, accessed 20 March 2009.

Bazan, L. and H. Schmitz (1997) 'Social Capital and Export Growth: An Industrial Community in Southern Brazil', IDS Discussion Paper no.361, Brighton: Institute of Development Studies.

Bebbington, A. (2000) 'Reencountering Development: Livelihood Transitions and Place Transformations in the Andes', *Annals of the Association of American Geographers*, vol.90, no.3, pp.495–520.

—— (2002a) 'Sharp Knives and Blunt Instruments: Social Capital in Development Studies', *Antipode*, vol.34, no.4, pp.796–9.

—— (2002b) 'Social Capital/Social Development/SDV', paper for workshop, 'Social Capital: The Value of the Concept and Strategic Directions for World Bank Lending', Washington, DC, March.

—— (2004) 'Social Capital and Development Studies I: Critique, Debate, Progress?', *Progress in Development Studies*, vol.4, no.4, pp.343–9.

—— (2007) 'Social Capital and Development Studies II: Can Bourdieu Travel to Policy?', *Progress in Development Studies*, vol.7, no.2, pp.155–62.

—— (2008) 'Social Capital and Development Studies III: Social Capital and the State (Seen from Peru)', *Progress in Development Studies*, vol.8, no.3, pp.271–80.

—— and T. Carroll (2002) 'Induced Social Capital and Federations of the Rural Poor in the Andes', in Grootaert and van Bastelaer (eds) (2002).

—— S. Guggenheim, E. Olson and M. Woolcock (2004) 'Grounding Discourse in Practice: Exploring Social Capital Debates at the World Bank', *Journal of Development Studies*, vol.40, no.5, pp.33–64.

—— Woolcock, M., Guggenheim, S., and E. Olson (eds) (2006) *The Search for Empowerment: Social Capital as Idea and Practice at the World Bank*, Bloomfield, CT: Kumarian Press.

Becker, G. (1996) *Accounting for Tastes*, Cambridge, MA: Harvard University Press.

Bellandi, M. (2001) 'Local Development and Embedded Large Firms', *Entrepreneurship and Regional Development*, vol.13, no.3, pp.189–210.

Benedict, P. (1996) 'Faith, Fortune and Social Structure in Seventeenth-Century Montpellier', *Past and Present*, no.152, pp.46–78.

Bennett, E. and W. Clerveaux (2005) 'Social Capital and Fisheries Management on Small Islands', *Aquatic Resources, Culture and Development*, vol.1, no.2, pp.109–18.

Bergeron, S. (2003) 'Economic Representations of Women in Development at the World Bank', *International Feminist Journal of Politics*, vol.5, no.3, pp.397–419.

Bertolini, P. and E. Giovannetti (2006) 'Industrial Districts and Internationalization: The Case of the Agri-Food Industry in Modena, Italy', *Entrepreneurship and Regional Development*, vol.18, no.4, pp.279–304.

Bestor, J. (1999) 'Marriage Transactions in Renaissance Italy and Mauss's Essay on the Gift', *Past and Present*, no.164, pp.6–46.

Bhattacharyya, H. (2002) *Making Local Democracy Work in India: Social Capital, Politics and Governance in West Bengal*, New Delhi: Vedams Books.

Bian, Y. (2001) 'Guanxi Capital and Social Eating: Theoretical Models and Empirical Analyses', in Lin et al. (eds) (2001)

Bina, C. and C. Davis (2000) 'Globalization, Technology, and Skill Formation in Capitalism', in Baiman et al. (2000).

—— and B. Yaghmaian (1991) 'Postwar Global Accumulation and the Transnationalization of Capital', *Capital and Class*, no.43, pp.107–30.

Blackshaw, T. and J. Long (2005) 'What's the Big Idea? A Critical Exploration of the Concept of Social Capital and its Incorporation into Leisure Policy Discourse', *Leisure Studies*, vol.24, no.3, pp.239–58.

Blakeley, G. (2002) 'Social Capital', in Bryson and Blakeley (2002).

Bloor, M. (2002) 'No Longer Dying for a Living: Collective Responses to Injury Risks in South Wales Mining Communities, 1900–47', *Sociology*, vol.36, no.1, pp.89–106.

Body-Gendrot, S. and M. Gittell (2003) 'Empowering Citizens: From Social Citizenshipship to Social Capital', in Body-Gendrot and Gittell (eds) (2003).

—— and M. Gittell (eds) (2003) *Social Capital and Social Citizenship*, Lanham, MD: Lexington Books.

Boggs, C. (2001) 'Social Capital and Political Fantasy: Robert Putnam's *Bowling Alone*', *Theory and Society*, vol.30, no.2, pp.281–97.

—— (2002) 'Social Capital as Political Fantasy', in McLean et al. (2002).

Bonnel, R. (2000) 'HIV/AIDS and Economic Growth: A Global Perspective', *South African Journal of Economics*, vol.68, no.5, pp.820–55.

Borcherding, T. and D. Filson (2002) 'Group Consumption, Free-Riding, and Informal Reciprocity Agreements', *Journal of Economic Behavior and Organization*, vol.47, no.3, pp.237–57.

Boreham, R. et al. (2002) *Health Survey for England, 2000: Social Capital and Health*, Norwich: HMSO.

Borgatti, S. and P. Foster (2003) 'The Network Paradigm in Organizational Research: A Review and Typology', *Journal of Management*, vol.29, no.6, pp.991–1013.

Borgida, E. et al. (2002) 'Civic Culture Meets the Digital Divide: The Role of Community Electronic Networks', *Journal of Social Issues*, vol.58, no.1, pp.125–42.

Boström, A.-K. (2002) 'Informal Learning in a Formal Context: Problematizing the Concept of Social Capital in a Contemporary Swedish Context', *International Journal of Lifelong Learning*, vol.21, no.6, pp.510–24.

Bourdieu, P. (1980) 'Le Capital Social: Notes Provisoires', *Actes de la Recherche en Sciences Sociales*, no.31, pp.2–3.

—— (1986) *Distinction: A Social Critique of the Judgement of Taste*, London: Routledge, first published in French in 1979.

—— and J. Coleman (eds) (1991) *Social Change for a Changing Society*, Boulder, CO: Westview Press.

Bowles, S. and H. Gintis (2002) 'Social Capital and Community Governance', *Economic Journal*, vol.112, no.483, pp. F419–36.

Bozionelos, N. and L. Wang (2006) 'The Relationship of Mentoring and Network Resources with Career Success in the Chinese Organizational Environment', *International Journal of Human Resource Management*, vol.17, no.9, pp.1531–46.

Bresnen, M. et al. (2005) 'Exploring Social Capital in the Construction Firm', *Building Research and Information*, vol.33, no.3, pp.235–44.

Brewer, G. (2003) 'Building Social Capital: Civic Attitudes and Behavior of Public Servants', *Journal of Public Administration Research and Theory*, vol.13, no.1, pp.5–26.

Brickner, B. (2000) 'The Promise Keepers as Social Capitalists and Architects of Civil Society', in McConkey and Lawler (2000).

Bridgen, P. (2006) 'Social Capital, Community Empowerment and Public Health: Policy Developments in the UK since 1997', *Policy and Politics*, vol.34, no.1, pp.27–50.

Brightman, R. (1996) 'The Sexual Division of Foraging Labor: Biology, Taboo, and Gender Politics', *Comparative Studies in Society and History*, vol.38, no.4, pp.687–729.

Brinton, M. (2000) 'Social Capital in the Japanese Youth Labor Market: Labor Market Policy, Schools, and Norms', *Policy Sciences*, vol.33, nos.3/4, pp.289–306

Broad, R. (2006) 'Research, Knowledge, and the Art of "Paradigm Maintenance": The World Bank's Development Economics Vice-Presidency (DEC)', *Review of International Political Economy*, vol.13, no.3, pp.387–419.

—— (2007) '"Knowledge Management": A Case Study of the World Bank's Research', *Development in Practice*, vol.17, nos.4/5, pp.700–8.

Brooks, A. (2005) 'Does Social Capital Make You Generous?', *Social Science Quarterly*, vol.86, no.1, pp.1–15.

—— and G. Lewis (2001) 'Giving, Volunteering, and Mistrusting Government', *Journal of Policy Analysis and Management*, vol.20, no.4, pp.765–70.

Bryer, R. (1997) 'The Mercantile Laws Commission of 1854 and the Political Economy of Limited Liability', *Economic History Review*, vol.50, no.1, pp.37–56.

Bryman, A. (1999) 'The Disneyization of Society', *Sociological Review*, vol.47, no.1, pp.25–47.

Brynin, M. and J. Schupp (2000) 'Education, Employment, and Gender Inequality amongst Couples: A Comparative Analysis of Britain and Germany', *European Sociological Review*, vol.16, no.4, pp.349–66.

Bryson, V. and G. Blakely (eds) (2002) *Contemporary Political Concepts: A Critical Introduction*, London: Pluto Press.

Buchanan, J. (1986) *Liberty, Market and State: Political Economy in the 1980s*, Brighton: Harvester Press.

Bull, A. and B. Jones (2006) 'Governance and Social Capital in Urban Regeneration: A Comparison between Bristol and Naples', *Urban Studies*, vol.43, no.4, pp.767–86.

Burt, R. (2002) 'The Social Capital of Structural Holes', in Guillén et al. (2002).

—— (2005) *Brokerage and Closure: An Introduction to Social Capital*, Oxford: Oxford University Press.

—— (ed.) (2001) *Social Capital: Theory and Research*, New York: Aldine de Gruyter.

Butler, T. (2003) 'Living in the Bubble: Gentrification and Its "Others" in North London', *Urban Studies*, vol.40, no.12, pp.2469–86.

—— and G. Robson (2001) 'Social Capital, Gentrification and Neighbourhood Change in London: A Comparison of Three South London Neighbourhoods', *Urban Studies*, vol.38, no.12, pp.2145–62.

Campbell, C. and C. McLean (2002) 'Ethnic Identities, Social Capital and Health Inequalities: Factors Shaping African–Caribbean Participation in Local Community Networks in the UK', *Social Science and Medicine*, vol.55, no.4, pp.643–57.

Campbell, J. (2003) 'Defining the Limits of a Discourse: "Social Capital" in Africa', in Mosley and Dowler (2003).

Carmona, J. and J. Simpson (1999) 'The "Rabassa Morta" in Catalan Viticulture: The Rise and Decline of a Long-Term Sharecropping Contract, 1670s–1920s', *The Journal of Economic History*, vol.59, no.2, pp.290–315.

Carp, B. (2001) 'Fire of Liberty: Firefighters, Urban Voluntary Culture, and the Revolutionary Movement', *The William and Mary Quarterly*, vol.58, no.4, pp.781–818.

Carpenter, J. (2000) 'Measuring Social Capital: Adding Field Experimental Methods to the Analytical Toolbox', mimeo, published in Isham et al. (2002).

—— et al. (2004) 'Social Capital and Trust in South-East Asian Cities', *Urban Studies*, vol.41, no.4, pp.853–74.

Carson, W. (2004) 'Is Communalism Dead? Reflections on the Present and Future Practice of Crime Prevention: Part One', *Australian and New Zealand Journal of Criminology*, vol.37, no.1, pp.1–21.

Carter, M. and J. Maluccio (2003) 'Social Capital and Coping with Economic Shocks: An Analysis of Stunting of South African Children', *World Development*, vol.31, no.7, pp.1147–63.

Carter, H. (2008) 'Building the Divided City: Race, Class and Social Housing in Southwark, 1945–1995', *London Journal*, vol.33, no.2, pp.155–85.

Castle, E. (2002) 'Social Capital: An Interdisciplinary Concept', *Rural Sociology*, vol.67, no.3, pp.331–49.

Cattell, V. (2001) 'Poor People, Poor Places, and Poor Health: The Mediating Role of Social Networks and Social Capital', *Social Science and Medicine*, vol.52, no.10, pp.1501–16.

Catterall, P. (1993) 'Morality and Politics: The Free Churches and the Labour Party between the Wars', *The Historical Journal*, vol.36, pp.667–85.

Catts, R. (2007) 'Quantitative Indicators of Social Capital: Measurement in a Complex Context', in Osborne et al. (2007).

Caughy, M. and P. O'Campo (2006) 'Neighborhood Poverty, Social Capital, and the Cognitive Development of African American Preschoolers', *American Journal of Community Psychology*, vol.37, nos.1/2, pp.141–54.

Champlin, D. (1999) 'Social Capital and the Privatization of Public Goods', *International Journal of Social Economics*, vol.26, nos.10/11, pp.1302–14.

Chandhoke, N. (2001) 'The "Civil" and the "Political" in Civil Society', *Democratization*, vol.8, no.2, pp.1–24.

Chang, H.-J. (ed.) (2003) *Rethinking Development Economics*, London: Anthem Press.

Chase, R. (2002) 'Supporting Communities in Transition: The Impact of the Armenian Social Investment Fund', *World Bank Economic Review*, vol.16, no.2, pp.219–40.

Cheshire, L. and G. Lawrence (2005) 'Neoliberalism, Individualisation and Community: Regional Restructuring in Australia', *Social Identities*, vol.11, no.5, pp.435–55.

Ciscel, D. and J. Heath (2001) 'To Market, to Market: Imperial Capitalism's Destruction of Social Capital and the Family', *Review of Radical Political Economics*, vol.33, no.4, pp.401–14.

Cleaver, F. (2005) 'The Inequality of Social Capital and the Reproduction of Chronic Poverty', *World Development*, vol.33, no.6, pp.893–906.

Coleman, J. (1988) 'Social Capital in the Creation of Human Capital', *American Journal of Sociology*, vol.94, pp.S95–S120, reproduced in Swedberg (1996).

—— (1990) *Foundations of Social Theory*, Cambridge, MA: Harvard University Press.

—— (1993) 'The Rational Reconstruction of Society', *American Sociological Review*, vol.58, no.6, pp.898–912.

Coletta, N. and M. Cullen (2002) 'Social Capital and Social Cohesion: Case Studies from Cambodia and Rwanda', in Grootaert and van Bastelaer (eds) (2002).

Collier, P. (2002) 'Social Capital and Poverty: A Microeconomic Perspective', in Grootaert and van Bastelaer (eds) (2002).

Collier, P. and J. Gunning (1999) 'Explaining African Economic Performance', *Journal of Economic Literature*, vol.37, no.1, pp.64–111.

Collin, S. et al. (2007) 'Gendered Career Rein: A Gender Analysis of the Certification Process of Auditors in Sweden', *International Journal of Auditing*, vol.11, no.1, pp.17–39.

Coole, D. (2009) 'Repairing Civil Society and Experimenting with Power: A Genealogy of Social Capital', *Political Studies*, vol.57, no.2, pp.374–96.

Cooper, B. (1995) 'Women's Worth and Wedding Gift Exchange in Maradi, Niger, 1907–89', *Journal of African History*, vol.36, no.1, pp.121–40.

Coulthard, M. et al. (2002) *People's Perceptions of Their Neighbourhood and Community Involvement*, Norwich: HMSO.

Couto, R. (1999) *Making Democracy Work Better: Mediating Structures, Social Capital, and the Democratic Prospect*, Chapel Hill, NC: University of North Carolina Press.

Craig, D. and D. Porter (2005) 'The Third Way and the Third World: Poverty Reduction and Social Inclusion Strategies in the Rise of "Inclusive" Liberalism', *Review of International Political Economy*, vol.12, no.2, pp.226–63.

Crenson, M. and B. Ginsberg (2006) 'Conclusion: The Declining Political Value of Social Capital', in Dilworth (2006).

Cross, W. (2003) 'Tracing the Historical Origins of Youth Delinquency and Violence: Myths and Realities about Black Culture', *Journal of Social Issues*, vol.59, no.1, pp.67–82.

Crowder, K. and S. South (2003) 'Neighborhood Distress and School Dropout: The Variable Significance of Community Context', *Social Science Research*, vol.32, no.4, pp.659–98.

Crozier, G. and J. Davies (2006) 'Family Matters: A Discussion of the Bangladeshi and Pakistani Extended Family and Community in Supporting the Children's Education', *Sociological Review*, vol.54, no.4, pp.678–95.

Dale, A. (2005a) 'Social Capital and Sustainable Community Development: Is There a Relationship?', in Dale and Onyx (2005).

—— (2005b) 'Conclusion: Reflections', in Dale and Onyx (2005).

—— and J. Onyx (eds) (2005) *A Dynamic Balance: Social Capital and Sustainable Community Development*, Vancouver: University of British Columbia Press.

Dannreuther, C. and W. Dolfsma (2003) 'Globalization, Social Capital, and Inequality: An Introduction', in Dannreuther and Dolfsma (eds) (2003).

—— (eds) (2003) *Globalization, Social Capital, and Inequality: Contested Concepts, Contested Experiences*, Cheltenham: Edward Elgar.

Das, R. (2004) 'Social Capital and Poverty of Wage Labourers: Problems with the Social Capital Theory', *Transactions of the Institute of British Geographers*, vol.29, no.1, pp.27–45.

—— (2005) 'Rural Society, the State and Social Capital in Eastern India: A Critical Investigation', *Journal of Peasant Studies*, vol.32, no.1, pp.48–87.

—— (2006) 'Putting Social Capital in Its Place', *Capital and Class*, no.92, pp.65–92.

Dash, S. (2004) *Social Capital and Public Policy*, New Delhi: Anmol Publications.

De Herdt, T. (2002) 'Economic Action and Social Structure: "Cambisme" in Kinshasa', *Development and Change*, vol.33, no.4, pp.683–732.

De Silva, D. and M. Yamaoi (2007) 'Effects of the Tsunami on Fisheries and Coastal Livelihood: A Case Study of Tsunami-Ravaged Southern Sri Lanka', *Disasters*, vol.31, no.4, pp.386–404.

Deacon, B. (2007) *Global Social Policy and Governance*, Los Angeles: Sage.

Deaton, A. et al. (2006) 'An Evaluation of World Bank Research, 1998–2005', available at http://siteresources.worldbank.org/DEC/Resources/ 84797-1109362238001/ 726454-1164121166494/RESEARCH-EVALUATION-2006-Main-Report.pdf

DeFilippis, J. (2001) 'The Myth of Social Capital in Community Development', *Housing Policy Debate*, vol.12, no.4, pp.781–806.

Delhey, J. and K. Newton (2003) 'Who Trusts? The Origins of Social Trust in Seven Societies', *European Societies*, vol.5, no.2, pp.93–137.

Dennison, T. and S. Ogilvie (2007) 'Serfdom and Social Capital in Bohemia and Russia', *Economic History Review*, vol.60, no.3, pp.513–44.

DesRoches, C. et al. (2007) 'Linking Forests and Economic Well-Being: A Four-Quadrant Approach', *Canadian Journal of Forest Research*, vol.37, no.10, pp.1821–31.

Deth, J. van (2003) 'Measuring Social Capital: Orthodoxies and Continuing Controversies', *International Journal of Social Research Methodology*, vol.6, no.1, pp.79–92.

Devine, F. and J. Roberts (2003) 'Alternative Approaches to Researching Social Capital: A Comment on van Deth's "Measuring Social Capital"', *International Journal of Social Research Methodology*, vol.6, no.1, pp.93–100.

D'Hernoncourt, J. and P. Méon (2008) 'The Not So Dark Side of Trust: Does Trust Increase the Size of the Shadow Economy?', Working Paper CEB 08-030.RS, Université Libre de Bruxelles, Solvay Business School, Centre Emile Bernheim (CEB), available at www.solvay.edu/EN/Research/Bernheim/documents/wp08030. pdf, accessed 20 March 2009.

Diani, M. (2001) 'Social Capital as Social Movement', in Edwards et al. (2001).

DiClemente, R. et al. (eds) (2002) *Emerging Theories in Health Promotion Practice and Research*, San Francisco: Jossey-Bass/Pfeiffer.

Dilworth, R. (ed.) (2006) *Social Capital in the City: Community and Civic Life in Philadelphia*, Philadephia: Temple University Press.

Dinovitzer, R. (2006) 'Social Capital and Constraints on Legal Careers', *Law and Society Review*, vol.40, no.2, pp.445–80.

Dodd, S. and G. Gotsis (2007) 'The Interrelationships between Entrepreneurship and Religion', *Entrepreneurship and Innovation*, vol.8, no.2, pp.93–104.

Dovey, K. and R. White (2005) 'Learning about Learning in Knowledge-Intense Organizations', *The Learning Organization*, vol.12, no.3, pp.246–60.

Dubé, Y. et al. (1957) *Housing and Social Capital*, Royal Commission on Canada's Economic Prospects, Ottawa.

Durlauf, S. (2002a) 'Review of "Bowling Alone: The Collapse and Revival of American Community"', *Journal of Economic Behavior and Organization*, vol.47, no.3, pp.259–73.

—— (2002b) 'On the Empirics of Social Capital', *Economic Journal*, vol.112, pp. F459–79.

—— and M. Fafchamps (2005) 'Social Capital', in Aghion and Durlauf (2005).

—— et al. (2004) 'Growth Econometrics', http://irving.vassar.edu/VCEWP/VCEWP61.pdf

—— et al. (2005) 'Growth Econometrics', in Aghion and Durlauf (2005).

Edelman, L. et al. (2004) 'The Benefits and Pitfalls of Social Capital: Empirical Evidence from Two Organizations in the United Kingdom', *British Journal of Management*, vol.15, no.1, pp.S59–S69.

Edwards, B. and M. Foley (2001) 'Civil Society and Social Capital: A Primer', in Edwards et al. (2001).

—— et al. (eds) (2001) *Beyond Tocqueville: Civil Society and the Social Capital Debate in Comparative Perspective*, Hanover, NH: University Press of New England.

Edwards, R. (2004) 'Present and Absent in Troubling Ways: Families and Social Capital Debates', *Sociological Review*, vol.52, no.1, pp.1–21.

Ehrenberg, J. (2002) 'Equality, Democracy, and Community from Tocqueville to Putnam', in McLean et al. (2002).

Elwitt, S. (1982) 'Education and the Social Questions: The Universités Populaires in Late Nineteenth Century France', *History of Education Quarterly*, vol.22, no.1, pp.55–72.

Engstrand, Å. and E. Stam (2002) 'Embeddedness and Economic Transformation of Manufacturing: A Comparative Research of Two Regions', *Economic and Industrial Democracy*, vol.23, no.3, pp.357–88.

Evans, B. et al. (2006) 'Governing Local Sustainability', *Journal of Environmental Planning and Management*, vol.49, no.6, pp.849–67.

Everett, J. (2008) 'Editorial Proximity Equals Publication Success: A Function of Rational Self-Interest or Good-Faith Economy?', *Critical Perspectives on Accounting*, vol.19, no.8, pp.1149–76

Everingham, C. (2003) *Social Justice and the Politics of Community*, Aldershot: Ashgate.

Fafchamps, M. and B. Minten (2002) 'Social Capital and the Firm: Evidence from Agricultural Traders in Madagascar', in Grootaert and van Bastelaer (eds) (2002).

Fagan, J. et al. (2007) 'The Relationship between Adolescent and Young Fathers' Capital and Marital Plans of Couples Expecting a Baby', *Family Relations*, vol.56, no.3, pp.231–43.

Farmer, A. and R. Kali (2007) 'Economic Progress, Social Regress?', *Journal of Public Economic Theory*, vol.9, no.3, pp.501–20.

Farr, J. (2004) 'Social Capital: A Conceptual History', *Political Theory*, vol.32, no.1, pp.6–33.

—— (2007) 'In Search of Social Capital', *Political Theory*, vol.35, no.1, pp.54–61.

Feldman, M. (2001) 'The Entrepreneurial Event Revisited: Firm Formation in a Regional Context', *Industrial and Corporate Change*, vol.10, no.4, pp.861–92.

Ferguson, B. and L. Roberts (eds) (2001) *Social Capital and Community in Canada and Germany*, Winnipeg: St. John's Press.

Ferguson, J. (2000) 'Economics and Barbarism: An Anthropological Comment on Pearson's "Homo Economicus"', *History of Political Economy*, vol.32, no.4, pp.991–8.

Ferguson, K. (2006) 'Social Capital Predictors of Children's School Status in Mexico', *International Journal of Social Welfare*, vol.15, no.4, pp.321–31.

Field, J. (2003) *Social Capital*, London: Routledge.

Fine, B. (1990) *The Coal Question: Political Economy and Industrial Change from the Nineteenth Century to the Present Day*, London: Routledge.

—— (1992a) *Women's Work and the Capitalist Family*, London: Routledge.

—— (1992b) 'Total Factor Productivity versus Realism: The South African Coal Mining Industry', *South African Journal of Economics*, vol.60, no.3, pp.277–92.

—— (1993) 'Economic Development and Technological Change: From Linkage to Agency', in Liodakis (1993).

—— (1995a) 'Towards a Political Economy of Anorexia?', *Appetite*, vol.24, no.3, pp.231–42.

—— (1995b) 'Flexible Production and Flexible Theory: The Case of South Africa', *Geoforum*, vol.26, no.2, pp.107–19.

—— (1998a) *Labour Market Theory: A Constructive Reassessment*, London: Routledge.

—— (1998b) *The Political Economy of Diet, Health and Food Policy*, London: Routledge.

—— (1999a) 'The Developmental State Is Dead: Long Live Social Capital?', *Development and Change*, vol.30, no.1, pp.1–19.

—— (1999b) 'From Becker to Bourdieu: Economics Confronts the Social Sciences', *International Papers in Political Economy*, vol.5, no.3, pp.1–43, reproduced with afterword in Arestis and Sawyer (2004).

—— (2000) 'Endogenous Growth Theory: A Critical Assessment', *Cambridge Journal of Economics*, vol.24, no.2, pp.245–65.

—— (2001a) *Social Capital versus Social Theory: Political Economy and Social Science at the Turn of the Millennium*, London: Routledge.

—— (2001b) 'It Ain't Social and It Ain't Capital', Research in Progress, no.1, Gender Institute, London School of Economics, edited by G. Morrow, pp.11–15.

—— (2001c) 'Social Capital and the Realm of the Intellect', *Economic and Political Weekly*, vol.36, no.9, pp.741–5.

—— (2002a) *The World of Consumption: The Material and Cultural Revisited*, London: Routledge.

—— (2002b) 'They F**k You up Those Social Capitalists', *Antipode*, vol.34, no.4, pp.796–9.

—— (2002c) 'It Ain't Social, It Ain't Capital and It Ain't Africa', *Studia Africana*, no.13, pp.18–33.

—— (2003a) 'From the Newer Economic History to Institutions and Development?', *Institutions and Economic Development*, vol.1, no.1, pp.105–36.

—— (2003b) 'New Growth Theory', in Chang (2003).

—— (2003c) 'Social Capital: The World Bank's Fungible Friend', *Journal of Agrarian Change*, vol.3, no.4, pp.586–603.

—— (2003d) 'Callonistics: A Disentanglement', *Economy and Society*, vol.32, no.3, pp.496–502.

—— (2004a) 'Examining the Idea of Globalisation and Development Critically: What Role for Political Economy?', *New Political Economy*, vol.9, no.2, pp.213–31.

—— (2004b) 'Economics and Ethics: Amartya Sen as Point of Departure', ABCDE conference, Oslo, 24–26 June 2002, published in *The New School Economic Review*, vol.1, no.1, pp.151–62, available at www.newschooljournal.com/files/NSER01/95-104.pdf, accessed 20 March 2009.

—— (2004c) 'Debating Production–Consumption Linkages in Food Studies', *Sociologia Ruralis*, vol.44, no.3, pp.332–42.

—— (2005a) 'Addressing the Consumer', in Trentmann (2005).

—— (2005b) 'Social Policy and Development: Social Capital as Point of Departure', in Mkandawire (2005).

—— (2006) 'New Growth Theory: More Problem than Solution', in Jomo and Fine (2006).

—— (2007a) 'Social Capital Goes to McDonald's', Plenary Address, Critical Management Studies conference, University of Manchester, July.

—— (2007b) 'Financialisation, Poverty, and Marxist Political Economy', Poverty and Capital conference, 2–4 July, University of Manchester.

—— (2007c) 'From Sweetness to McDonald's: How Do We Manufacture (the Meaning of) Foods?', *The Review of Social and Economic Studies*, vol.29, no.2, pp.247–71.

—— (2007d) 'Social Capital', *Development in Practice*, vol.17, nos.4/5, pp.566–74.

—— (2007e) 'Eleven Hypotheses on the Conceptual History of Social Capital', *Political Theory*, vol.35, no.1, pp.47–53.

—— (2007f) 'The Historical Logic of Economics Imperialism and Meeting the Challenges of Contemporary Orthodoxy: Or Twelve Hypotheses on Economics, and What Is to Be Done', paper presented at EAEPE conference, 1–3 November, Porto, Portugal.

—— (2007g) 'The General Impossibility of the New Institutional Economics: Or Does Bertrand Russell Deserve a Nobel Prize for Economics?', https://eprints.soas.ac.uk/5683/1/GeneralImpossibilityofNeoclassicalEconomics.pdf, accessed 20 March 2009.

—— (2008a) 'Social Capital in Wonderland: The World Bank behind the Looking Glass', *Progress in Development Studies*, vol.8, no.3, pp.261–9.

—— (2008b) 'Social Capital versus Social History', *Social History*, vol.33, no.4, pp.442–67.

—— (2008c) 'Social Capital and Health: The World Bank through the Looking Glass after Deaton', available at www.soas.ac.uk/cdpr/seminars/43279.pdf, accessed 20 March 2009.

—— (2008d) 'Zombieconomics: The Living Death of the Dismal Science in the Age of Neo-Liberalism', paper for ESRC Neoliberalism seminar, 1 April, to appear revised in seminar series volume, available at https://eprints.soas.ac.uk/5621/1/Zombiekean.pdf, accessed 20 March 2009.

—— (2008e) 'Development as Zombieconomics in the Age of Neo-Liberalism', keynote paper for the 35th anniversary conference for the Center for International Development Issues, CIDIN, Radboud University, Nijmegen, Netherlands, September 2008, to appear in special issue of *Third World Quarterly*.

—— and E. Leopold (1993) *The World of Consumption*, London: Routledge.

—— and D. Milonakis (2003) 'From Principle of Pricing to Pricing of Principle: Rationality and Irrationality in the Economic History of Douglass North', *Comparative Studies in Society and History*, vol.45, no.3, pp.120–44.

—— and D. Milonakis (2009) *From Economics Imperialism to Freakonomics: The Shifting Boundaries Between Economics and Other Social Sciences*, London: Routledge.

—— and A. Saad-Filho (2004) *Marx's Capital*, 4th edn., London: Pluto Press.

—— et al. (1996) *Consumption in the Age of Affluence: The World of Food*, London: Routledge.

—— et al. (eds) (2001) *Development Policy in the Twenty-First Century: Beyond the Post-Washington Consensus*, London: Routledge.

Finke, R. and K. Dougherty (2002) 'The Effects of Professional Training: The Social and Religious Capital Acquired in Seminaries', *Journal for the Scientific Study of Religion*, vol.41, pp.103–20.

Fischbach, M. (2001) 'Britain and the Ghawr Abi 'Ubayda Waqf Controversy in TransJordan', *International Journal of Middle Eastern Studies*, vol.33, no.4, pp.525–44.

Fischer, G. et al. (2004) 'Fostering Social Creativity by Increasing Social Capital', in Huysman and Wulf (2004).

Flap, H. and B. Völker (2001) 'Goal Specific Social Capital and Job Satisfaction: Effects of Different Types of Networks on Instrumental and Social Aspects of Work', *Social Networks*, vol.23, no.4, pp.297–320.

—— (eds) (2004) *Creation and Returns of Social Capital: A New Research Program*, London: Routledge.

Flint, J. and A. Kearns (2006) 'Housing, Neighbourhood Renewal and Social Capital: The Case of the Registered Social Landlords in Scotland', *European Journal of Housing Policy*, vol.6, no.3, pp.31–54.

—— and R. Rowlands (2003) 'Commodification, Normalisation and Intervention: Cultural, Social and Symbolic Capital in Housing Consumption and Governance', *Journal of Housing and the Built Environment*, vol.18, no.3, pp.213–32.

Foley, M. and D. Hoge (2007) *Religion and the New Immigrants: Social Capital, Identity, and Civic Engagement*, Oxford: Oxford University Press.

—— et al. (2001) 'Social Capital Reconsidered', in Edwards et al. (2001).

Fonchingong, C. (2006) 'Expanding Horizons: Women's Voices in Community-Driven Development in the Cameroon Grasslands', *GeoJournal*, vol.65, no.3, pp.137–49.

Forrest, R. and A. Kearns (2001) 'Social Cohesion, Social Capital and the Neighbourhood', *Urban Studies*, vol.38, no.12, pp.2125–43.

Forsman, M. (2005) *Development of Research Networks: The Case of Social Capital*, Åbo: Åbo Akademi University Press.

Fox, J. and J. Gershman (2000) 'The World Bank and Social Capital: Lessons from Ten Rural Development Projects in the Philippines and Mexico', *Policy Sciences*, vol.33, nos.3/4, pp.399–419

Franklin, J. (ed.) (2004) 'Politics, Trust and Networks: Social Capital in Critical Perspective', Families and Social Capital ESRC Research Group, London South Bank University, April.

Franklin, V. (2002) '"Location, Location, Location": The Cultural Geography of African Americans: Introduction to a Journey', *Journal of African American History*, vol.87, no.1, pp.1–11.

Fraser, N. (1989) *Unruly Practices: Power, Discourse, and Gender in Contemporary Social Theory*, Minneapolis: University of Minnesota Press.

Freitag, M. (2003) 'Beyond Tocqueville: The Origins of Social Capital in Switzerland', *European Sociological Review*, vol.19, no.2, pp.217–32.

—— (2004) 'Method and Mysticism: Comment on Dominique Joye's Suggestions and Advices', *Swiss Political Science Review*, vol.10, no.2, pp.133–5.

Frey, S. et al. (2008) 'Noblesse Oblige? Determinants of Survival in a Life and Death Situation', CREMA Working Paper Series 2008-21, Center for Research in Economics, Management and the Arts, Munich.

Fried, A. (2002) 'The Strange Disappearance of Alexis de Tocqueville in Putnam's Analysis of Social Capital', in McLean et al. (2002).

Friedemann-Sánchez, G. (2006) 'Assets in Intrahousehold Bargaining among Women Workers in Colombia's Cut-Flower Industry', *Feminist Economics*, vol.12, nos.1/2, pp.247–69.

Frost, T. and C. Zhou (2005) 'R&D Co-Practice and "Reverse" Knowledge Integration in Multinational Firms', *Journal of International Business Studies*, vol.36, no.6, pp.676–87.

Fukuyama, F. (1999) 'Social Capital and Civil Society', IMF conference on Second Generation Reforms, Institute of Public Policy, George Mason University, October 1.

—— (2001) 'Social Capital, Civil Society and Development', *Third World Quarterly*, vol.22, no.1, pp.7–20.

—— (2002) 'Social Capital and Development: The Coming Agenda', *SAIS Review*, vol.22, no.1, pp.23–38.

—— (2004) 'Social Capital and Development: The Coming Agenda', in Atria and Siles (2004).

Fuller, S. (2005) 'What Makes Universities Unique? Updating the Ideal for an Entrepreneurial Age', *Higher Education Management and Policy*, vol.17, no.3, pp.17–42.

Furstenberg, F. (2005) 'Banking on Families: How Families Generate and Distribute Social Capital', *Journal of Marriage and Family*, vol.67, no.4, pp.809–21.

Fyfe, N. (2005) 'Making Space for "Neo-Communitarianism"? The Third Sector, State and Civil Society in the UK', *Antipode*, vol.37, no.3, pp.536–57.

—— and C. Milligan (2003) 'Out of the Shadows: Exploring Contemporary Geographies of Voluntarism', *Progress in Human Geography*, vol.27, no.4, pp.397–413.

Gabrielson, T. (2006) 'Woman-Thought, Social Capital, and the Generative State: Mary Austin and the Integrative Civic Idea in Progressive Thought', *American Journal of Political Science*, vol.50, no.3, pp.650–63.

Gaggio, D. (2004) 'Do Social Historians Need Social Capital?', *Social History*, vol.29, no.4, pp.499–513.

—— (2007) *In Gold We Trust: Social Capital and Economic Change in the Italian Jewelry Towns*, Princeton, NJ: Princeton University Press.

Galab, S. et al. (2006) 'Exploring Linkages between Maternal Social Capital and Children's Nutritional Status in Andhra Pradesh', Working Paper no.32, London: Save the Children, available at www.younglives.org.uk/pdf/publication-section-pdfs/working-paper-pdfs/wp32_linkages.pdf, accessed 20 March 2009.

Gallent, N. (2007) 'Second Homes, Community and a Hierarchy of Dwelling', *Area*, vol.39, no.1, pp.97–106.

Gewirtz, S. et al. (2005) 'The Deployment of Social Capital Theory in Education Policy and Provision: the Case of Education Action Zones in England', *British Educational Research Journal*, vol.31, no.6, pp.651–73.

Ghazali, S. (2003) '*Kut* (Informal Rotating Credit) in the Livelihood Strategies of Urban Households in Penang, Malaysia', *Area*, vol.35, no.2, pp.183–94.

Gidengil, E. and B. O'Neill (2006) 'Gender, Social Capital, and Political Engagement: Findings and Future Directions', in O'Neill and Gidengil (2006).

Gillies, V. and H. Lucey (2006) '"It's a Connection You Can't Get away from": Brothers, Sisters and Social Capital', *Journal of Youth Studies*, vol.9, no.4, pp.479–93.

Glaeser, E. and B. Sacerdote (2000) 'The Social Consequences of Housing', *Journal of Housing Economics*, vol.9, nos.1/2, pp.1–23.

Godechot, O. (2008) 'What Do Heads of Dealing Rooms Do? The Social Capital of Internal Entrepreneurs', *Sociological Review*, vol.56, suppl.1, pp.145–61.

Goetz, S. and A. Rupasingha (2006) 'Wal-Mart and Social Capital', *American Journal of Agricultural Economics*, vol.88, no.5, pp.1304–10.

Gomez, R. et al. (2002) 'Comparing Youth and Adult Desire for Unionization in Canada', *British Journal of Industrial Relations*, vol.40, no.3, pp.521–42.

Goodhand, J. et al. (2000) 'Social Capital and the Political Economy of Violence: A Case Study of Sri Lanka', *Disasters*, vol.24, no.4, pp.390–406

Granovetter, M. (1985) 'Economic Action and Social Structure: The Problem of Embeddedness', *American Journal of Sociology*, vol.91, no.3, pp.481–510.

Gray, I. et al. (2005) 'Rural Community and Leadership in the Management of Natural Resources: Tensions between Theory and Policy', *Journal of Environmental Policy and Planning*, vol.7, no.2, pp.125–39.

Grenier, P. and K. Wright (2006) 'Social Capital in Britain', *Policy Studies*, vol.27, no.1, pp.27–35.

Griffiths, D. et al. (2005) *Refugee Community Organisations and Dispersal: Networks, Resources and Social Capital*, Bristol: The Policy Press.

Griswold, M. and M. Nichols (2006) 'Social Capital and Casino Gambling in U.S. Communities', *Social Indicators Research*, vol.77, no.3, pp.369–94.

Grix, J. (2001) 'Social Capital as a Concept in the Social Sciences: The Current State of the Debate', *Democratization*, vol.8, no.3, pp.189–210.

Grootaert, C. (1997) 'Social Capital: The Missing Link?', in World Bank (1997), reproduced as World Bank, Social Capital Initiative, Working Paper no.3.

—— and T. van Bastelaer (2002) 'Introduction and Overview', in Grootaert and van Bastelaer (eds) (2002).

—— (eds) (2002) *The Role of Social Capital in Development: An Empirical Assessment*, Cambridge, MA: Harvard University Press.

Gugerty, M. and M. Kremer (2002) 'The Impact of Development Assistance on Social Capital: Evidence from Kenya', in Grootaert and van Bastelaer (eds) (2002).

Guillén, M. et al. (eds) (2002) *The New Economic Sociology: Developments in an Emerging Field*, New York: Russell Sage.

Hadiz, V. (2004) 'Decentralization and Democracy in Indonesia: A Critique of Neo-Institutionalist Perspectives', *Development and Change*, vol.35, no.4, pp.697–718.

Hadjimichalis, C. (2006) 'Non-Economic Factors in Economic Geography and in "New Regionalism": A Sympathetic Critique', International Journal of Urban and Regional Research, vol.30, no.3, pp.690–704.

Hagan, J. and J. Coleman (2001) 'Returning Captives of the American War on Drugs: Issues of Community and Family Reentry', *Crime and Delinquency*, vol.47, no.3, pp.352–67.

Hall, J. and F. Trentmann (2005) 'Contests over Civil Society: Introductory Perspectives', in Hall and Trentmann (eds) (2005).

—— (eds) (2005) *Civil Society: A Reader in History, Theory and Global Politics*, Basingstoke: Palgrave.

Halpern, D. (2005) *Social Capital*, London: Polity.

Hanifan, L. J. (1916) 'The Rural School Community Center', *Annals of the American Academy of Political and Social Science*, vol.67, no.1, pp.130–8.

Harrigan, J. and H. El-Said (2008) *Economic Liberalisation, Social Capital and Islamic Welfare Provision*, Basingstoke: Palgrave Macmillan.

Harrison, J. (2006) 'Re-Reading the New Regionalism: A Sympathetic Critique', *Space and Polity*, vol.10, no.1, pp.21–46.

Harvey, M. et al. (2003) 'Global Account Management: A Supply-Side Managerial View', *Industrial Marketing Management*, vol.32, no.7, pp.563–71.

Hauser, C. (2007) 'The Learning Region: The Impact of Social Capital and Weak Ties on Innovation', *Regional Studies*, vol.41, no.1, pp.75–88.

Hays, R. (2002) 'Habitat for Humanity: Building Social Capital through Faith-Based Service', *Journal of Urban Affairs*, vol.24, no.3, pp.247–69.

Hean, S. et al. (2003) 'The M–C–M' Cycle and Social Capital', *Social Science and Medicine*, vol.56, no.5, pp.1061–72.

Heffron, J. (2000) 'Beyond Community and Society: The Externalities of Social Capital Building', *Policy Sciences*, vol.33, nos.3/4, pp.477–94.

Heller, P. (1995) 'From Class Struggle to Class Compromise: Redistribution and Growth in a South Indian State', *Journal of Development Studies*, vol.31, no.5, pp.645–72.

—— (1996) 'Social Capital as a Product of Class Mobilization and State Intervention: Industrial Workers in Kerala, India', *World Development*, vol.24, no.6, pp.1055–72.

—— (1999a) *The Labor of Development: Workers and the Transformation of Capitalism in Kerala, India*, Ithaca, NY: Cornell University Press.

—— (1999b) 'Social Capital and the Developmental State: Industrial Workers in Kerala', in Parayil (ed.) (2000).

Hemenway, D. et al. (2001) 'Firearm Prevalence and Social Capital', *Annals of Epidemiology*, vol.11, no.7, pp.484–90.

Hero, R. (2007) *Racial Diversity and Social Capital: Equality and Community in America*, New York: Cambridge University Press.

Herreros, F. (2004) *The Problem of Forming Social Capital: Why Trust?* Basingstoke: Palgrave.

Hess, A. (2007) 'The Social Bonds of Cooking Gastronomic Societies in the Basque Country', *Cultural Sociology*, vol.1, no.3, pp.383–407.

Hewison, K. (2002) 'The World Bank and Thailand: Crisis and Social Safety Nets', *Public Administration and Policy*, vol.11, no.1, pp.1–22.

Heying, C. (1997) 'Civic Elites and Corporate Delocalization: An Alternative Explanation for Declining Civic Engagement', *American Behavioral Scientist*, vol.40, no.5, pp.657–68.

—— (2001) 'Civic Elites and Corporate Delocalization: An Alternative Explanation for Declining Civic Engagement', in Edwards et al. (2001).

Holland, J. et al. (2007) 'Transitions, Networks and Communities: The Significance of Social Capital in the Lives of Children and Young People', *Journal of Youth Studies*, vol.10, no.1, pp.97–116.

Honig, B. et al. (2006) 'Social Capital and the Linkages of High-Tech Companies to the Military Defense System: Is there a Signaling Mechanism?', *Small Business Economics*, vol.27, nos.4/5, pp.419–37.

Hooghe, M. and D. Stolle (eds) (2003) *Generating Social Capital: Civic Society and Institutions in Comparative Perspective*, Basingstoke: Palgrave.

Hope Cheong, P. (2006) 'Communication Context, Social Cohesion and Social Capital Building among Hispanic Immigrant Families', *Community, Work and Family*, vol.9, no.3, pp.367–87.

Hospers, G.-J. (2006) 'Jane Jacobs: Her Life and Work', *European Planning Studies*, vol.14, no.6, pp.723–32.

—— and M. van Lochem (2002) 'Social Capital and Prosperity', *New Economy*, vol.9, no.1, pp.52–6.

Hunter, M. (2002) '"If You're Light You're Alright": Light Skin Color as Social Capital for Women of Color', *Gender and Society*, vol.16, no.2, pp.175–93.

Hüppi, R. and P. Seemann (2001) *Social Capital: Securing Competitive Advantage in the New Economy*, London: Prentice Hall.

Huysman, M. and V. Wulf (2006) 'IT to Support Knowledge Sharing in Communities, Towards a Social Capital Analysis', *Journal of Information Technology*, vol.21, no.1, pp.40–51.

—— (eds) (2004) *Social Capital and Information Technology*, Cambridge, MA: MIT Press.

Hyggen, C. (2006) 'Risks and Resources: Social Capital among Social Assistance Recipients in Norway', *Social Policy and Administration*, vol.40, no.5, pp.493–508.

Idahosa, P. and B. Shenton (2006) 'The Layers of Social Capital', *African Studies*, vol.65, no.1, pp.63–77.

Inkeles, A. (2000) 'Measuring Social Capital and Its Consequences', *Policy Sciences*, vol.33, nos.3/4, pp.245–68.

Isham, J, and S. Kähkönen (2002) 'How Do Participation and Social Capital Affect Community-Based Water Projects? Evidence from Central Java, Indonesia', in Grootaert and van Bastelaer (eds) (2002).

—— et al. (eds) (2002) *Social Capital and Economic Development: Well-Being in Developing Countries*, Cheltenham: Edward Elgar.

Islam, M. (2005) *Decentralisation, Transparency, Social Capital and Development*, New Delhi: Mittal Publications.

Islam, N. (2003) 'What Have We Learnt from the Convergence Debate?', *Journal of Economic Surveys*, vol.17, no.3, pp.309–61.

Ito, S. (2003) 'Microfinance and Social Capital: Does Social Capital Help Create Good Practice?', *Development in Practice*, vol.13, no.4, pp.322–32.

Jack, S. et al. (2004) 'Social Structures and Entrepreneurial Networks: The Strength of Strong Ties', *International Journal of Entrepreneurship and Innovation*, vol.5, no.2, pp.107–20.

Jackson, C. (2000) 'Men at Work', *European Journal of Development Research*, vol.12, no.2, pp.1–22.

Jacobs, K. and J. Kemp (2002) 'Exploring Accounting Presence and Absence: Case Studies from Bangladesh', *Accounting, Auditing and Accountability Journal*, vol.15, no.2, pp.143–61.

Jamal, A. (2007) *Barriers to Democracy: The Other Side of Social Capital in Palestine and the Arab World*, Princeton, NJ: Princeton University Press.

James, E. (2000) 'Race-Related Differences in Promotions and Support: Underlying Effects of Human and Social Capital', *Organization Science*, vol.11, no.5, pp.493–508.

Jayasuriya, K. and A. Rosser (2001) 'Economic Orthodoxy and the East Asian Crisis', *Third World Quarterly*, vol.22, no.3, pp.381–96.

Jeffrey, A. (2007) 'The Geopolitical Framing of Localized Struggles: NGOs in Bosnia and Herzegovina', *Development and Change*, vol.38, no.2, pp.251–74.

Jóhannesson, G. et al. (2003) 'Coping with Social Capital? The Cultural Economy of Tourism in the North', *Sociologia Ruralis*, vol.43, no.1, pp.1–16.

John, P. (2005) 'The Contribution of Volunteering, Trust, and Networks to Educational Performance', *Policy Studies Journal*, vol.33, no.4, pp.635–56.

Johns, J. and P. Ormerod (2008) 'The Unhappy Thing about Happiness Economics', *Real-World Economics Review*, no.46, available at www.paecon.net/PAEReview/issue46/JohnsOrmerod46.pdf, accessed 20 March 2009.

Johnston, G. and J. Percy-Smith (2003) 'In Search of Social Capital', *Policy and Politics*, vol.31, no.3, pp.321–34.

Jomo, K. and B. Fine (eds) (2006) *The New Development Economics: After the Washington Consensus*, Delhi: Tulika and London: Zed Press.

Jones, M. and A. Gray (2001) 'Social Capital, or Local Workfarism? Reflections on Employment Zones', *Local Economy*, vol.16, no.3, pp.178–86.

Käärläinen, J. and H. Lehtonen (2006) 'The Variety of Social Capital in Welfare State Regimes: A Comparative Study of 21 Countries', *European Societies*, vol.8, no.1, pp.27–57.

Kaika, M. (2003) 'The Water Framework Directive: A New Directive for a Changing Social, Political and Economic European Framework', *European Planning Studies*, vol.11, no.3, pp.303–20.

Kanazawa, S. (2002) 'Bowling with Our Imaginary Friends', *Evolution and Human Behavior*, vol.23, no.3, pp.167–72.

Kanji, N. (2002) 'Trading and Trade-Offs: Women's Livelihoods in Gorno-Badakhshan, Tajikistan', *Development in Practice*, vol.12, no.2, pp.138–52.

Kapteijns, L. (1995) 'Gender Relations and the Transformation of the Northern Somali Pastoral Tradition', *International Journal of African Historical Studies*, vol.28, no.2, pp.241–59.

Kapucu, N. (2007) 'Non-Profit Response to Catastrophic Disasters', *Disaster Prevention and Management*, vol.16, no.4, pp.551–61.

Kay, A. (2006) 'Social Capital, the Social Economy and Community Development', *Community Development Journal*, vol.41, no.2, pp.160–73.

Keating, M. (2001) 'Rethinking the Region: Culture, Institutions and Economic Development in Catalonia and Galicia', *European Urban and Regional Studies*, vol.8, no.3, pp.217–34.

Keele, L. (2005) 'Macro Measures and Mechanics of Social Capital', *Political Analysis*, vol.13, no.2, pp.139–56.

Kelso, M. (1936) 'The Inception of the Modern French Labor Movement (1871–79): A Reappraisal', *The Journal of Modern History*, vol.8, no.2, pp.173–93.

Khan, B. (2000) 'Commerce and Cooperation: Litigation and Settlement of Civil Disputes on the Australian Frontier, 1860–1900, *The Journal of Economic History*, vol.60, no.4, pp.1088–119.

Khan, H. and R. Muir (eds) (2006) *Sticking Together: Social Capital and Local Government, the Results and Implications of the Camden Social Capital Surveys 2002 and 2005*, London: IPPR and the London Borough of Camden.

Kilpatrick, S. et al. (2003) 'Social Capital: An Analytical Tool for Exploring Lifelong Learning and Community Development', *British Educational Research Journal*, vol.29, no.3, pp.417–33.

Kipnis, A. (1996) 'The Language of Gifts: Managing Guanxi in a North China Village', *Modern China*, vol.22, no.3, pp.285–314.

Kisby, B. (2007) 'New Labour and Citizenship Education', *Parliamentary Affairs*, vol.60, no.1, pp.84–101.

Klabbers, J. (2001) 'The Emerging Field of Simulation and Gaming: Meanings of a Retrospect', *Simulation and Gaming*, vol.32, no.4, pp.471–80.

Kliksberg, B. (1999) 'Social Capital and Culture: Master Keys to Development', *CEPAL Review*, no.69, pp.83–101.

Klooss, W. (2001) 'Setting the Table: Food and Community Construction in English-Canadian Writing', in Ferguson and Roberts (2001).

Knack, S. (2002) 'Social Capital, Growth, and Poverty: A Survey of Cross-Country Evidence', in Grootaert and van Bastelaer (eds) (2002).

Knight, J. and L. Yueh (2008) 'The Role of Social Capital in the Labour Market in China', *Economics of Transition*, vol.16, no.3, pp.389–414.

Knorringa, P. and I. van Staveren (2007) 'Beyond Social Capital: A Critical Approach', *Review of Social Economy*, vol.65, no.1, pp.1–9.

Kornai, J. et al. (eds) (2004) *Creating Social Trust in Post-Socialist Transition*, Basingstoke: Palgrave.

Korosteleva, E. (2006) 'Can Theories of Social Capital Explain Dissenting Patterns of Engagement in the New Europe?', *Contemporary Politics*, vol.12, no.2, pp.175–91.

Korupp, E. and M. Szydlik (2005) 'Causes and Trends of the Digital Divide', *European Sociological Review*, vol.21, no.4, pp.409–22.

Kovách, I. and E. Kučerová (2006), 'The Project Class in Central Europe: The Czech and Hungarian Cases', *European Society for Rural Sociology*, vol.46, no.1, pp.3–21.

Kreuter, M. and N. Lezin (2002) 'Social Capital Theory: Implications for Community-Based Health Promotion', in DiClemente et al. (2002).

Krippner, G. et al. (2004) 'Polanyi Symposium: A Conversation on Embeddedness', *Socio-Economic Review*, vol.2, no.1, pp.109–35.

—— (2001) 'Moving from the Stock of Social Capital to the Flow of Benefits: The Role of Agency', *World Development*, vol.29, no.6, pp.925–44.

—— (2002a) *Active Social Capital: Tracing the Roots of Development and Democracy*, New York: Columbia University Press.

—— (2002b) 'Enhancing Political Participation in Democracies: What is the Role of Social Capital?', *Comparative Political Studies*, vol.35, no.4, pp.437–60.

—— (2007) 'How Does Social Capital Grow? A Seven-Year Study of Villages in India', *Journal of Politics*, vol.69, no.4, pp.941–56.

—— and N. Uphoff (2002) 'Mapping and Measuring Social Capital through Assessment of Collective Action to Conserve and Develop Watersheds in Rajasthan, India', in Grootaert and van Bastalaer (eds) (2002).

Kunitz, S. (2004) 'Social Capital and Health', *British Medical Bulletin*, vol.69, no.1, pp.1–13.

Kusakabe, K. et al. (2001) *Social Capital of Women Micro-Vendors in Phnom Penh (Cambodia) Markets: A Study of Vendors' Association*, United Nations Urban Management Programme, Asia Occasional Paper no.53.

La Ferrara, E. (2002) 'Inequality and Group Participation: Theory and Evidence from Rural Tanzania', *Journal of Public Economics*, vol.85, no.2, pp.235–73.

Laird, P. (2006) *Pull: Networking and Success since Benjamin Franklin*, Cambridge, MA: Harvard University Press.

Lam, P. (2002) 'As the Flocks Gather: How Religion Affects Voluntary Association Participation', *Journal for the Scientific Study of Religion*, vol.41 no.3, pp.405–22.

Lamoreaux, N. (1998) 'Economic History and the Cliometric Revolution', in Molho and Wood (1998).

Langbein, L. and R. Bess (2002) 'Sports in School: Source of Amity or Antipathy?', *Social Science Quarterly*, vol.83, no.2, pp.436–54.

Larance, L. (2001) 'Fostering Social Capital through NGO Design: Grameen Bank Membership in Bangladesh', *International Social Work*, vol.44, no.1, pp.7–18.

Lazega, E. and P. Pattison (2001) 'Social Capital as Social Mechanisms and Collective Assets: The Example of Status Auctions among Colleagues', in Burt (2001).

Lebow, R. (2005) 'Reason, Emotion and Cooperation', *International Politics*, vol.42, no.3, pp.283–313.

Lee, F. (2007) 'The Research Assessment Exercise, the State and the Dominance of Mainstream Economics in British Universities', *Cambridge Journal of Economics*, vol.31, no.2, pp.309–25.

Leeder, S. (1998) 'Social Capital and Its Relevance to Health and Family Policy', available at www.ahpi.health.usyd.edu.au/pdfs/srlpres1998/asocialcapital98.pdf, accessed 20 March 2009.

Leeuwen, M. van (1994) 'Logic of Charity: Poor Relief in Preindustrial Europe', *Journal of Interdisciplinary History*, vol.24, no.4, pp.589–613.

Lei, L. et al. (2008) 'The Turtle–Hare Race Story Revisited: Social Capital and Resource Accumulation for Firms from Emerging Economies', *Asia Pacific Journal of Management*, vol.25, no.2, pp.251–75.

Lelieveldt, H. and M. Gaiani (2007) 'The Political Role of Associations', in Maloney and Rossteutscher (2007).

Letki, N. (2006) 'Investigating the Roots of Civic Morality: Trust, Social Capital, and Institutional Performance', *Political Behavior*, vol.28, no.4, pp.305–25.

Levi, M. (1996) 'Social and Unsocial Capital: A Review Essay of Robert Putnam's "Making Democracy Work"', *Politics and Society*, vol.24, no.1, pp.45–55.

Lichterman, P. (2006) 'Social Capital or Group Style? Rescuing Tocqueville's Insights on Civic Engagement', *Theory and Society*, vol.35, nos.5/6, pp.529–63.

Lin, N. (2001) *Social Capital: A Theory of Social Structure and Action*, Cambridge: Cambridge University Press.

—— K. Cook and R. Burt (eds) (2001) *Building a Network Theory of Social Capital*, Hawthorne, NY: Aldine de Gruyter.

—— and B. Erickson (2008) 'Theory, Measurement, and the Research Enterprise on Social Capital', in Lin and Erickson (eds) (2008).

—— (eds) (2008) *Social Capital: An International Research Program*, New York: Oxford University Press.

—— et al. (2001) 'Preface', in Lin et al. (eds) (2001).

Linda, P. (2006) 'Mum and Dad Prefer Me to Speak Bengali at Home: Code Switching and Parallel Speech in a Primary School Setting', *Literacy*, vol.40, no.3, pp.137–45.

Liodakis, G. (ed.) (1993) *Society, Technology and Restructuring of Production*, Athens: V. Papazissis (in Greek).

Lister, R. (2003) 'Investing in the Citizen–Workers of the Future: Transformations in Citizenship and the State under New Labour', *Social Policy and Administration*, vol.37, no.5, pp.427–43.

Liverani, A. (2007) *Civil Society in a Weak State: The Political Functions of Associational Life in Algeria, 1987–2005*, Ph.D. thesis, University of London.

Livingston, G. (2006) 'Gender, Job Searching, and Employment Outcomes among Mexican Immigrants', *Population Research and Policy Review*, vol.25, no.1, pp.43–66.

Lofors, J. and K. Sundquist (2007) 'Low-Linking Social Capital as a Predictor of Mental Disorders: A Cohort Study of 4.5 Million Swedes', *Social Science and Medicine*, vol.64, no.1, pp.21–34.

Logan, I. and K. Mengisteab (1993) 'IMF–World Bank Adjustment and Structural Transformation in Sub-Saharan Africa', *Economic Geography*, vol.69, no.1, pp.1–24.

Lorenzen, M. (2007) 'Social Capital and Localised Learning: Proximity and Place in Technological and Institutional Dynamics', *Urban Studies*, vol.44, no.4, pp.799–817.

Loury, G. (1977) 'A Dynamic Theory of Racial Income Differences', in Wallace and Le Mund (1977).

—— (1987) 'Why Should We Care about Group Inequality', *Social Philosophy and Policy*, vol.5, no.1, pp.249–71.

Lovell, A. (2002) 'Risking Risk: The Influence of Types of Capital and Social Networks on the Injection Practices of Drug Users', *Social Science and Medicine*, vol.55, no.5, pp.803–21.

Lowndes, V. (2004) 'Getting on or Getting by? Women, Social Capital and Political Participation', *British Journal of Politics and International Relations*, vol.6, no.1, pp.45–64.

—— and D. Wilson (2001) 'Social Capital and Local Governance: Exploring the Institutional Design Variable', *Political Studies*, vol.49, no.4, pp.629–47.

—— et al. (2006a) 'Local Political Participation: The Impact of Rules-in-Use', *Public Administration*, vol.84, no.3, pp.539–61.

—— et al. (2006b) 'Diagnosing and Remedying the Failings of Official Participation Schemes: The CLEAR Framework', *Social Policy and Society*, vol.5, no.2, pp.281–91.

Lyons, M. and S. Snoxell (2005) 'Creating Urban Social Capital: Some Evidence from Informal Traders in Nairobi', *Urban Studies*, vol.42, no.7, pp.1077–97.

MacHardy, K. (1992) 'The Rise of Absolutism and Noble Rebellion in Early Modern Habsburg Austria, 1570 to 1620', *Comparative Studies in Society and History*, vol.34, no.3, pp.407–38.

—— (1999) 'Cultural Capital, Family Strategies and Noble Identity in Early Modern Habsburg Austria 1579–1620', *Past and Present*, no.163, pp.36–75.

MacKian, S. (2002) 'Complex Cultures: Rereading the Story about Health and Social Capital', *Critical Social Policy*, vol.22, no.2, pp.203–25.

Majewski, J. et al. (1993) 'Responding to Relative Decline: The Plank Road Boom of Antebellum New York', *Journal of Economic History*, vol.53, no.1, pp.106–22.

Malinvaud, E. (2003) 'The Legacy of Knut Wicksell to Capital Theory', *Scandinavian Journal of Economics*, vol.105, no.4, pp.507–25.

Maloney, W. and S. Rossteutscher (eds) (2007) *Social Capital and Associations in European Democracies: A Comparative Analysis*, London: Routledge.

Marger, M. (2001) 'The Use of Social and Human Capital among Canadian Business Immigrants', *Journal of Ethnic and Migration Studies*, vol.27, no.3, pp.439–54.

Marjoribanks, K. and M. Mboya (2001) 'Family Capital and South African Young Adults' Self-Concept', *Journal of Comparative Family Studies*, vol.32, no.1, pp.127–39.

Marsh, R. (2005) 'Social Capital and Democracy in a New Democracy', *Sociological Quarterly*, vol.46, no.4, pp.593–615.

Marshall, B. and A. Witz (eds) (2004) *Engendering the Social: Feminist Encounters with Sociological Theory*, Maidenhead: Oxford University Press.

Marsiglio, W. and R. Hinojosa (2007) 'Managing the Multifather Family: Stepfathers as Father Allies', *Journal of Marriage and Family*, vol.69, no.3, pp.845–62.

Marysse, S. (1999) 'Social Capital in the Context of Crisis-Ridden Africa', Faculty of Applied Economics, UFSIA-University of Antwerp, Research Paper no.99-014, May.

Mayer, M. (2003) 'The Onward Sweep of Social Capital: Causes and Consequences for Understanding Cities, Communities and Urban Movements', *International Journal of Urban and Regional Research*, vol.27, no.1, pp.110–32.

Mayoux, L. (2001) 'Tackling the Down Side: Social Capital, Women's Empowerment and Micro-Finance in Cameroon', *Development and Change*, vol.32, no.3, pp.435–64.

McAreavey, R. (2006) 'Getting Close to the Action: the Micro-Politics of Rural Development', *Sociologia Ruralis*, vol.46, no.2, pp.85–103.

McCarthy, B. and J. Hagan (2001) 'When Crime Pays: Capital, Competence and Criminal Success', *Social Forces*, vol.79, no.3, pp.1035–60.

McClenaghan, P. (2000) 'Social Capital: Exploring the Theoretical Foundations of Community Development Education', *British Educational Research Journal*, vol.26, no.5, pp.565–82.

—— (2003) 'Response to "Social Capital: An Analytical Tool for Exploring Lifelong Learning and Community Development"', *British Educational Research Journal*, vol.29, no.3, pp.435–9.

McConkey, D. and P. Lawler (eds) (2000) *Social Structures, Social Capital, and Personal Freedom*, Westport, CT: Praeger.

McDougall, D. (1966) 'Discussion of Shoyama and Davis and Legler Papers', *Journal of Economic History*, vol.26, no.4, pp.553–5.

McGhee, D. (2003) 'Moving to "Our" Common Ground: A Critical Examination of Community Cohesion Discourse in Twenty-First Century Britain', *Sociological Review*, vol.51, no.3, pp.376–404.

McGonigal, J. et al. (2007) 'Social Capital, Social Inclusion and Changing School Contexts: A Scottish Perspective', *British Journal of Educational Studies*, vol.55, no.1, pp.77–94.

McIntosh, M. (1998) 'Response', *Journal of British Studies*, vol.37, no.3, pp.291–305.

—— (1999) 'The Diversity of Social Capital in English Communities, 1300–1640 (with a Glance at Modern Nigeria)', *Journal of Interdisciplinary History*, vol.19, no.3 pp.459–90.

McLean, S. (2002a) 'Patriotism, Generational Change, and the Politics of Sacrifice', in McLean et al. (2002).

—— (2002b) 'Afterword', in McLean et al. (2002).

—— (2007/8) 'Diverse Communities: The Problem With Social Capital', *Political Science Quarterly*, vol.122, no.4, pp.683–5.

—— et al. (eds) (2002) *Social Capital: Critical Perspectives on Community and 'Bowling Alone'*, New York: New York University Press.

McNamee, S. and R. Miller (2004) *The Meritocracy Myth*, Lanham, MD: Rowman & Littlefield.

McPhee, W. and D. Wheeler (2006) 'Making the Case for the Added-Value Chain', *Strategy and Leadership*, vol.34, no.4, pp.39–46.

Meadowcroft, J. and M. Pennington (2007) *Rescuing Social Capital from Social Democracy*, London: Institute of Economic Affairs.

Meagher, K. (2006) 'Social Capital, Social Liabilities, and Political Capital: Social Networks and Informal Manufacturing in Nigeria', *African Affairs*, vol.105, no.421, pp.553–82.

Menguc, B. and T. Barker (2005) 'Re-Examining Field Sales Unit Performance: Insights from the Resource-Based View and Dynamic Capabilities Perspective', *European Journal of Marketing*, vol.39, nos.7/8, pp.885–909.

Merrett, C. (2001) 'Declining Social Capital and Nonprofit Organizations: Consequences for Small Towns after Welfare Reform', *Urban Geography*, vol.22, no.5, pp.407–23.

Merton, R. (1957) *Social Theory and Social Structure*, New York: Free Press.

Messner, S. et al. (2004) 'Dimensions of Social Capital and Rates of Criminal Homicide', *American Sociological Review*, vol.69, no.6, pp.882–907.

Meulemann, H. (2008a) 'Introduction', in Meulemann (ed.) (2008).

—— (2008b) 'Social Capital and Empowerment at the Work Place', in Meulemann (ed.) (2008).

—— (ed.) (2008) *Social Capital in Europe: Similarity of Countries and Diversity of People? Multi-level Analyses of the European Social Survey, 2002*, Leiden: Brill.

Mihaylova, D. (2004) *Social Capital in Central and Eastern Europe*, Budapest: Central European University.

Miller, B. et al. (2006) 'Gender and Science in Developing Areas: Has the Internet Reduced Inequality?', *Social Science Quarterly*, vol.87, no.3, pp.679–89.

Milonakis, D. and B. Fine (2007) 'Douglass North's Remaking of Economic History: A Critical Appraisal', *Review of Radical Political Economics*, vol.39, no.1, pp.27–57.

—— (2009) *From Political Economy to Economics: Method, the Social and the Historical in the Evolution of Economic Theory*, London: Routledge.

—— (forthcoming) *Reinventing the Economic Past: Method and Theory in the Evolution of Economic History*, London: Routledge.

Milone, P. and F. Ventura (2000) 'Theory and Practice of Multi-Product Farms: Farm Butcheries in Umbria', *Sociologia Ruralis*, vol.40, no.4, pp.452–65.

Mitchell, C. and M. LaGory (2002) 'Social Capital and Mental Distress in an Impoverished Community', *City and Community*, vol.1, no.2, pp.199–222.

Mitlin, D. (2001) 'Civil Society and Urban Poverty: Examining Complexity', *Environment and Urbanization*, vol.13, no.2, pp.151–73.

Miyata, K. and T. Kobayashi (2008) 'Causal Relationship between Internet Use and Social Capital in Japan', *Asian Journal of Social Psychology*, vol.11, no.1, pp.42–52.

Mkandawire, T. (ed.) (2005) *Social Policy in a Development Context*, UNRISD, Basingstoke: Palgrave MacMillan.

Moerbeek, H. and A. Need (2003) 'Enemies at Work: Can They Hinder Your Career?', *Social Networks*, vol.25, no.1, pp.67–82.

Mogues, T. and M. Carter (2005) 'Social Capital and the Reproduction of Economic Inequality in Polarized Societies', *Journal of Economic Inequality*, vol.3, no.3, pp.193–219.

Mohan, G. and J. Mohan (2002) 'Placing Social Capital', *Progress in Human Geography*, vol.26, no.2, pp.191–210.

Molho, A. and G. Wood (eds) (1998) *Imagined Histories: American Historians Interpret the Past*, Princeton, NJ: Princeton University Press.

Molina-Morales, F. (2005) 'The Territorial Agglomerations of Firms: A Social Capital Perspective from the Spanish Tile Industry', *Growth and Change*, vol.36, no.1, pp.74–99.

—— and M. Martínez-Fernández (2006) 'Industrial Districts: Something More than a Neighbourhood', *Entrepreneurship and Regional Development: An International Journal*, vol.18, no.6, pp.503–24.

Möllering, G. (2001) 'The Nature of Trust: From Georg Simmel to a Theory of Expectation, Interpretation and Suspension', *Sociology*, vol.35, no.2, pp.403–20.

—— (2006) *Trust: Reason, Routine, Reflexivity*, Amsterdam: Elsevier.

Molyneux, M. (2002) 'Gender and the Silences of Social Capital: Lessons from Latin America', *Development and Change*, vol.33, no.2, pp.167–88.

Montero, J. and M. Torcal (2006) 'Some Basic Conclusions about Political Disaffection in Contemporary Democracies', in Torcal and Montero (2006).

Montgomery, J. (2000) 'Social Capital as a Policy Resource', *Policy Sciences*, vol.33, nos.3/4, pp.227–43.

Mooney, G. and N. Fyfe (2006) 'New Labour and Community Protests: The Case of the Govanhill Swimming Pool Campaign, Glasgow', *Local Economy*, vol.21, no.2, pp.136–50.

Moore, M. (2001) 'Empowerment at Last', *Journal of International Development*, vol.13, no.3, pp.321–9.

Morgan, B. (2002) 'Higher Education and Regional Economic Development in Wales: An Opportunity for Demonstrating the Efficacy of Devolution in Economic Development', *Regional Studies*, vol.26, no.1, pp.65–73.

Morgan, M. et al. (2006) 'Attitudes to Kidney Donation and Registering as a Donor among Ethnic Groups in the UK', *Journal of Public Health*, vol.28, no.3, pp.226–34.

Morokvasic, M. (2004) '"Settled in Mobility": Engendering Post-Wall Migration in Europe', *Feminist Review*, vol.77, no.1, pp.7–25.

Morris, M. (1998) 'Social Capital in India', Institute of Development Studies, Working Paper no.61, January.

Morrison, N. (2003) 'Neighbourhoods and Social Cohesion: Experiences from Europe', *International Planning Studies*, vol.8, no.2, pp.115–38.

Morrow, V. (1999) 'Conceptualising Social Capital in Relation to the Well-Being of Children and Young People: A Critical Review', *Sociological Review*, vol.47, no.4, pp.744–65.

Mosley, P. and E. Dowler (eds) (2003) *Poverty and Social Exclusion in North and South*, London: Routledge.

Mouritsen, P. (2003) 'What's the Civil in Civil Society? Robert Putnam, Italy and the Republican Tradition', *Political Studies*, vol.51, no.4, pp.650–68.

Mowbray, M. (2005) 'Community Capacity Building or State Opportunism?', *Community Development Journal*, vol.40, no.3, pp.255–64.

Muldrew, C. (2001) '"Hard Food for Midas": Cash and Its Social Value in Early Modern England', *Past and Present*, no.170, pp.78–120.

Mullis, R. et al. (2003) 'Predictors of Academic Performance during Early Adolescence: A Contextual View', *International Journal of Behavioral Development*, vol.27, no.6, pp.541–8.

Muntaner, C. (2004) 'Commentary: Social Capital, Social Class, and the Slow Progress of Psychosocial Epidemiology', *International Journal of Epidemiology*, vol.33, no.4, pp.674–80.

—— et al. (2001) 'Social Capital, Disorganised Communities, and the Third Way: Understanding the Retreat from Structural Inequalities in Epidemiology and Public Health', *International Journal of Health Services*, vol.31, no.2, pp.213–37.

Murphy, J. (2002) 'Networks, Trust, and Innovation in Tanzania's Manufacturing Sector', *World Development*, vol.30, no.4, pp.591–619.

Mutti, A. (2000) 'Particularism and the Modernization Process in Southern Italy', *International Sociology*, vol.15, no.4, pp.579–90.

Myant, M. and S. Smith (2006) 'Regional Development and Post-Communist Politics in a Czech Region', *Europe–Asia Studies*, vol.58, no.2, pp.147–68.

Nahapiet, J. and S. Ghoshal (1998) 'Social Capital, Intellectual Capital, and the Organizational Advantage', *Academy of Management Review*, vol.23, no.2, pp.242–66.

Nast, J. (2000) 'Mapping the "Unconscious": Racism and the Oedipal Family', *Annals of the Association of American Geographers*, vol.90, no.2, pp.215–55.

Navarro, V. (2002) 'A Critique of Social Capital', *International Journal of Health Services*, vol.81, no.3, pp.423–32.

Nel, E. et al. (2001) 'Community-Based Development, Non-Governmental Organizations and Social Capital in Post-Apartheid South Africa', *Geografiska Annaler*, series B, vol.83, no.1, pp.3–14.

Némedi, D. (2005) 'The Kabyle Paradigm', *Review of Sociology of the Hungarian Sociological Association*, vol.11, no.1, pp.35–48.

Newman, L. and A. Dale (2005) 'The Role of Agency in Sustainable Local Community Development', *Local Environment*, vol.10, no.5, pp.477–86.

Newton, K. (2001) 'Trust, Social Capital, Civil Society, and Democracy', *International Political Science Review*, vol.22, no.2, pp.201–14.

—— (2006) 'Institutional Confidence and Social Trust: Aggregate and Individual Relations', in Torcal and Montero (2006).

Norchi, C. (2000) 'Indigenous Knowledge as Intellectual Property', *Policy Sciences*, vol.33, nos.3/4, pp.387–98.

Novicevic, M. and M. Harvey (2001) 'The Emergence of the Pluralism Construct and the Inpatriation Process', *International Journal of Human Resource Management*, vol.12, no.3, pp.333–56.

O'Connell, M. (2003) 'Anti "Social Capital": Civic Values versus Economic Equality in the EU', *European Sociological Review*, vol.19, no.3, pp.241–8.

O'Connor, J. (1973) *The Fiscal Crisis of the State*, New York: St Martin's Press.

OECD (2006a) 'Financial Support to Fisheries: Implications for Sustainable Development: Social Capital and Fisheries Subsidy Reform', *OECD Agriculture and Food*, vol.2006, no.13, pp.274–97.

—— (2006b) 'Local Economic and Employment Development Business Clusters Promoting Enterprise in Central and Eastern Europe: Social Capital: A Key Ingredient for Clusters in Post-Communist Societies', *OECD Industry, Services and Trade*, vol.2005, no.22, pp.30–53.

Ogilvie, S. (2003) *A Bitter Living: Women, Markets, and Social Capital in Early Modern Germany*, Oxford: Oxford University Press.

—— (2004) 'Guilds, Efficiency, and Social Capital: Evidence from German Proto-Industry', *Economic History Review*, vol.57, no.2, pp.286–333.

O'Neill, B. and E. Gidengil (eds) (2006) *Gender and Social Capital*, New York: Routledge.

Oishi, T. (2001) *The Unknown Marx: Reconstructing a Unified Perspective*, London: Pluto Press.

Onion, The (2005) '"Not Quite Perfect" McDonald's Opens in Illinois Outlet Mall', no.41.9, 11 May, available at www.theonion.com/content/news/not_quite_perfect_mcdonalds_opens, accessed 20 March 2009.

Onyx, J. (2005) 'Introduction', in Dale and Onyx (2005).

Ooka, E. (2001) 'Social Capital and Income Attainment among Chinese Immigrant Entrepreneurs in Toronto', *Asian and Pacific Migration Journal*, vol.10, no.1, pp.123–44.

Oorschot, W. van et al. (2005) 'Welfare State Effects on Social Capital and Informal Solidarity in the European Union: Evidence from the 1999/2000 European Values Study', *Policy and Politics*, vol.33, no.1, pp.35–56.

Osborne, M. et al. (eds) (2007) *Social Capital, Lifelong Learning and the Management of Place*, London: Routledge.

Oxendine, A. et al. (2007) 'The Importance of Political Context for Understanding Civic Engagement: A Longitudinal Analysis', *Political Behavior*, vol.29, no.1, pp.31–67.

Pagett, L. (2006) 'Mum and Dad Prefer Me to Speak Bengali at Home: Code Switching and Parallel Speech in a Primary School Setting', *Literacy*, vol.40, no.3, pp.137–45.

Paldam, M. (2000) 'Social Capital: One or Many? Definition and Measurement', *Journal of Economic Surveys*, vol.14, no.5, pp.629–54.

—— and G. Svendsen (2004) 'Social Capital and Economics', in Flap and Völker (2004).

Parayil, G. (ed.) (2000) *Kerala: The Development Experience, Reflections on Sustainability and Replicability*, London: Zed Books.

Parcel, T. and M. Dufur (2001) 'Capital at Home and at School: Effects on Child Social Adjustment', *Journal of Marriage and the Family*, vol.63, no.1, pp.32–47.

Pargal, S. et al. (2002) 'Does Social Capital Increase Participation in Voluntary Solid Waste Management? Evidence from Dhaka, Bangladesh', in Grootaert and van Bastelaer (eds) (2002).

Park, C. (2007) 'Gender in Academic Career Tracks: The Case of Korean Biochemists', *Sociological Forum*, vol.22, no.4, pp.452–73.

Pattussi, M. et al. (2006) 'The Potential Impact of Neighborhood Empowerment on Dental Caries among Adolescents', *Community Dentistry and Oral Epidemiology*, vol.34, no.5, pp.344–50.

Pavey, B. (2006) 'Human Capital, Social Capital, Entrepreneurship and Disability: An Examination of Some Current Educational Trends in the UK', *Disability and Society*, vol.21, no.3, pp.217–29.

Pawar, M. (2006) '"Social" "Capital"'? *Social Science Journal*, vol.43, no.2, pp.211–26.

Pellow, D. (1991) 'The Power of Space in the Evolution of an Accra Zongo', *Ethnohistory*, vol.38, no.4, pp.414–50.

Perna, L. (2005) 'Sex Differences in Faculty Tenure and Promotion: The Contribution of Family Ties', *Research in Higher Education*, vol.46, no.3, pp.277–307.

Peterson, T. et al. (2006) 'To Play the Fool: Can Environmental Conservation and Democracy Survive Social Capital?', *Communication and Critical/Cultural Studies*, vol.3, no.2, pp.116–140.

Phillipson, J. et al. (2006) 'Local Business Co-operation and the Dilemmas of Collective Action: Rural Micro-Business Networks in the North of England', *Sociologia Ruralis*, vol.46, no.1, pp.40–60.

Piazza-Georgi, B. (2002) 'The Role of Human and Social Capital in Growth: Extending Our Understanding', *Cambridge Journal of Economics*, vol.26, no.4, pp.461–79.

Pichler, F. and C. Wallace (2009) 'Social Capital and Social Class in Europe: The Role of Social Networks in Social Stratification', *European Sociological Review*, vol.25, no.3, pp.319–32.

Pietrykowski, B. (2004) 'You Are What You Eat: The Social Economy of the Slow Food Movement', *Review of Social Economy*, vol.62, no.3, pp.307–21.

Pinnock, A. (2007) 'New Development: The Infrastructural Aspect of Social Capital. Suggestions for a Bridge between Concept and Policy', *Public Money and Management*, vol.27, no.5, pp.345–50.

Podolny, J. and J. Baron (1997) 'Resources and Relationships: Social Networks and Mobility in the Workplace', *American Sociological Review*, vol.62, no.5, pp.673–93.

Polèse, M. and R. Shearmur (2006) 'Why Some Regions Decline: A Canadian Case Study with Thoughts on Local Development Strategies', *Papers in Regional Science*, vol.85, no.1, pp.23–46.

Pomerantz, A. (2002) 'Language Ideologies and the Production of Identities: Spanish as a Resource for Participation in a Multilingual Marketplace', *Multilingua*, vol.21, nos.2/3, pp.275–302.

Porter, G. and F. Lyon (2006) 'Social Capital as Culture: Promoting Cooperative Action in Ghana', in Radcliffe (2006).

Portes, A. (1998) 'Social Capital: Its Origins and Applications in Modern Sociology', *Annual Review of Sociology*, vol.24, pp.1–24.

Pouwels, R. (2002) 'Eastern Africa and the Indian Ocean to 1800: Reviewing Relations in Historical Perspective', *International Journal of African Historical Studies*, vol.35, nos.2/3, pp.385–425.

Prabhakar, R. (2002) 'Capability, Responsibility, Human Capital and the Third Way', *Political Quarterly*, vol.73, no.1, pp.51–7.

Pretty, J. and H. Ward (2001) 'Social Capital and the Environment', *World Development*, vol.29, no.2, pp.209–27.

Purdue, D. (2001) 'Neighbourhood Governance: Leadership, Trust and Social Capital', *Urban Studies*, vol.38, no.12, pp.2211–24.

Putnam, R. (1993) *Making Democracy Work: Civic Traditions in Modern Italy*, Princeton, NJ: Princeton University Press.

—— (1995) 'Bowling Alone: America's Declining Social Capital', *Journal of Democracy*, vol.6, no.1, pp.65–78.

—— (2000) *Bowling Alone: The Collapse and Revival of American Community*, New York: Simon & Schuster.

—— (2002) 'Bowling Together', *American Prospect*, vol.13, no.3, available at www.prospect.org/cs/articles?article=bowling_together, accessed 20 March 2009.

—— (2007) '*E Pluribus Unum*: Diversity and Community in the Twenty-First Century. The 2006 Johan Skytte Prize Lecture', *Scandinavian Political Studies*, vol.30, no.2, pp.137–74.

—— (ed.) (2002) *Democracies in Flux: The Evolution of Social Capital in Contemporary Society*, Oxford: Oxford University Press.

—— and K. Goss (2002) 'Introduction', in Putnam (ed.) (2002).

Quan-Haase, A. and B. Wellman (2004) 'How Does the Internet Affect Social Capital?', in Huysman and Wulf (2004).

Quinn, J. (2005) 'Belonging in a Learning Community: The Re-Imagined University and Imagined Social Capital', *Studies in the Education of Adults*, vol.37, no.1, pp.4–17.

Quinones, B. and H. Seibel (2000) 'Social Capital in Microfinance: Case Studies in the Philippines', *Policy Sciences*, vol.33, nos.3/4, pp.421–34.

Radcliffe, S. (2004) 'Geography of Development: Development, Civil Society and Inequality – Social Capital Is (Almost) Dead?', *Progress in Human Geography*, vol.28, no.4, pp.517–27.

—— (ed.) (2006) *Culture and Development in a Globalizing World: Geographies, Actors, and Paradigms*, London: Routledge.

Rai, P. et al. (2006) 'To Play the Fool: Can Environmental Conservation and Democracy Survive Social Capital?', *Communication and Critical/Cultural Studies*, vol.3, no.2, pp.116–40.

Rankin, K. (2002) 'Social Capital, Microfinance, and the Politics of Development', *Feminist Economics*, vol.8, no.1, pp.1–24.

Rao, V. and M. Woolcock (2007) 'Disciplinary Monopolies in Development Research: A Response to the Research Evaluation Process', available at http://siteresources.worldbank.org/INTPOVRES/Resources/DisciplinaryMonopoly.pdf.

Ray, G. et al. (2001) 'Increasing Returns to Scale in Affluent Knowledge-Rich Economies', *Growth and Change*, vol.32, no.4, pp.491–510.

Raymond, L. (2006) 'Cooperation without Trust: Overcoming Collective Action Barriers to Endangered Species Protection', *Policy Studies Journal*, vol.34, no.1, pp.37–57.

Reagans, R. and E. Zuckerman (2001) 'Networks, Diversity, and Productivity: The Social Capital of Corporate R&D Teams', *Organization Science*, vol.12, no.4, pp.502–17.

Riesman, D. et al. (1953) *The Lonely Crowd: A Study of the Changing American Character*, New York: Doubleday.

Ritzer, G. (1993) *The McDonaldization of Society: An Investigation into the Changing Character of Contemporary Social Life*, 5th edn., Thousand Oaks, CA: Pine Forge Press.

—— (2003) *The Globalization of Nothing*, 2nd edn., London: Pine Forge Press.

Roberts, J. (2004) 'What's "Social" about "Social Capital"?', *British Journal of Politics and International Relations*, vol.6, no.4, pp.471–93.

—— and F. Devine (2004) 'Some Everyday Experiences of Voluntarism: Social Capital, Pleasure, and the Contingency of Participation', *Social Politics*, vol.11, no.2, pp.280–96.

Robison, L. and J. Flora (2003) 'The Social Capital Paradigm: Bridging across Disciplines', *American Journal of Agricultural Economics*, vol.85, no.5, pp.1187–93.

—— et al. (2002) 'Is Social Capital Really Capital?', *Review of Social Economy*, vol.60, no.1, pp.1–22.

Robison, R. (2003) 'Looking Back on the Asian Crisis: The Question of Convergence', *Asian Journal of Social Science*, vol.31, no.2, pp.162–71.

—— (2004) 'Neoliberalism and the Future World: Markets and the End of Politics', *Critical Asian Studies*, vol.36, no.3, pp.405–23.

Rodriguez, F. (2006) 'Growth Empirics When the World Is Not Simple', available at www.un.org/esa/policy/backgroundpapers/rodriguez_2.pdf, accessed 20 March 2009.

Rossteutscher, S. (2002) 'Advocate or Reflection? Associations and Political Culture', *Political Studies*, vol.50, no.3, pp.514–28.

Rotberg, R. (ed.) (2001) *Patterns of Social Capital: Stability and Change in Historical Perspective*, Cambridge: Cambridge University Press.

Rothstein, B. (2000) 'Social Capital and Institutional Legitimacy', paper prepared for the Annual Meeting of the American Political Science Association, Washington, DC, September.

—— (2001) 'Social Capital in the Social Democratic Welfare State', *Politics and Society*, vol.29, no.2, pp.207–42.

—— and D. Stolle (2002) 'How Political Institutions Create and Destroy Social Capital: An Institutional Theory of Generalized Trust', paper presented at Collegium Budapest, Project on Honesty and Trust, 22–23 November, available at www.colbud.hu/honesty-trust/rothstein/pub03.doc, accessed 29 July 2009.

——(2003) 'Introduction: Social Capital in Scandinavia', *Scandinavian Political Studies*, vol.26, no.1, pp.1–26.

Runnymede Trust (2005) *Social Capital, Civil Renewal and Ethnic Diversity*, London: Runnymede Trust.

Rycroft, R. (2003) 'Technology-Based Globalization Indicators: The Centrality of Innovation Network Data', *Technology in Society*, vol.25, no.3, pp.299–317.

Sabatini, F. (2007) 'The Empirics of Social Capital and Economic Development: A Critical Perspective', in Osborne et al. (2007).

Sacks, M. et al. (2001) 'Global Institutions and Networks: Contingent Change in the Structure of World Trade Advantage, 1965–1980', *American Behavioral Scientist*, vol.44, no.10, pp.1579–601.

Saegert, S. (2006) 'Building Civic Capacity in Urban Neighbourhoods: An Empirically Grounded Anatomy', *Journal of Urban Affairs*, vol.28, no.3, pp.275–94.

—— et al. (eds) (2001) *Social Capital and Poor Communities*, New York: Russell Sage Foundation.

—— et al. (2002) 'Social Capital and Crime in New York City's Low-Income Housing', *Housing Policy Debate*, vol.13, no.1, pp.189–226.

Sagas, M. and G. Cunningham (2004) 'Does Having "the Right Stuff" Matter? Gender Differences in the Determinants of Career Success Among Intercollegiate Athletic Administrators', *Sex Roles*, vol.50, nos.5/6, pp.411–21.

Samal, K. (2007) *Poverty, Social Capital and Natural Resource Management*, Jaipur: Rawat Publications.

Sánchez, D. (2007) 'Explaining Union Membership of Temporary Workers in Spain: The Role of Local Representatives and Workers' Participative Potential', *Industrial Relations Journal*, vol.38, no.1, pp.51–69.

Sander, T. with R. Putnam (2006) 'Social Capital and Civic Engagement of Individuals over Age Fifty in the United States', in Wilson et al. (2006).

Sato, H. (2005) 'Total Factor Productivity vs. Realism Revisited: The Case of the South Korean Steel Industry,' *Cambridge Journal of Economics*, vol.29, no.4, pp.635–55.

Savage, M. et al. (2005) 'Social Capital and Social Trust in Britain', *European Sociological Review*, vol.21, no.2, pp.109–23.

Saxton, G. and M. Benson (2005) 'Social Capital and the Growth of the Nonprofit Sector', *Social Science Quarterly*, vol.86, no.1, pp.16–35.

Schafft, K. and D. Brown (2003) 'Social Capital, Social Networks, and Social Power', *Social Epistemology*, vol.17, no.4, pp.329–42.

Scheepers, P. et al. (2002) 'Welfare States and Dimensions of Social Capital: Cross-National Comparisons of Social Contacts in European Countries', *European Societies*, vol.4, no.2, pp.185–207.

Schmid, A. (2002) 'Using Motive to Distinguish Social Capital from Its Outputs', *Journal of Economic Issues*, vol.36, no.3, pp.747–68.

Schoen, R. and P. Tufis (2003) 'Precursors of Nonmarital Fertility in the United States', *Journal of Marriage and Family*, vol.65, no.4, pp.1030–40.

Schoenbrun, D. (1997) 'Gendered Histories between the Great Lakes: Varieties and Limits', *International Journal of African Historical Studies*, vol.29, no.3, pp.461–92.

Schuller, T. (2007) 'Reflections on the Use of Social Capital', *Review of Social Economy*, vol.65, no.1, pp.11–28.

Schultz, D. (2002) 'The Phenomonology of Democracy: Putnam, Pluralism, and Voluntary Associations', in McLean et al. (2002).

Schuurman, F. (2003) 'Social Capital: The Politico-Emancipatory Potential of a Disputed Concept', *Third World Quarterly*, vol.24, no.6, pp.991–1010.

Schwadel, P. (2005) 'Individual, Congregational, and Denominational Effects on Church Members' Civic Participation', *Journal for the Scientific Study of Religion*, vol.44, no.2, pp.159–71.

Scott, C. (2006) 'Museums: Impact and Value', *Cultural Trends*, vol.15, no.1, pp.45–75.

Secor, A. and J. O'Loughlin (2005) 'Social and Political Trust in Istanbul and Moscow: A Comparative Analysis of Individual and Neighbourhood Effects', *Transactions of the Institute of British Geographers*, vol.30, no.1, pp.66–82.

Selin, S. and C. Pierskalla (2005) 'Next Step: Strengthening the Social Science Voice in Environmental Governance', *Society and Natural Resources*, vol.18, no.10, pp.933–6.

Seppola, R. (2004) *Social Capital in International Business Networks: Confirming a Unique Type of Governance Structure*, doctoral dissertation, Helsinki School of Economics.

Servon, L. (2003) 'Social Capital, Identity Politics, and Social Change', in Body-Gendrot and Gittell (eds) (2003).

Shane, S. and T. Stuart (2002) 'Organizational Endowments and the Performance of University Start-Ups', *Management Science*, vol.48, no.1, pp.154–70.

Shetler, J. (1995) 'A Gift for Generations to Come: A Kiroba Popular History from Tanzania and Identity as Social Capital in the 1980s', *International Journal of African Historical Studies*, vol.28, no.1, pp.69–112.

Shortall, S. (2004) 'Social or Economic Goals, Civic Inclusion or Exclusion? An Analysis of Rural Development Theory and Practice', *European Society for Rural Sociology*, vol.44, no.1, pp.109–23.

Siisiäinen, M. (2000) 'Two Concepts of Social Capital: Bourdieu vs. Putnam', paper presented at the International Society for Third Sector Research, fourth international conference on 'The Third Sector: For What and For Whom', Trinity College, Dublin, July 5–8.

Silverman, R. (2002) 'Vying for the Urban Poor: Charitable Organizations, Faith-Based Social Capital, and Racial Reconciliation in a Deep South City', *Sociological Inquiry*, vol.72, no.1, pp.151–65.

Simon, J. (1983) 'The Effects of Population on Nutrition and Economic Well-Being', *Journal of Interdisciplinary History*, vol.14, no.2, pp.413–37.

Skocpol, T. (2008) 'Bringing the State Back In: Retrospect and Prospect', *Scandinavian Political Studies*, vol.31, no.2, pp.109–24.

Smith, C. (1995) 'Race–Class–Gender Ideology in Guatemala: Modern and Anti-Modern Forms', *Comparative Studies in Society and History*, vol.37, no.4, pp.723–49.

Smith, D. (1980) 'Tonypandy 1910: Definitions of Community', *Past and Present*, no.87, pp.158–84.

Smith, G. (2004) 'Faith in Community and Communities of Faith? Government Rhetoric and Religious Identity in Urban Britain', *Journal of Contemporary Religion*, vol.19, no.2, pp.185–204.

—— et al. (2004) 'Building Social Capital in Cities: Scope and Limitations', *Political Studies,* vol.52, no.3, pp.508–30.

Smith, S. and J. Kulynych (2002a) 'It May Be Social, but Why Is It Capital? The Social Construction of Social Capital and the Politics of Language', *Politics and Society*, vol.30, no.1, pp.149–86.

—— (2002b) 'Liberty, Equality, and ... Social Capital', in McLean et al. (2002).

Snyder, R. (2002) 'Social Capital: The Politics of Race and Gender', in McLean et al. (2002).

Soubeyran, A. and S. Weber (2002) 'District Formation and Local Social Capital: A (Tacit) Co-Opetition Approach', *Journal of Urban Economics*, vol.52, no.1, pp.65–92.

Staber, U. (2007) 'Contextualizing Research on Social Capital in Regional Clusters', *International Journal of Urban and Regional Research*, vol.31, no.3, pp.505–21.

Starkey, K. and S. Tempest (2004) 'Bowling Along: Strategic Management and Social Capital', *European Management Review*, vol.1, no.1, pp.78–83.

Steffensmeier, D. and J. Ulmer (2006) 'Black and White Control of Numbers Gambling: A Cultural Asset–Social Capital View', *American Sociological Review*, vol.71, no.1, pp.123–56.

Steger, M. (2002) 'Robert Putnam, Social Capital and A Suspect Named Globalization', in McLean et al. (2002).

Stein, H. (2001) 'Institutions, Institutional Theory and Institutional Development: Filling the "Black Box" of Social Capital?', paper presented to DANIDA workshop on 'Social Capital in the Theory and Practice of Development', University of Copenhagen, March.

Stevens, D. et al. (2006) 'Local News Coverage in a Social Capital Capital: Election 2000 on Minnesota's Local News Stations', *Political Communication*, vol.23, no.1, pp.61–83.

Stolle, D. (2003) 'The Sources of Social Capital: Theoretical and Empirical Insights', in Hooghe and Stolle (2003).

—— and M. Hooghe (2004) 'The Roots of Social Capital: Attitudinal and Network Mechanisms in the Relation between Youth and Adult Indicators of Social Capital', *Acta Politica*, vol.39, no.4, pp.422–41.

Stone, C. (2001) 'Civic Capacity and Urban Education', *Urban Affairs Review*, vol.36, no.5, pp.595–619.

Strathdee, R. (2005) *Social Exclusion and the Remaking of Social Networks*, Aldershot: Ashgate.

Sullivan, J. et al. (2002) 'Social Capital and Community Electronic Networks: For-Profit versus For-Community Approaches', *American Behavioral Scientist*, vol.45, no.5, pp.868–86.

Sundar, N. (2001) 'Is Devolution Democratization?', *World Development*, vol.29, no.12, pp.2007–24.

Sunderland, D. (2007) *Social Capital, Trust and the Industrial Revolution, 1780–1880*, London: Routledge.

Svendsen, A. et al. (2003) *Stakeholder Relationships, Social Capital and Business Value Creation: Research Report*, Canadian Institute of Chartered Accountants: Toronto.

Svendsen, G. and G. Svendsen (2003) 'On the Wealth of Nations: Bourdieuconomics and Social Capital', *Theory and Society*, vol.32, nos.5/6, pp.607–31.

—— (2004) *The Creation and Destruction of Social Capital: Entrepreneurship, Cooperative Movements and Institutions*, Cheltenham: Edward Elgar.

Swartz, D. (1997) *Culture and Power: The Sociology of Pierre Bourdieu*, Chicago: University of Chicago Press.

Swedberg, R. (ed.) (1990) *Economics and Sociology, Redefining Their Boundaries: Conversations with Economists and Sociologists*, Princeton, NJ: Princeton University Press.

—— (ed.) (1996) *Economic Sociology*, Cheltenham: Edward Elgar.

Szreter, S. (2002a) 'Health, Class, Place and Politics: Social Capital and Collective Provision in Britain', *Contemporary British History*, vol.16, no.3, pp.27–57.

—— (2002b) 'The State of Social Capital: Bringing Back in Power, Politics, and History', *Theory and Society*, vol.31, no.5, pp.573–621.

Takahisa, O. (2001) *The Unknown Marx: Reconstructing a Unified Perspective*, London: Pluto Press.

Takhar, S. (2006) 'South Asian Women, Social Capital and Multicultural (Mis) Understandings', *Community, Work and Family*, vol.9, no.3, pp.291–307.

Taylor, M. (2002) 'Enterprise, Embeddedness and Exclusion: Business and Development in Fiji', *Tijdschrift voor Economische en Sociale Geografie*, vol.93, no.3, pp.302–15.

—— and S. Leonard (eds) (2002) *Embedded Enterprise and Social Capital: International Perspectives*, Aldershot: Ashgate.

Temin, P. (1997) 'Is It Kosher to Talk about Culture?', Journal of Economic History, vol.57, no.2, pp.267–87.

Temple, J. (2001) 'Growth Effects of Education and Social Capital in the OECD', *OECD Economic Studies*, no.33, pp.57–100.

Thompson, G. (2003) *Between Hierarchies and Markets: The Logic and Limits of Network Forms of Organization*, Oxford: Oxford University Press.

Thomson, I. (2005) 'The Theory That Won't Die: From Mass Society to the Decline of Social Capital', *Sociological Forum*, vol.20, no.3, pp.421–48.

Timberlake, S. (2005) 'Social Capital and Gender in the Workplace', *Journal of Management Development*, vol.24, no.1, pp.34–44.

Tindall, D. and B. Wellman (2001) 'Canada as Social Structure: Social Network Analysis and Canadian Sociology', *Canadian Journal of Sociology*, vol.26, no.3, pp.265–308.

Tittensor, D. (2007) 'Social Capital and Public Policy: The Current Challenge Facing the Victorian Government', *Australian Journal of Public Administration*, vol.66, no.4, pp.512–18.

Tomer, J. (2002) 'Human Well-Being: A New Approach Based on Overall and Ordinary Functionings', *Review of Social Economy*, vol.60, no.1, pp.23–46.

Torcal, M. and J. Montero (eds) (2006) *Political Disaffection in Contemporary Democracies: Social Capital, Institutions, and Politics*, London: Routledge.

Torell, E. (2002) 'From Past to Present: The Historical Context of Environmental and Coastal Management in Tanzania', *Development Southern Africa*, vol.19, no.2, pp.273–88.

Torsvik, G. (2000) 'Social Capital and Economic Development: A Plea for the Mechanisms', *Rationality and Society*, vol.12, no.4, pp.451–76.

Trask, H. (2000) 'Native Social Capital: The Case of Hawaiian Sovereignty and Ka Lahui Hawaii', *Policy Sciences*, vol.33, nos.3/4, pp.375–86.

Trentmann, F. (ed.) (2005) *The Making of the Consumer: Knowledge, Power and Identity in the Modern World*, Oxford: Berg.

Trigilia, C. (2001) 'Social Capital and Local Development', *European Journal of Social Theory*, vol.4, no.4, pp.427–42.

Tschoegl, A. (2007) 'McDonald's: Much Maligned, But an Engine of Economic Development', *Global Economy Journal*, vol.7, no.4, pp.1–16.

Tuan, T. et al. (2005) 'Validity of a Social Capital Measurement Tool in Vietnam', *Asian Journal of Social Science*, vol.33, no.2, pp.208–22.

Udovitch, A. (1962) 'At the Origins of the Western *Commenda*: Islam, Israel, Byzantium?', *Speculum*, vol.37, no.2, pp.198–207.

Unruh, H. and R. Sider (2005) *Saving Souls, Serving Society: Understanding the Faith Factor in Church-Based Social Ministry*, Oxford: Oxford University Press.

Urry, J. (2002) 'Mobility and Proximity', *Sociology*, vol.36, no.2, pp.255–74.

Uslaner, E. and G. Badescu (2003) 'Legacies and Conflicts: The Challenges to Social Capital in the Democratic Transition', in Badescu and Uslaner (2003).

Valentine, S. and G. Fleischman (2003) 'The Impact of Self-Esteem, Machiavellianism, and Social Capital on Attorneys' Traditional Gender Outlook', *Journal of Business Ethics*, vol.43, no.4, pp.323–5.

Van Waeyenberge, E. (2007) *Exploring the Emergence of a New Aid Regime: Selectivity, Knowledge and the World Bank*, Ph.D. thesis, University of London.

Varese, F. (2004) 'Mafia Transplantation', in Kornai et al. (2004).

Vasileiou, K. and J. Morris (2006) 'The Sustainability of the Supply Chain for Fresh Potatoes in Britain', *Supply Chain Management: An International Journal*, vol.11, no.4, pp.317–27.

Vreese, C. de (2007) 'Digital Renaissance: Young Consumer and Citizen?', *Annals of the American Academy of Political and Social Science*, vol.611, no.1, pp.207–16.

Wade, R. (2009) 'From Global Imbalances to Global Reorganisations', *Cambridge Journal of Economics*, vol.33, no.4, pp.539–62.

Waldinger, R. (1995) 'The "Other Side" of Embeddedness: A Case-Study of the Interplay of Economy and Ethnicity', *Ethnic and Racial Studies*, vol.18, no.3, pp.555–80.

Walker, C. (2002) 'Philanthropy, Social Capital or Strategic Alliance? The Involvement of Senior UK Business Executives with the Voluntary Sector and Implications for Corporate Fundraising', *International Journal of Nonprofit and Voluntary Sector Marketing*, vol.7, no.3, pp.219–28.

Wallace, P. and A. Le Mund (eds) (1977) *Women, Minorities, and Employment Discrimination*, Lexington, MA: Lexington Books.

Walters, W. (2002) 'Social Capital and Political Sociology: Re-imagining Politics?', *Sociology*, vol.36, no.2, pp.377–97.

Warde, A. and G. Tampubolon (2002) 'Social Capital, Networks and Leisure Consumption', *Sociological Review*, vol.50, no.2, pp.155–80.

Warr, D. (2006) 'Gender, Class, and the Art and Craft of Social Capital', *Sociological Quarterly*, vol.47, no.3, pp.497–520.

Warren, M. et al. (2001) 'The Role of Social Capital in Combating Poverty', in Saegert et al. (2001).

Watts, M. (2006) 'Culture, Development, and Global Neo-liberalism', in Radcliffe (2006).

Wellman, B. et al. (2001) 'Does the Internet Increase, Decrease, or Supplement Social Capital? Social Networks, Participation, and Community Commitment', *American Behavioral Scientist*, vol.45, no.3, pp.436–55.

Westlund, H. and R. Bolton (2003) 'Local Social Capital and Entrepreneurship', *Small Business Economics*, vol.21, no.2, pp.77–113.

White, L. (2002) 'Connection Matters: Exploring the Implications of Social Capital and Social Networks for Social Policy', *Systems Research and Behavioral Science*, vol.19, no.3, pp.255–69.

White, M. (1982) 'Reading and Rewriting: The Production of an Economic Robinson Crusoe', *Southern Review*, vol.15, no.2, pp.115–42.

Wieloch, N. (2002) 'Collective Mobilization and Identity from the Underground: The Deployment of "Oppositional Capital" in the Harm Reduction Movement', *Sociological Quarterly*, vol.43, no.1, pp.45–72.

Williams, C. (2003) 'Harnessing Social Capital: Some Lessons From Rural England', *Local Government Studies*, vol.29, no.1, pp.75–90.

Williams, D. (2006) 'On and Off the 'Net: Scales for Social Capital in an Online Era', *Journal of Computer-Mediated Communication*, vol.11, no.2, pp.593–628.

Williams, J. and R. Sickles (2002) 'An Analysis of the Crime as Work Model: Evidence from the 1958 Philadelphia Birth Cohort Study', *Journal of Human Resources*, vol.37, no.3, pp.479–509.

Williams, P. and P. de Mola (2007) 'Religion and Social Capital Among Mexican Immigrants in Southwest Florida', *Latino Studies*, vol.5, no.2, pp.233–53.

Willman, P. et al. (2006) 'Noise Trading and the Management of Operational Risk: Firms, Traders and Irrationality in Financial Markets', *Journal of Management Studies*, vol.43, no.6, pp.1363–74.

Wilson, L. et al. (eds) (2006) *Civic Engagement and the Baby Boomer Generation: Research, Policy, and Practice Perspectives*, New York: Haworth Press.

Wilson, S. (1976) 'A View of the Past: *Action Française* Historiography and Its Socio-Political Function', *The Historical Journal*, vol.19, no.1, pp.135–61.

Witz, A. and B. Marshall (2004) 'Introduction: Feminist Encounters with Sociological Theory', in Marshall and Witz (2004).

Wølneberg, K. (2002) 'Supply Chains, Embeddedness and the Restructuring of Argentina's Tanning Industry', in Taylor and Leonard (2002).

Wong, K. (2003) 'Empowerment as a Panacea for Poverty – Old Wine in New Bottles? Reflections on the World Bank's Conception of Power', *Progress in Development Studies*, vol.3, no.4, pp.307–22.

Wood, C. et al. (2007) 'Protestantism and Child Mortality in Northeast Brazil, 2000', *Journal for the Scientific Study of Religion*, vol.46, no.3, pp. 405–16.

Wood, L. et al. (2005) 'The Pet Connection: Pets as a Conduit for Social Capital?', *Social Science and Medicine*, vol.61, no.6, pp.1159–73.

—— et al. (2007) 'More Than a Furry Companion: The Ripple Effect of Companion Animals on Neighborhood Interactions and Sense of Community', *Society and Animals*, vol.15, no.1, pp.43–56.

Woolcock, M. (1998) 'Social Capital and Economic Development: Toward a Theoretical Synthesis and Policy Framework', *Theory and Society*, vol.27, no.2, pp.151–208.

—— (2002) 'Social Capital in Theory and Practice', in Isham et al. (2002).

—— and D. Narayan (2000) 'Social Capital: Implications for Development Theory, Research, and Policy', *World Bank Research Observer*, vol.15, no.2, pp.225–49.

World Bank (1997) *Expanding the Measure of Wealth: Indicators of Environmentally Sustainable Development*, Washington: World Bank.

—— (2001) *Attacking Poverty*, World Development Report 2000/2001, Oxford: Oxford University Press.

Wuthnow, R. (2002) 'Religious Involvement and Status-Bridging Social Capital', *Journal for the Scientific Study of Religion*, vol.41, no.4, pp.669–84.

Yang, M. (1989) 'The Gift Economy and State Power in China', *Comparative Studies in Society and History*, vol.31, no.1, pp.25–54.

Yli-Renko, H. et al. (2001) 'Social Capital, Knowledge Acquisition, and Knowledge Exploitation in Young Technology-Based Firms', *Strategic Management Journal*, vol.22, nos.6/7, pp.587–614.

Zhao, Y. (2002) 'Measuring the Social Capital of Laid-Off Chinese Workers', *Current Sociology*, vol.50, no.4, pp.555–71.

Zobler, L. (1962) 'An Economic-Historical View of Natural Resource Use and Conservation', *Economic Geography*, vol.38, no.3, pp.189–94.

Index

Compiled by Sue Carlton